Withdrawn from Collection

An Unauthorized Biography of
GORDIE HOWE

GORDIE
A HOCKEY LEGEND

Roy MacSkimming

GREY*S*TONE BOOKS
Douglas & McIntyre Publishing Group
Vancouver/Toronto/Berkeley

To the memory of my father, William MacSkimming

Copyright © 1994, 2003 by Roy MacSkimming
First paperback edition 1995
Revised paperback edition 2003
First US edition published in 2003
07 08 09 10 11   11 10 9 8 7

All rights reserved. No part of this book may be reproduced, stored in a retrieval
system or transmitted, in any form or by any means, without the prior written
consent of the publisher or a licence from The Canadian Copyright Licensing Agency
(Access Copyright). For a copyright licence, visit www.accesscopyright.ca or call
toll free to 1-800-893-5777.

Greystone Books
A division of Douglas & McIntyre Ltd.
2323 Quebec Street, Suite 201
Vancouver, British Columbia
Canada V5T 4S7
www.greystonebooks.com

NATIONAL LIBRARY OF CANADA CATALOGUING IN PUBLICATION DATA
MacSkimming, Roy, 1944–
   Gordie : a hockey legend / Roy MacSkimming.-Rev. ed.

   Includes index.
   ISBN-13: 978-1-55054-719-1 · ISBN-10: 1-55054-719-4

   1. Howe, Gordie, 1928– 2. Hockey players—Canada—Biography. I. Title
GV848.5.H6M32 2003   796.962′092   C2003-910796-5

Library of Congress Cataloging-in-Publication data is available.

Editing by Barbara Pulling
Cover design by Jessica Sullivan
Text design by Tom Brown
Cover photograph by The Detroit News
Typeset by Brenda and Neil West, BN Typographics West

Printed and bound in Canada by Friesens
Printed on acid-free paper
Distributed in the U.S. by Publishers Group West

Every reasonable care has been taken to trace ownership of copyrighted visual
material. Information that will enable the publisher to rectify any reference or credit
is welcome.

We gratefully acknowledge the financial support of the Canada Council for the Arts,
the British Columbia Arts Council, the Province of British Columbia through the
Book Publishing Tax Credit, and the Government of Canada through the Book
Publishing Industry Development Program (BPIDP) for our publishing activities.

Contents

Introduction to the New Edition

EVEN FOR A HOCKEY GOD whose career is measured in super-latives, 2003 should have been a landmark year for Gordie Howe. It marked sixty years since he'd begun his last season in hometown Saskatoon before departing for stardom in the east. It marked thir-ty years since he'd amazed the sports world by coming out of retirement to play for the Houston Aeros alongside two of his sons. And it marked the seventy-fifth birthday of a man who con-tinued playing the game he loved until he was a fifty-two-year-old grandfather.

At three-quarters of a century old, despite knee replacements, brain surgery, assorted lost teeth, a catalogue of fractures and a daily diet of searing arthritic pain that most of us can only imagine, Gordie Howe was in robust health, physically and mentally. Since the death in 2000 of his once-hated rival and belated friend, Maurice (Rocket) Richard, Howe was indisputably the greatest liv-ing link to the glories of the National Hockey League's six-team era. For that reason, as much as for his abundance of scoring records, most of them exceeded only by Wayne Gretzky, Howe has remained an icon. Witnessing his appearances at card-show signings or NHL all-star weekends, you never cease to be amazed by his magnetic star power in attracting around-the-block line-ups of old and young.

But there's even more to the Howe mystique. He's not only revered for his achievements but beloved, in a time of million-dollar salaries paid to players who couldn't carry his skates, for his old-fashioned honour, humour and humility. He still has that rare gift for reaching out to an awestruck kid, as he once did to eleven-year-old Gretzky, and making him or her laugh. Just take a look at the photographs in the pages within.

To crown 2003, Howe would also be celebrating the golden anniversary of his marriage to his agent, business manager and biggest all-time booster, Colleen Howe. But one terrible sadness would cast a shadow over the family's celebrations: Colleen would be there more in body than in mind or spirit. The year before, at the age of seventy, she'd been diagnosed with a form of dementia known as Pick's disease—a degenerative ailment related to Alzheimer's, with similar symptoms of forgetfulness and problems in judgement. Pick's disease is incurable. Colleen, to whom family has always been paramount, sometimes has difficulty recognizing her children and closest friends.

An emotional man, Howe is devastated by the drastic changes in the woman whose practical judgement he always relied on. The active, even hectic existence they once shared as partners in business as well as life is shattered. "I've never had so many worries in my life," he told a reporter. "I'm home all the time now. You have to be constantly aware. We have an alarm system, and whenever a door opens there's a ring. I go like hell when it rings."

A photograph rich in pathos appeared in *The Detroit News* showing the couple smiling bravely, Gordie in his Red Wings sweater extending his arm protectively around his wife's shoulder. The image poignantly expressed vanished glories. At the same time, it portrayed an indomitable courage in facing up to life's cruel surprises.

Not so very long before, Colleen Howe had been running the couple's business enterprises as president of Power Play International, Inc. in Michigan. She'd been indefatigable in pursuing her twin objectives: promoting the Howe legend and fundraising for children's causes through the Howe Foundation.

No one had ever doubted the sincerity of the couple's charitable work. Yet many had shaken their heads over Colleen's occasional excesses in managing Gordie's retirement. Because hockey's toughest practitioner always accepted Colleen's judgment in worldly matters, his trust sometimes landed him in strange places. Howe is the most modest of heroes (his old teammate Marty Pavelich says later in this book, "he's as humble today as the day I met him"), so it was ironic that some of the Howes' retirement capers contained an immodest amount of self-promotion. More than anything, this reflected Colleen's ambitions for them both. During 1993 she promoted a sixty-five-city North American tour to celebrate the sixty-fifth birthday of "Mr. Hockey®," a trademark that "Mrs. Hockey®" arranged to have legally registered. Although many in professional hockey viewed the birthday tour as grandiose showmanship, it also pulled in money for children's charities—nearly $1 million, according to the Howes.

Four years later, on October 3, 1997, they grabbed media attention again. Gordie, then aged sixty-nine, stepped onto the ice for a single shift during a home game of the minor-league Detroit Vipers of the International Hockey League. The idea was to make him the only human on the planet to have "played" professional hockey in six decades. His illustrious career hardly needed such a spurious postscript.

The stunt's only benefit may have been boosting sales of Howe-related products. Some time later, on the *mrhockey.com* Web site operated by Power Play International, the avid collector could purchase, for only US$499, an autographed replica of the Vipers sweater Howe had worn. If the price seemed high, it made the US$599 price tag for a replica of his original Detroit Red Wings sweater seem like a bargain. In either case, a signed photograph of Howe in the act of autographing your sweater would be thrown in free. Also available through the Web site were autographed pucks, photographs, lithographs, hockey sticks and Gordie Howe bobble-head dolls, available in home or away sweaters. The new millennium also saw the unveiling of two limited-edition breakfast cereals: Mr. Hockey® Honey Nut Toasted Oats and Gordie Howe® Frosted Flakes. Fans could enjoy the ultimate communion with Gordie by sitting down to a bowl of "his" cereal. By that point, the commodification of Mr. Hockey® had got a bit out of hand.

Yet in a way, you can hardly blame the Howes. After many years of being exploited financially by NHL owners, Gordie and other retired players of his generation had to mount an extended legal battle in the 1990s just to recover pension funds long owed to them. It's understandable they'd become anxious to extract the maximum benefit from their fame. Ever since 1968, when Gordie discovered Red Wings management had been lying about his being the best-paid player in the league, Colleen had been negotiating on his behalf and driving the best possible bargain for his services: a role Gordie heartily approved of. The Howes were bound and determined that Gordie would never be taken advantage of again. And so Colleen engineered the US$2-million four-year deal taking Gordie, Marty and Mark Howe to Houston and the World Hockey Association.

The Howes' wariness of exploitation extends to authors seeking to write about Gordie. As one of those, I was troubled that on publication of this book in 1994, the Howes went on record as saying it was intended as a "spoiler," detracting from the book they planned to produce themselves. In truth, my publisher and I had previously but unsuccessfully proposed to the Howes a collaboration on an authorized biography of Gordie. But in the end, the two books that appeared within a year of each other could hardly have been more different.

This one is a hockey biography, pure and simple, focusing on Gordie's playing career. The volume that the Howes self published in 1995, *and...Howe!,* subtitled *An Authorized Autobiography* by Gordie and Colleen Howe with Tom DeLisle, is a kind of family album consisting of edited interviews with various members of the Howe clan. In it, Gordie's voice is only one among many; and his hockey career is only one subject among many, surrounded by the reminiscences of Colleen and their four children. It's the kind of book that Colleen had told me she wanted to see published, rather than a straight biography of Gordie. Living in his shadow all those years had been tough for her and the kids, she'd said at the time, and now they too deserved their share of the limelight.

and...Howe! was sold in Canada exclusively through the Zellers department store chain, for which Gordie modelled a line of men's casual wear. The book's highlight is the photographs. Amid portraits of Colleen as bathing queen, Republican candidate and business executive, some rare portraits reward the patient fan:

Gordie's dirt-poor yet proud parents in their wedding finery in 1918; the ramshackle farmhouse where he was born in Floral, Saskatchewan; the twenty-year-old budding NHL star perched on the hood of his first car, a 1948 Chev; a handsome, youthful Gordie during the off-season, fishing or wearing the uniform of the Saskatoon Gems baseball team.

Occasionally, the Howes' book yields nuggets of new information or revealing insights. In Colleen's version of the family's move from Detroit to Houston, we hear the fierce mother lion defending her cubs when she asserts: "Once Gordie got drafted by the Aeros, everybody forgot about how young Marty and Mark were, how good they were.... Suddenly the story is 'Gordie's Comeback.' It was as if Marty and Mark were tagging along with Gordie instead of Gordie tagging along with them, which is what really happened." And we learn, in previously undisclosed detail, how Gordie's playing career *really* ended, once and for all, in 1980.

Nobody was surprised by his retirement from the Hartford Whalers after a phenomenal thirty-two professional seasons. Not only had Howe been playing the world's fastest, roughest sport at an incredibly advanced age, he'd also just completed a sub-par season. But rather than making a considered decision to retire gracefully, Gordie reveals that he quit in a huff. He'd gone to see the Whalers' general manager, Jack Kelley, to say he wanted to play one more year while doubling as an assistant coach. According to Howe, Kelley declined the offer and said the team would be going with youth instead: "I think they had my retirement all planned before I went to meet Jack. I got so ticked off that I said, on the spot, 'Well, then you can shove it, I quit,' and I walked out."

When Gordie arrived home, Colleen was angry too. She was "infuriated" that he hadn't consulted her first and that he hadn't left himself any other option. The team immediately called a news conference to announce his retirement the next day. "So he robbed himself of controlling one of the most monumental moments of his life," as Colleen put it in *and...Howe!* She continued, "I always felt personally robbed of feeling good about the last time Gordie would put on a pair of skates.... He'll always regret what happened, because he did not want to quit that year."

Gordie, of course, concurred with Colleen's opinion. He accused himself of "screwing up royally."

All that doesn't seem so important now. Transcending such matters is Howe's immutable, untouchable genius as a player. In the nine years since this book appeared, it's become possible to discern even more clearly his true place in hockey.

The sport has undergone immense change since Howe retired: arguably more change overall than any other major-league sport. Today professional hockey is faster, richer and far more international than it has ever been. The historic eight-game series between Canada and the former Soviet Union in 1972, followed by multinational confrontations in the Canada Cup showdowns, dismantled barriers that were both athletic and political. International competition allowed Canadian, American, Russian, Swedish, Czech and Finnish players to learn from each other's distinct styles and raise their game to new levels of speed and skill. In turn, the influx of foreign talent into the NHL fuelled the league's expansion to thirty cities, twenty-four of them in the United States. The demand for talent and the growing access to lucrative American markets and television contracts drove salaries into the stratosphere.

Although expansion's early days extended his career, and although he did play in a mini–Summit Series between the Soviets and the WHA all-stars in 1974, Howe belongs to an earlier era of hockey: an era he personally embodies more than any other player, simply because he was the best. It was a time when only six teams vied for the Stanley Cup, icing a total of only 120 players, and virtually all those players were Canadian. The sport was then played at a furious clip sometimes, but often at a more leisurely speed: the pace of each game more modulated, varied and unpredictable than now, allowing individual brilliance like Howe's or Richard's to stand out more boldly and decide an outcome more dramatically. It was an era when players didn't jump to a different city every two or three years for the lure of bigger money but often remained with a team throughout their entire career, putting down deep personal roots in a city, so that fans identified with them and called them *theirs*. Trading a local hero was often a scandal that triggered public shock and outrage. And it was a time before helmets and visors, so that on the ice a player's features were familiar, his emotions apparent, his scale human, rather than being an anonymous armoured behemoth churning up the rink in only one gear—high.

Of course, it's easy to romanticize hockey's underpaid past. The fact is, Howe helped set in motion many of the changes we see today. In the early 1950s, he arrived at the top of his game just as television arrived, becoming one of the first authentic superstars of televised hockey. His fame while playing for an American franchise contributed enormously, as former NHL president Clarence Campbell once said, to converting a Canadian game into a North American game. And after playing twenty-five seasons in Detroit, he became one of the earliest big-money players by joining the exodus from the NHL in pursuit of WHA cash.

As Ken Dryden memorably put it, the golden age of hockey is always whoever was playing when you were ten. Those who were ten when Howe was in the ascendancy are now heading toward sixty themselves; the time will come when they too will no longer be here to witness how superbly Gordie played. By then, all that will remain to attest to his brilliance will be books and videotapes. And so let it be recorded here that Gordie Howe was as graceful and instinctual, as inventive and multi-skilled, as mean and dominant on the ice as they all said.

But was he the greatest? Of all time? That's impossible to determine, finally—unless you've witnessed as a mature observer every last player of the past hundred years, and none of us can say that. In search of some objective standard for ranking players of different eras, hockey analysts have used various schemes for measuring Howe against the player with whom he's most often compared, the Great One. The simplest method (and the one favoured by Howe himself) is to go beyond NHL scoring records, where Gretzky reigns supreme, by adding NHL and WHA totals. By that measure, Howe had 975 regular-season goals, whereas Gretzky had 940.

More complex methods attempt to allow for different conditions in different eras by adjusting the figures. According to one system used in *Total Hockey: The Official Encyclopedia of the NHL*, an adjusted calculation gives Howe 988 NHL goals to 779 for Gretzky.

Using another system, two *Detroit News* hockey writers, Vartan Kupelian and Mike O'Hara, compared Howe's twenty-five seasons with the Red Wings with Gretzky's twenty NHL seasons and computed their total goals as a percentage of all goals scored in the league during those years (in Gretzky's case, they limited the calculation to the top six teams, in order to mirror conditions in Howe's time). The result: Howe scored a percentage of .0259 of all goals scored, to Gretzky's .0236.

The point is not whether these tortured statistical comparisons prove anything, but the fact that people make them at all. Howe's rightful place at the pinnacle of hockey is unquestioned, even if he shares it with his younger heir and admirer.

Howe set the gold standard by which all others are evaluated, and that's why we call him a legend. If he is now becalmed at home, caring for his wife in her illness, it simply means that hockey's immortal has become mortal after all, with worries the rest of us can understand. Meanwhile, the legend endures.

R.M.
Perth, Ontario
May 2003

Getting to Gordie

"Hockey is real life."
—Ken Dryden and Roy MacGregor, *Home Game*

MY OLDEST MEMORY OF GORDIE HOWE is all wrapped up with my oldest friendship. In the bone-chilling month of February 1955, I was eleven years old. After a house-league game on the outdoor rink at school, I was walking home at dusk with my best friend, Larry—glasses, freckles, a little pudgy at that stage, but brainy and quick with his mouth, especially at my expense. Both of us were wearing woollen toques and carrying our sticks on our shoulders, the stick blades shoved through our skates. Pausing under a pool of light from a street lamp at the corner, we aimed slow, rhythmic kicks at a snowbank that came up to eye-level and talked about how we should have won the game.

That winning goal of theirs had just been a damn fluke, I said. For once, Larry agreed with me.

Encouraged, I said with greater vehemence, "It was a real *garbage* goal."

"Yeah," he said again, aiming another hard kick at the snowbank, "you're not kidding—like one of those Rocket Richard goals."

Very slowly, I turned to stare at him. I'd been a Montreal Canadiens fan forever, and he knew it. Maurice (Rocket) Richard was my original and only hero. The Rocket's greatness was unequalled. Indisputable. Larry's disparagement of it suddenly brought us to the edge of a vast divide.

The moment required exceptional eloquence, but all I could think to say was, "Whaddaya mean 'Rocket Richard goals'?"

"You've got TV, don't you?"

Of course I did—our house had been one of the first on the street to have a television set.

"So, you've seen Richard hanging around in front of the other team's net, waiting for a garbage goal! He doesn't pass, he doesn't forecheck, doesn't backcheck, all he does is wait for the puck to *come* to him. That's why he scores so much."

I wanted to cite brilliant, irrefutable counter-arguments, but in the adrenalin of anger, my mind had gone blank. I was grateful for a huge Plymouth that came rumbling slowly towards us, drowning out conversation, allowing me to gather my thoughts. Watching the Plymouth's taillights recede through swirls of exhaust, I burst out with, "So what about fifty goals in one season?"

"Fifty garbage goals? What's so great about that?"

"They weren't garbage goals! Fifty is still the all-time record, *jerk*. And Richard did it in fifty games and now they play seventy. So who's greater than the Rocket? Name *one*."

Larry had been grinning at my discomfort, but now his grin became an outright laugh. "It's so obvious. The best player in the National Hockey League, the best player in the *world*, is Gordie Howe. He can do everything. He can skate, stick-handle, pass, check, kill penalties, fight, you name it—*and* score. All Richard can do is score. Oh yeah, and get penalties, I forgot about that."

Larry looked serious again, and I realized he believed it. The effect of this was worse than being bugged, worse than the irritation he regularly provoked in me: this time he'd transgressed my faith. I remembered that Larry was Catholic and I was Protestant. It had never seemed to matter before.

We picked up our sticks, turned our backs on each other and trudged off in our separate directions, not even saying good-bye. I still seethed inwardly. I considered hurling a well-aimed snowball at his retreating back—he was still within my range, and I was beyond his puny arm—but decided that would be a childish thing to do.

Although we didn't realize it at the time, Larry and I had been engaging, in our eleven-year-old way, in a classic debate of the Canadian psyche: Howe vs. Richard. English vs. French. Reason vs. passion. The debate would continue across the country for years, far beyond the Rocket's retirement and Howe's two retirements and far beyond our own boyhoods, and in a few arenas and rec rooms and Legion halls—although increasingly fewer, no doubt—it continues still.

A few weeks after our argument, in a game in the Boston Garden on March 13, 1955, Richard capped a fight with the Bruins' Hal Laycoe by slugging an official twice in the face.

The NHL held a private hearing into the incident, and league president Clarence Campbell suspended Richard not only for the rest of the season, with three games left to play, but for the entire Stanley Cup playoffs. The league said the Rocket's conduct was either "the product of temperamental instability or wilful defiance of the authority of the game." In other words, he was either crazy or rebellious, and neither would be tolerated by the NHL owners or their mouthpiece. At the next game in Montreal, a riot ensued inside and outside the Forum: "the Richard Riot," as it became known, although the Rocket hadn't called for it.

Before the suspension, Richard had been heading for his first scoring title. But during those final three games, he lost the title yet again, and Montreal again lost first place to Detroit. In the bitterly fought Stanley Cup finals that year, the Red Wings defeated the Rocket-less Canadiens in seven games. Throughout the series, Gordie Howe was indisputably brilliant, indeed dominant. He scored the Cup-winning goal and established a record with 20 playoff points, and he and linemates Ted Lindsay and Earl Reibel set a record for total points by a forward line.

Larry used all this against me, of course. To his face, I never ceased defending the Rocket; but in truth, during the whole time Richard was suspended, I lost heart a little. My hero had let his emotions get the better of him. He'd let himself and our team down. As Larry persisted in pointing out, you couldn't imagine Gordie Howe doing a thing like that.

My conversion, however, still wasn't quite complete. That would take another four years until, with a precious ticket to Maple Leaf Gardens in my pocket, I travelled alone on the bus down highway 401 to watch the newly rejuvenated Leafs against the Red Wings. Finally I would see Howe play in person.

At first I thrilled simply to the spectacle of the teams weaving their intricate patterns across the milky, luminous ice in full colour instead of the pallid greys of television. Even the sounds of the game were sharper: the *clack* of the puck against stick blades, the throaty *wump* of a stop by Johnny Bower's pads, the electrifying *ping* of a shot caroming off the post, all seemingly amplified by the arena's acoustics. There was no constant blare of rock music in those days.

But ultimately, what I received that night, like a gift, was a vision of how majestically hockey can be played—how one player, like a great filmmaker, can direct certain scenes in a game, as if in command not only of his own teammates but of the other team too.

I focussed on Howe, even when he didn't have the puck. There was just so much to watch: his sly stick-work; his tender way of relieving Toronto players of the puck; his endlessly inventive playmaking; his constant, fluid skating into spaces that the Leafs couldn't seem to help leaving open, no matter how closely they checked him. He managed it all so calmly, without fanfare or heroics, that he might have been a magician lulling the senses of his subjects as he prepared them for hypnosis.

On his first goal, he circled with the puck in a wide, lazy arc about twenty feet out in front of Bower. Giving no hint of his destination, he studied with interest the maelstrom of players jostling furiously for position; holding his fire, he watched for that merest glimpse of an open net through the screen of bodies. Finally Bower became so agitated he couldn't stand it. Thinking he'd anticipated Howe's intent, he lunged for the expected shot, overcommitting himself and surrendering even more net than his old fishing buddy had been expecting. In a deceptively lackadaisical motion, Howe's wrist shot flicked the puck high and hard over Bower's prostrate pad, and the netting bulged like a bullfrog's throat. The partisan crowd gave a collective gasp, then a low collective groan. Finally there was a light, grudging but sincere scattering of applause, coming from those aficionados who just had to acknowledge the moment of grace.

Before scoring his other goal that night, Howe banked the puck off a Leaf defenseman's skate—it may have been Allan Stanley's or Tim Horton's—as if off the boards. Recovering it, he veered in on net from right wing. One of the Leaf defenders draped himself all over Howe, who powered ahead regardless, simply outmuscling the other man and carrying him along for the ride like an old raincoat he'd forgotten to discard. With a fiendishly complicated motion involving his head, shoulders and knees, he deked Bower into a puzzle of futility, swept the puck swiftly to his backhand and sunk it up high in the top left-hand corner. Bower just stood there, his stick dangling uselessly from one hand. The best goalie in the world couldn't have denied Howe that one.

In hockey, as in life, timing may be everything. But to do what Howe did that night, a player would have to have such exquisite timing, and simultaneously be master of so many different skills, that you could only wonder how in the world he'd put it all together. I walked out of the Gardens onto Carlton Street enveloped in a sweet haze. I was aware I'd been privileged to witness a unique and sublime and, in some way, godlike performance. And I came around to admitting Larry had probably been right on that cold February afternoon four years earlier. Considering the amazing course of Howe's continuing career over the next two decades, I had little choice.

CHAPTER ONE

Living the Legend

"This is home. It always will be home.
I'm very proud of it."
—Gordie Howe, Saskatoon, 1993

SEPTEMBER 25, 1993, IS A CHILLY SATURDAY in Saskatoon. The wind is gusting, the skies threatening. On a busy downtown corner across the street from Sears, Gordie Howe turns sharply on his skates, looks over his left shoulder for a pass and raises a massive elbow to ward off unwary opponents. Wearing his Red Wings uniform, he is only a block away from the old Arena, now demolished, where he first impressed NHL scouts at the age of fifteen. He is large as life and solid as bronze. Howe may have left Saskatoon behind, but Saskatoon has just brought him back home, permanently. Back where even he, at times, feels he belongs.

The flesh-and-blood Gordie Howe, still reigning at this point as the National Hockey League's all-time goals scorer, grins appreciatively at his bronze double while a large throng of admirers applauds. The statue's unveiling, accompanied by the martial skirl of bagpipes, is a highlight of a gala three-day homecoming for Howe. Following visits to three other cities in his native province, Regina, Moose Jaw and Prince Albert, the homecoming is part of a sixty-five-city North American tour conceived by Howe's wife, promoter and business partner, Colleen Howe, to celebrate his sixty-fifth birthday.

Saskatonians keep a strong grip on their prairie identity. They like to memorialize their past, and so they've erected statues all over town: a young, bronze John Diefenbaker sells a newspaper to a top-hatted Sir Wilfrid Laurier at the corner of First Avenue and Twenty-first Street; Metis general Gabriel Dumont and current Governor General Ray Hnatyshyn stand alongside the broad sweep of the South Saskatchewan River. Now another local hero, who hasn't lived here for half a century, has his statue, too.

The hundreds of kids among the spectators don't realize it, but right where they're standing, the CNR tracks used to divide the city between east and west; on his way to the Arena, young Gordie often walked with his skates and stick across a wooden bridge that spanned those tracks. Of course, old Gordie, real-life Gordie, remembers. But he doesn't talk about it, just steps right up to the statue and mugs playfully for the cameras, patting the menacing elbow approvingly.

Still tall and lanky, Howe moves stiffly and a touch bowleggedly and turns his long head aside in a lifelong gesture of shyness. Seen close up, his face is a long-familiar icon come to life. It's tanned the colour of soft cowhide from hours spent out on golf courses and fishing lakes, and it makes a startling contrast with the pure white silk of his hair, which in turn contrasts with the youthfulness of his features. His hazel eyes blink involuntarily from time to time, the famous twitch inherited from his father, which stuck him with the nickname "Blinky" early in his career.

But the most striking landmark on his face is the nose. Long and pointed, it curls precipitously downwards like a Stuka dive bomber. It is not a nose to trifle with. It reminds you of Hemingway's line about what is broken becoming stronger at the broken places.

The statue doesn't quite capture the ornery aggressiveness of that nose. The likeness was created by Michael Martin, a local carpenter who sculpts on the side, and formerly languished for months in a farmer's field. In town for a celebrity hockey game during 1992, Howe drove out to see the sculpture, observing, "The head is too fat," and suggesting it resembled his younger brother Vic. So Martin recast the head but still couldn't find a purchaser.

Finally veteran sports broadcaster Lloyd Saunders lamented the statue's fate on the air, and sports columnist Ken Juba wrote a feature in the Saskatoon *StarPhoenix*, concluding: "Just like it

might have been fifty years ago, Howe is spending the Saskatchewan winter in a snowy field, waiting for somebody to come
and discover him." The story caught the imagination of Peter
Zakreski, a senior vice-president of Federated Co-operatives Ltd.
and chair of the Spirit of Service Committee, a civic-minded
group that raised the money to buy the sculpture and ended up
organizing the entire homecoming visit.

Colleen has conceived her husband's birthday tour on a grand,
even grandiose, scale: every one of the twenty-six NHL cities is to
be included, plus many minor-league cities, for a total of sixty-five
over a two-year period. The idea is for Howe to appear at a
hockey game and a fund-raising event, typically a big-ticket
luncheon or dinner, with the money raised to go to a local charity
and to the Howe Foundation, which is dedicated to improving the
quality of life for children.

Already the tour has run into a few snags. Not all NHL teams
consider it a good investment of their time, effort and money.
Nothing against Gordie personally, some have said, but they have
Hall of Famers of their own to celebrate, many of whom wouldn't
appreciate their team honouring an old enemy who clobbered
them year after year. This has been the reaction, for example, of
the Toronto Maple Leafs.

Other teams have a hard time seeing the point of the tour.
Evidently they don't buy the "Mr. Hockey" label pinned on
Howe years ago and used by his wife as a sort of brand name. The
Howes' daughter, Cathy, handling details of the tour, has told the
New York Times she's surprised by some of the rejections: "One
NHL team said Gordie wasn't synonymous with hockey . . . Los
Angeles said yes, but they called me last week and said no." Howe
himself has cited the cold shoulder from Indianapolis as one of the
funnier putdowns: "Indianapolis told us, 'If the San Diego
Chicken cancels, we'll call you.'" And one of Howe's oldest team-
mates has told this author, on condition of anonymity, "I love the
man—he's the greatest who ever played the game, he's as humble
today as the day I met him, and I'd never say anything to hurt him.
But I think he's retired enough times."

Nonetheless, the show has gone on. It's been a hit (not unexpectedly) in Detroit, in Montreal during the 1993 NHL all-star

weekend, in Ottawa and in Hamilton, where the tour raised significant money for a local children's hospital. But Saskatoon has outdone them all.

After the unveiling ceremony is complete, the crowd flocks into the welcome warmth of Midtown Plaza for birthday cake and autographs. Kids line up as far as the eye can see and applaud as Howe slices a gigantic birthday cake, the first of several that weekend. One by one, they step up to meet the legend face-to-face. And one by one, to the last kid, they receive his autograph—on scraps of paper, hockey cards, hats, T-shirts, hockey sticks or hands—accompanied by a friendly bit of conversation, always different, always personal to the individual.

Howe gives his fans full value. For one boy, this means getting tapped on the head with his own scarred stick before having it autographed "Gordon Howe" in an elegantly flowing script. For another, it means being gently ribbed about wearing an earring: "If you wear that in your nose, it's better." Another, presenting for autographing purposes a photograph of himself in his hockey uniform, receives some free coaching:

"You have trouble shooting?"

"Well, no . . ."

"Yes, you do. You miss the puck sometimes?"

"Sometimes . . ."

"You know why? 'Cause you have your hand way up here. See that? It's like putting one hand in your pocket before trying to shoot. That hand's gotta be down farther."

The autograph session lasts over two hours. Yet Howe never seems to tire or cease enjoying himself. Among these folks, he is perfectly content and at home, just as he is later in the evening at sleek, modern Sask Place, home of the Saskatoon Blades juniors of the Western Hockey League, where he attends the Blades' season opener and skates out to centre ice under a dramatic spotlight in the pre-game ceremonies, wearing a yellow, white and blue Blades jersey with a big number nine on the back. Seated in the stands during the game against Prince Albert, mobbed by youngsters, Howe is steadily besieged for autographs until the final whistle.

He does find time during the weekend to stop being public property for a while and revert to being plain Gordie Howe, private citizen. His schedule leaves him one afternoon for a reunion with the family he left behind so long ago.

As one of his sisters, Joan Clark, explains afterwards, this is a rare occurrence. "Before he married Colleen, he used to drive back here from Detroit after the season ended. But this was the first time he'd spent so much time with us for years. We had him for the whole afternoon," she exclaims.

The Howe relatives gather in the party room of the townhouse development where Mrs. Clark's daughter, Pat, lives. "When Gord came into the party room, it was full of people," Mrs. Clark says later. "He didn't know a lot of them. Of course, they all knew him. He got to meet his nieces and nephews and grand-nieces and grand-nephews."

Usually when her brother visits Saskatoon, it's on business of some sort—the business of being Mr. Hockey—making paid appearances on behalf of some corporate client, or starring at a sports-card show, or playing in an old-timers' game for charity. But this time it's different. "He was really thrilled about the homecoming," Mrs. Clark says.

On the morning of his last day in Saskatoon, Howe revisits his old public school. King George Community School is a five-storey, red-brick castle on Avenue K. Built in 1912, it's an inner-city institution attended by poor kids, just as it was in his boyhood. By now, the King George student body is even more disadvantaged, containing about 50 per cent Native and Metis children. Like young Howe during the Depression, many of these pupils come from families that can't afford to pay for sports equipment, books, field trips or other extracurricular activities. A King George Legacy Fund was created some years ago to enrich the children's education, and now the fund has been designated to receive the $18,000 raised during Howe's homecoming.

As he enters the school's front doors, Howe walks past a glass showcase containing one of his old Northland hockey sticks—autographed, of course—with only the slightest curve in the blade. Hanging above the stick is a portrait collage of him, done in heroic style by artist James Lumbers. It depicts three stages in Howe's life: the famous moment when young Gordie got his first skates; the adolescent Gordie skating—a misty, ghostlike figure—

out of the prairies, a grain elevator at his back; and the adult Howe in the foreground, wearing number nine for the Red Wings and chasing a puck to glory. The showcase is a shrine to King George's most famous old boy, who never made it out of grade eight.

In a ceremony in the gym, principal Lynda McLean-Woodward and one of her students present Howe with a grade-eight graduation diploma. Although family and friends remember that he did graduate, school records indicate Howe still hadn't received a diploma when he left King George forty-nine years earlier, in 1944.

For his part, the returning legend seems genuinely touched by his old school's gesture. For his thank-you speech, he gives the students his much-practised inspirational talk about staying in school and giving 100 per cent to your studies, as well as 100 per cent to sports. He confesses to getting into scrapes at King George: there was the time he proved he could kick a football onto the school roof, then had to copy out ten pages of history before climbing up to retrieve the ball, and the time he broke the rule about running in the halls, and tripped and destroyed two storm windows. He inscribes a photo of himself, saying, "If the spelling's wrong, it's because this is where I learned to write." He goes on a walkabout of the hallways and classrooms with Colleen, clowns around with the kids, teases them relentlessly, poses for photographs, plays ball hockey in his shirtsleeves with the third-graders, and slices yet another giant birthday cake.

Afterwards, the principal can't praise him highly enough. "He had a marvellous rapport with the kids," McLean-Woodward says. "He always had time for each of them. And they just loved him."

His school visit and family reunion are in the forefront of Howe's mind later that day, when he's back on public view for the final event of the homecoming. In a reflective mood, he addresses four hundred guests at a fund-raising luncheon in his honour at the Ramada Renaissance Hotel. Delivering a rambling talk in his relaxed, genial drawl, he stumbles just once, suddenly choking on emotion.

He's been speaking about how good it feels to come home, how wholehearted Saskatoon's welcome has been, and how he might have remained part of this warm, closely knit community if life

11

had turned out differently. In a quietly moving admission, he acknowledges: "But what I didn't realize at the time, because of my ambition and excitement over becoming a professional hockey player, was that I gave up the friendship of an en- . . . excuse me . . . of an entire family . . . because of where I was playing, and where they were. Since then, we've gotten together a few times, thank God. Because it *is* a big price to pay."

A price paid willingly, even eagerly. But a price nonetheless. Being a legend doesn't come cheaply.

"Hockey legend" is a much devalued term, inflated from long overuse. But it almost seems invented to describe Gordie Howe.

For decades now, he has embodied a collective idea—call it a myth, since it's impossible to tell exactly where the reality ends and the illusion begins—that English Canadians entertain about themselves. This is all the more remarkable (and all the more Canadian) given that Howe played his entire professional career on American teams.

It's the myth of the quintessential hockey player. Supremely skilled on the ice, rugged physically, resourceful mentally, tough, even mean when need be, a man who can handle himself so well his opponents keep their distance out of respect, he is at the same time an unassuming gentleman off the ice—modest, decent, self-deprecating, and always, always a credit to his sport, his family and himself. That model has been replicated thousands of times over the years, in small Canadian towns and large Canadian cities. And no one fulfils it better than Howe.

Canadians approve of such an unlikely combination of virtues. And they approve of the fact that, during nearly fifty years in the public eye, Howe has never visibly disgraced himself. It's unthinkable that he'd ever behave like a mere mortal hockey star: insulting the fans like Ted Lindsay, say, or slugging a referee like Maurice Richard; becoming embroiled in media controversies over wife-battering or implicated in sexual misdemeanours; getting charged with drunk driving or spitting beer at a woman on a dance floor.

Howe's image has been so clean-cut, so virtuous, that we forget he can flash a deliciously wicked sense of humour occasionally, such as the time talk-show host Dick Cavett asked him why he didn't wear a helmet to protect his head while playing—after all, he wore an athletic protector, didn't he?—and Howe is remembered to have said, "Sure, but you can always pay people to do your *thinking* for you."

The Howe legend wouldn't exist in the first place if it weren't for his genius on the ice. For many people, he long ago settled the debate about himself and Richard: Howe is generally accepted as the greatest all-round player ever to compete in the NHL, or in any other league, anywhere.

Although Wayne Gretzky came along and shattered Howe's scoring records in an era of more wide-open, offensive hockey, Howe rewrote the record book against some of the finest goaltending the sport has ever seen. He held sway during the golden age of defensive hockey, when twenty goals a season was the standard of scoring excellence. And Howe, in addition to lasting far longer than Gretzky is likely to, never required the services of a bodyguard. He wasn't only great, he was tough. He stood up to them all, bar none.

The most glowing accolades ever bestowed on Howe have come from those in the best position to know, the real experts— his opponents.

Jean Beliveau once said, "As far back as I can remember, Gordie Howe has been the greatest hockey player." Johnny Bower called him "the greatest hockey player I have ever played against." While still active in the NHL, Bobby Orr remarked, "Before I started playing hockey, Gordie Howe was my idol. Now he's still my idol." Crusty Ted Lindsay, who hasn't hesitated to criticize his old buddy and linemate over the years, told *Sport* magazine, "Gordie Howe is still the greatest all-round player."

And the Great One himself has written in his autobiography, "When I was a kid, I wanted to play, talk, shoot, walk, eat, laugh, look and be like Gordie Howe. He was far and away my favourite player . . . He's the best player ever."

Vigorous claims are still made for the Rocket. But even Richard has personally acknowledged, "I wasn't the best player in the league. I knew that." Although he occasionally claimed his biggest rival wasn't enough of a money player, Richard was once quoted as saying, "Howe is a better all-around player than I was . . . Sincerely, I have never seen a greater hockey player. I mean a more complete player. Gordie Howe does everything and does it well."

There is also the objective evidence of the record book. But even his longstanding records for career points (1,850, passed by Gretzky on October 15, 1989) and career goals (801, passed by Gretzky on March 23, 1994), or his six Art Ross trophies as leading scorer and six Hart trophies as most valuable player, only begin to hint at Howe's greatness. For consistently exceptional performance over time, he is unparalleled. While most athletic records are made to be broken, it is unlikely that anyone will ever exceed Howe's record of twenty-one all-star picks—certainly not Gretzky, with thirteen, at this late stage of his career—or Howe's phenomenal achievement of finishing in the top five NHL scorers for twenty consecutive seasons, 1950 to 1969 inclusive.

Howe's endurance records could remain unmatched in our lifetimes, given the ruinous damage today's players inflict on each other. Breaking in with Detroit in 1946 at the age of eighteen, he played twenty-five seasons with the Red Wings through 1970-71, already a record. After a two-year retirement, he emerged to play six more seasons in the World Hockey Association, then added a final season in the NHL in 1979-80 after the WHA folded, for a record twenty-six NHL seasons and a staggering 1,767 regular-season NHL games. In all, he played a grand total of thirty-two seasons—a career twice as long as the Rocket's, three times longer than Orr's.

Such longevity in professional sports is unsurpassed. Only baseball pitcher Satchel Paige, of indeterminate vintage, and English football great Sir Stanley Matthews, who played into his early fifties, have rivalled Howe's playing age by the time he retired permanently—fifty-two. George Blanda kicked field goals in the National Football League until he was forty-eight, and big-league pitcher Hoyt Wilhelm lasted until he was forty-nine. But none of these geriatric wonders competed in a sport as physically demanding or punishing as hockey.

For hockey fans over the generations, Howe has been a fixed reference point in a world of rapid, violent and unnerving change. His continuing visibility today, most recently during the retired players' triumphant court battle to recover their pension money, is a reminder that, despite all the babble about NHL market demographics and merchandising strategies and million-dollar salaries and strikes and criminal charges, hockey still belongs to those of us who love the game. If we know what hockey is *really* about, it's because we've seen Howe and the other greats in their prime, their transitory gifts leaving indelible memories of how the game can and should be played.

Unquestionably, Gordie Howe is a living legend. But behind the legend, there is a life.

CHAPTER TWO

A Little Help from His Friends

"I never thought he'd amount to anything."
—Albert Howe, exact date unknown

AS JUST ABOUT EVERYBODY KNOWS, Gordie Howe hails from Floral, Saskatchewan, a handful of homes surrounding a grain elevator nine miles east of Saskatoon. It's one of those reliable Canadian facts, neatly symbolizing the heroic journey Howe had to make, geographically and spiritually, down the railway tracks from his humble prairie origins to big-league stardom in Detroit.

"The farm boy from Floral": both Canadian and American media regularly recycle the image. The trouble is, Howe doesn't really come from Floral at all. He was born there, true enough, in his parents' farmhouse about three miles from the grain elevator. But by the time he was nine days old, the Howes would move right into Saskatoon, where Gordie would remain until leaving home to pursue his hockey destiny in the east. Howe is a Saskatoon boy, period.

In fact, his father had already begun looking for a house in the city before Gordie was born. Albert (Ab) Howe was a big, bluff labourer from Minnesota who had come across the border into Canada as a young man, seeking work and land. He was hard-working, hard-bitten and outspoken: a plain, blunt character who had no difficulty making his views known.

In some ways, Ab Howe could scarcely have been more different from the young Saskatchewan woman he married. Katherine Schultz, the soft-spoken daughter of German immigrants, worked as a domestic before her marriage. She's remembered by all as a gentle, affectionate and devoted mother. But Katherine was also tremendously hardworking, and as strong beneath her soft demeanour as Ab was on the outside. The pair shared a hardy stubbornness and an instinct for survival, which saw them through a punishing Depression (even more dragged out on the prairies than elsewhere in the country), the raising of nine children through adversity and deprivation, and a lifelong marriage. It's unlikely either Ab or Katherine dreamed of producing an athletic superstar, much less a national icon. They just wanted to get by, and to teach their kids to stand on their own two feet. There were times when they wondered whether their sixth-born, Gordon, would ever make it.

If Gordie Howe is a more complex and even contradictory man than he at first appears, or than his public image suggests, it's because of his very mixed legacy from these two people. He is by turns self-deprecating and proud; introverted and outgoing; kindly and aggressive; excessively dependent and boldly risk-taking; guilelessly naive and shrewdly down-to-earth. He acquired these potent contradictions from Katherine and Ab, and combined them with his own natural gifts to create two fairly distinct personalities—his Ab side typically on display on the ice, his Katherine side off the ice. It would be a rank cliché to compare Gordie Howe to Jekyll and Hyde. But it wouldn't be so far off the mark.

In interviews, Howe has accorded his father an almost heroic status as a horseman, hunter and provider. He likes to retell family tales about Ab's hunting prowess, dating from before Gordie was born, when Ab used to earn money selling animal pelts. Ab would ride out from the Floral farm to hunt coyotes, and on days when he was too broke to buy shells for his shotgun, he'd run a coyote down on horseback, lean over in the saddle to disable it by slashing its hind leg with a hunting knife, crack its skull with a rock or fence post, and take it back to the farm to skin it. The pelts brought between $12 and $20. Hunting gophers for a one-cent bounty was far less lucrative, but a lot easier, since they could be killed down in their holes; with enough gopher corpses, Ab could at least afford to buy more shells.

Later, after the family had moved into Saskatoon, Ab worked on construction jobs and eventually became an auto mechanic, a foreman on road gangs, and finally superintendent of maintenance for the city works department. Howe has often recounted how hard his father had to work to support the large, hungry family. The old man refused to go on social assistance, and the only time he took a holiday was during harvest season, so he could earn some more money.

As a result, Gordie in his youth had a starkly different experience from most hockey-playing sons today: different, too, from young Wayne Gretzky, whose father, Walter, maintained a backyard rink and worked closely and constantly at his son's side as his first coach and mentor. By contrast, Howe's development as a hockey player was his own doing, totally independent of his father—owing more, as we'll see, to his mother and to friends and kindly neighbours. In fact, Ab was so busy, or so preoccupied, that he almost never went to watch his son's hockey games in Saskatoon. It would be many years after Gordie had become an NHL star before Ab actually saw him play in person.

Gordie Howe's entry into this world had a touch of peril about it—not unusual for that time and place.

The day he was born in Floral, March 31, 1928, his father was off earning money with his team of horses on excavation jobs in Saskatoon. The Depression hadn't begun in earnest yet, but Ab Howe was fed up with subsistence farm life, scraping a living from uncooperative soil. He was also looking for a house he could afford. Nothing fancy, not even a place with indoor plumbing, just something closer to people and work and a half-decent living for his burgeoning family.

Katherine Howe was at the farm, without benefit of doctor or midwife or telephone, when she felt her labour pains begin. In fact, she was outside chopping wood. Having already given birth five times, Katherine knew what she had to do. She drew water from the well, set it to boil on the wood stove, and made herself comfortable in bed. She gave birth right there, without adult assistance. With the newborn lying at her side, she cut the umbilical cord herself. While he slept and she waited for her husband to return, she struggled painfully out of bed and shifted packing cases around to prepare for the family's anticipated move into town.

Ab had located a suitable house. But by the time he arrived back at the farm with the horses, Katherine had begun to hemorrhage and was in serious distress. Ab mounted up and galloped to the home of his sister-in-law, Mary, whom he brought back to attend to his wife and keep an eye on the baby. Fortunately, Katherine's bleeding was quickly brought under control. When she was out of danger, she and the child travelled to Mary's home to recover, while Ab moved the rest of the family to their new place on the northwestern edge of Saskatoon. Little wonder Gordie Howe later called his mother "the strongest woman I have ever known."

After Gordie came another brother and two more sisters to round out the family, a total of four boys and five girls: in order of birth, Gladys, Vernon, Norman, Violet, Edna, Gordon, Victor, Joan and Helen. So Gordie had neither the burden of responsibility placed on the eldest children in a large family, nor the spoiling often bestowed on the youngest. As a middle child, he might easily have been overlooked or neglected, but that didn't happen—partly because his mother was such a warm and caring woman, incapable of neglecting any of her kids, and partly because he contracted various health problems requiring medical attention.

Paradoxically, the athlete who developed into such an extraordinary tower of strength and endurance well into midlife was frail and sometimes sickly as a young boy. His problems were caused principally by poverty ("poorness," Howe sometimes prefers to call it) and inadequate nutrition. The family finances were so tight that for a while they all subsisted on oatmeal porridge, eating it two or three times a day.

By the age of five or six, Gordie had developed a calcium deficiency that affected his bone density and bone marrow, particularly in his spine. He remembers the family doctor warning Mrs. Howe that if her son took a heavy blow to the body, it might break his back. Gordie was put on a regime of vitamin supplements. And in a simple, homemade but evidently effective form of physiotherapy, the doctor instructed him to exercise regularly by hanging from the top of a doorway by his arms, swinging from side to side from the hips down, to straighten his spine and strengthen his back muscles. Gordie did as he was told; a former classmate remembers him regularly chinning himself in doorways at school. "That's why my arms are so long," he jokes today. He also suffered from a goiter, an enlargement of the thyroid gland in the neck, for which he had to take iodine pills.

Howe was just five and a half when one of the most storied incidents in Canadian popular myth took place: he got his first pair of skates. It's the earliest stage in the Howe legend, and the Canadian equivalent (to stretch a point only slightly) of little George Washington cutting down the cherry tree. It's a tale that was already being told in elementary school readers a generation ago; and it illustrates not only the economic desperation of the times and the necessity for mutual help among neighbours, but the crucial role Katherine Howe played in launching her son's hockey career—not out of any particular ambition for him but through her instinctive thoughtfulness.

At the very bottom of the Depression, a poor woman came knocking at the Howes' door . . . But better to let Mrs. Howe tell the story herself, as related to former *Globe and Mail* sports editor Jim Vipond a few years before her death in 1971:

"There were a lot of people on social aid . . . A neighbour lady, whose husband was sick, came to the door with a grain sack filled with things and asked me if I would buy it to help her feed her baby. I didn't have much to offer but I reached into my milk money and gave her a dollar and a half. We dumped the contents of the sack on the floor. Out fell a pair of skates. Of course Gord pounced on them.

" 'They're mine!' he yelled. They were too big. Edna, his younger sister, and Gord each tried on a skate. They put on several pairs of stockings and out they went. The old Hudson Bay slough ran behind our house and the kids could skate for miles right out to what is now the airport. They kept coming in cold, bruised and crying but they'd go out again. Gord kept pestering Edna for the other skate until after a week he offered to buy it from her for ten cents. I gave him the dime to make the deal."

The skates were men's size six. In another interview at about the same time, Mrs. Howe added: "When Gordie first tried to skate with both of them on, he was happy but exhausted. A couple of years later I traded a package of his father's cigarettes for the next pair of skates . . . A man had brought them to the door." (We don't know what Ab thought about the trade.)

As the story of the neighbour lady and the grain sack was retold over the years, the amount Mrs. Howe paid increased with inflation. However little she spent in terms of today's dollars, she wasn't only offering charity; her family was large and poor enough that they could use some of the belongings in the sack, such as used clothing—as well, of course, as those famous skates.

Some hockey observers have reported hearing a variant of the story. In that version, it's the lady appearing at the door who is offering charity, saying, "I'm sure someone here could use these skates." But Howe himself corroborates his mother's version, in all but the detail of how he acquired the second skate. In a 1992 interview for the program *June Callwood's National Treasures*, aired on Vision-TV, he recalled, "They always say if you give, you'll get twice as much back. It was through the kindness of my mother— she took a couple of hard-earned dollars, either one or two or whatever it was. There was a lady who was trying to feed her family during the Depression and she needed some milk money, so my mother gave it to her. She in return gave her a gunny sack, and when that was dropped out onto the linoleum, there was a pair of skates fell out. My sister grabbed one, I grabbed one, and we went outside. We skated around on the pond at the back of the house. She got cold and went in and took the skate off, and that was the last she ever saw of it. I fell in love with hockey that day. I couldn't get enough of it. On the weekends, I never took the skates off."

On those weekends, Gordie and thirty or forty other kids would play on the frozen slough as long as they could. Using weighted-down jam tins for goalposts, they'd chase a puck up and down the immense natural ice surface and endure ravening cold that routinely descended to 25°F or 30°F below zero. The chill would be heightened by fierce prairie winds whipping into their faces and clothing, and whenever Gordie and his brothers or sisters caught a touch of frostbite, Mrs. Howe treated it with cold water on cheeks, fingers and toes. But weather was just weather. It didn't deter Gordie from playing the game he'd fallen in love with.

"I think I was immune to the cold," he says now. His mother would put newspapers down on the kitchen linoleum so that he and his brothers and friends wouldn't have to remove their skates while eating lunch. Then they'd go back outside onto the ice for hours.

But Gordie didn't have an easy time of it during those early years; he'd developed into a painfully shy child. Sometimes his sensitivity and self-consciousness were so extreme that he was nearly crippled socially. For a CBC radio documentary in 1966, Katherine Howe described her young son's difficulties in dealing with the other boys. "He was a little clumsy and awkward, you know, because he was growing so fast. The other boys used to tell him, 'Get out of the road!' or something, and he'd come home crying. And I'd say, 'Well, don't cry, you're strong enough, just get out there and look after yourself, because I can't be around all the time.'"

Somehow during those years, with all she had to do at home, Mrs. Howe did find time to encourage her son and even to be his playmate occasionally. She once told a Saskatoon television interviewer that Gordie would say, "C'mon, Mom, let's play hockey," and they'd find a couple of sticks and knock a stone around for a puck. Today Howe says he doesn't remember such times—perhaps the only point in recent memory on which he's contradicted his mother.

Ab Howe was less patient with his son. On the radio documentary just mentioned, Ab spoke in his gravelly voice, in the homespun style of a born raconteur, about his own memory of Gordie's "backwardness":

"He was awful backward, you know, awful backward. Even after he played hockey, he wouldn't go into a store and buy an ice-cream cone. We was going to stop for a drink one night, and we give him a quarter: 'Go on in and get yourself a pop or an ice cream.' And he come out, and we said, 'Did you get your ice cream, Gordon?' And he said, 'No. You go get it.' And I said, 'You'll wait a long time, boy—you got to get in there and hustle for yourself.'"

This was Ab's ruling principle, the primary lesson he felt he had to teach his bashful son. Just as young Gordie strengthened his

physical backbone with exercise and, later, hard labour on construction sites, Ab tried to ensure, in the only way he knew, that
Gordie strengthened his emotional backbone. With characteristic
forthrightness, Ab stated his approach in another interview in the
early 1960s. "The first time [Gordie] tried to join one of the small
teams here they sent him home because he wasn't dressed properly
or something and I was hopping mad. Ever since then I've always
told him to never take any dirt from nobody, because if you do,
they'll keep throwing it in on you. That's the way life is."

The old man's dictum eventually took—on the ice, at least.
Howe was to make it his very own. No player ever took less dirt in
the NHL, or so excelled at repaying dirty hits with interest.

But in a different sense, Ab's brusque approach could very well
have had a negative, discouraging influence, to judge from another
published remark: "[Gordie] was clumsy and backward and bashful. That's why I never thought he'd amount to anything."

If this assumption filtered down to young Gordie, as it inevitably must have, the fact that he later "amounted" to so much
suggests a tremendous inner strength, a proud, stubborn deter-
mination to overcome the limits his father had placed on him.

Evidently Ab's negative attitude was picked up by at least some
other family members. Ab himself once told a reporter, "I can
recall his brother Vic always yelling at him, 'Gordie, when are you
going to learn to stand on your own two feet?' "

To some extent, this family attitude reinforced Gordie's learning
difficulties and low self-esteem at school. Katherine Howe remembered other students nicknaming him "Doughhead." He's often
confirmed this childhood insult, and even now will drop the occasional comment seeming to belittle his own intelligence, as if out of
long habit, even though, as his mother attested, he was always much
brighter than people thought. "That ['doughhead'] means 'stupid',"
Mrs. Howe remarked, "or someone who doesn't know anything,
and Gordie was never stupid. It used to bother him, too, but he'd
never fight with the kids because he was so much bigger than most
of them and he was always aware of that advantage."

The worst of the disparaging taunts came during his years at
Westmount public school, which he attended from grades one
through four. He was required to repeat grade three twice, there

being no policy of automatic promotion in those days. The frustration he experienced as a result of his apparent learning disability was compounded by his reluctance to put himself forward to seek help.

The way his mother described it, "He always tried, but the second time he failed the third grade it took the heart right out of him. I remember seeing him coming down the street crying. 'Is the work too difficult?' I asked him. 'Don't you understand the teacher? Do you ask her questions about what you don't understand?'

" 'No, Ma, I don't want to bother her.' Then we both had a good long cry."

Howe discussed these humiliations on television with June Callwood, acknowledging that they helped him sympathize with a former NHL opponent, Eddie Shack. Although Shack has achieved considerable business success in spite of his handicap, he is severely dyslexic. Howe never suffered a disability as serious as Shack's, but he did have to endure the ridicule of classmates: "I was a little slow at the start, then things fell into line, so I know a little bit what Eddie went through. We had to get up in front of the class and read, and they used to laugh, and that *really* bothered me."

Howe likes to joke that the other kids decided he was smart enough after all when he grew so much bigger than they were. But, as his mother had noted, he actually hesitated to take advantage of his size. The real reason for his growing self-confidence as he neared adolescence was that he began discovering and using his natural athletic gifts—especially his exceptional eye-hand coordination, which is another form of intelligence, and which he'd term later in life "a God's gift." It's what enabled him to shoot a puck, kick a soccer ball, hit a baseball, golf, ski, water-ski, and cast a fly so much better, and with so much more success, than ordinary mortals.

As he developed those gifts through games and sports, young Howe gradually acquired a stronger belief in himself. Even though his athletic successes didn't eradicate his shyness, they increasingly enabled him to make friends, attract praise and have fun. Little by little, life wasn't such a struggle after all. He could be happy.

Howe and his boyhood friends had plenty of happy days growing up in Saskatoon in the late 1930s and early '40s. In the summer, there was the South Saskatchewan River to swim or fish in, or to navigate on big logs floating downstream beneath the high walls of the chateau-like Bessborough Hotel. One friend recalled how the boys would steal "old Doc Bolton's crabapples and entertain his nurses at night" by lobbing the crabapples at windows. Or they'd walk across the old Grand Trunk Railway bridge over the river to the golf course, hiding in the bushes waiting for drives gone astray, then pouncing on the balls before the golfers arrived and selling the balls back to them three holes later. They'd raid the Chinese market garden, returning across the bridge with their pockets full of vegetables, until they heard a train coming: "You'd have to dive for a water barrel, and water barrels were few and far between on the bridge. It meant sometimes you'd have to get off and hang onto the trestle. If our parents had ever seen us, they'd have skinned us alive."

Contrary to his social shyness and agonizing self-consciousness at school, young Gordie had a daredevil's courage. Sometimes he'd accept a dare to swing from a rope suspended under the steelwork of the Grand Trunk bridge. Once he was playing in a barn with some other boys, jumping from one crossbar to another under the eaves, and lost his footing; he fell to the floor and was knocked unconscious, and a friend ran to the house screaming in panic, "Mrs. Howe, Mrs. Howe, Gordie has killed hisself!"

On another occasion, he built himself a pair of stilts, but Ab warned him to stay off them because they weren't safe. Unable to resist the temptation to try out his handiwork, Gordie was humping down the street on the stilts when he saw his father coming towards him. Fearing Ab's anger and punishment, he was suddenly seized with alarm, lost his balance and fell over onto an iron fence, impaling himself on a railing. He barely escaped serious and possibly permanent injury.

As he grew older, Gordie spent more and more time playing team sports, in pickup games and in organized leagues at the school and community levels. He was emerging as a superb natural athlete who excelled year-round at softball, soccer, track and field, and any other sport he attempted. But hockey was his abiding passion.

Even in the summers he'd prepare for the hockey season. He'd practise his shot endlessly, improving its speed and accuracy by shooting at a barrel with the ends removed that he'd set against the side of the family home. The siding on the house, constructed of wooden shingles, got bombarded so heavily by pucks and tennis balls that many of the shingles ended up lying on the ground—too many to suit Ab, who administered the strap to his son's behind as punishment for damaging rented property. Later, Ab thought better of it and helped Gordie obtain a large piece of plywood as a backstop.

In utter contrast to today's norm of artificial ice and technically sophisticated hockey gear, Gordie and his pals played with nothing but the most minimal, primitive equipment. If nobody owned a puck, anything would do as a substitute: a chunk of ice, a tennis ball (although they got awfully heavy when frozen rock-hard) or what the kids called "road apples"—nice and spherical and hardening quickly after being deposited steaming on the street by the horses drawing the milk wagons. Howe says he and his pals "used to kid about chasing a horse for the next puck."

Hockey sticks and skates were at a premium, especially for West End boys, and secondhand equipment was better than none. Howe and his buddies would jump at a broken stick discarded by some better-off kid, repair it as best they could with tape, and play with it as long as it lasted. Sticks left untended by careless owners soon disappeared. And as young feet outgrew their skates, it wasn't simply a matter of going shopping for a bigger pair; sometimes Gordie had to wear blades strapped onto an old pair of shoes.

Hockey pads were rich kids' luxuries. Magazines or Eaton's catalogues took the place of shin pads, and hockey gloves or shoulder pads were things you could only dream about. A boyhood friend of Howe's recalled on radio, "As far as equipment was concerned, you had a pair of skates and a stick, if you were lucky. You'd borrow your dad's mitts and you'd be out on that school rink from the time day broke until it was dark."

Howe related how a friend's misfortune was once his ticket onto a Saskatoon peewee team, after he'd been rejected earlier for not having the equipment. "A friend fell through the ice of the Hudson Bay slough and caught a terrible case of pneumonia on the way home. He had these skates with a terrific pair of nickel-plated blades. My friend's dad said, 'Are you trying out for peewee?' and

I said, 'No, I don't have the equipment,' and he said, 'Well, you do now.' He gave me the whole sack and I went down and made the peewee Red Wing club."

It wouldn't be the last time Gordie and his career benefited from the kindness and concern of neighbours. Over the next few years, until the very day he left Saskatoon for good, his development as a hockey player would depend, in addition to his own great talent and hard work, on just such acts of generosity.

Throughout Howe's youth, his most influential benefactors were female. His mother's support was crucial. At least two other caring women, Frances Hodges and Doris Crawford, also made a vital difference by understanding and appreciating the big, clumsy kid, whose "backwardness" seemed to irritate men while attracting maternal protectiveness.

Mrs. Crawford died in 1972, but Mrs. Hodges, now in her eighties, still resides in Saskatoon. Howe's sister, Joan Clark, recalls that, of all the adults who played a part in his early hockey career, it was Mrs. Hodges "who helped Gord the most."

There was a relative absence of male coaches and role models at the time because of the war. After 1939, many Saskatoon men, including Gordie's two older brothers, Vern and Norm, were away serving in the armed forces; others were like Ab Howe, working long hours to make ends meet in an era of scarcity. Hence the women were more likely to be available to help a boy growing up. This was the case with Frances Hodges, whose husband, Bert, was one of the organizers and coaches of the King George Athletic Club; since Bert's job with Canadian National Railways often took him away from home, Frances assumed his hockey duties more often than not.

With two hockey-playing sons of their own, the Hodges maintained a regulation-size rink in their backyard, near the small, two-storey frame house where the Howes now lived at 633 Avenue L South, kitty-corner from King George school. The Howes' house was cramped, and the children still living at home had to double up in the bedrooms. Mrs. Clark remembers her brother spending all his spare time on the Hodges' ice, playing shinny or just practising his moves. And as she also recalls,

"Us girls wanted to play too, but we were never welcome—the guys wouldn't let us."

Mrs. Hodges, now a widow, retains crystal-clear images of "Gordon" from the age of about ten—images of his single-minded devotion to hockey and of his appealing personality. Indeed, if single-mindedness is one of the attributes of genius, Howe displayed it from an early age.

"We'd wake up in the morning to see Gordon out there skating on the rink," she recalled recently, "all by himself. He was a beautiful skater. Sometimes he had to clear the snow off first, but he didn't mind."

Circling the Hodges' ice, picking up speed as he perfected that rather peculiar kinesthetic process known as stick-handling—skating while moving a puck back and forth between opposite sides of a stick blade and simultaneously propelling it forward—the young Howe could leave his school difficulties and classroom humiliations so far behind that for a blissful while they ceased to exist. On the sanctuary of the ice, he was fulfilled, so totally absorbed by the pleasures of hockey that he often stayed on the Hodges' rink long after dark.

"He knew what he wanted, and he got it," Mrs. Hodges said. "It could be the coldest night of the year, but Gordon would be out there practising all by himself."

In Mrs. Hodges's memory, Gordie was likeable as well as determined. His nature still shines for her down through the years: "He was a very quiet, gentlemanly young man, no trouble at all. You didn't have to ask him to do anything, like carrying the sticks for the team—he'd just pick them up and shoulder them." She attributes his considerate behaviour to his upbringing by his mother, describing her as "a wonderful lady, a very friendly, nice person who influenced Gordon a lot."

Since he could never get enough of hockey, Howe belonged to as many different teams as he could. Between the ages of ten and fourteen, in addition to school hockey and the Kinsmen's peewee league, he played in a house league run by the King George Athletic Club, a year-round community organization providing boys in the West End with sports activities—baseball in the summer and hockey in the winter. Mrs. Hodges was the club's treasurer and chief organizer, and she coached one of the hockey teams along with her husband. Another coaching couple were the Crawfords: Buck, still living in Saskatoon, and his late wife, Doris.

According to Buck Crawford, the athletic club set up a rink with boards, overhead lighting and a wooden shack on a vacant lot at the corner of Avenue J and Seventeenth Street, not far from the Howe residence, across from a fuel company selling coal and wood. The company donated coal for the club to burn in an old potbellied stove inside the shack, where the boys could put on their skates and warm up between periods—or, when it was 30°F or 40°F below, between shifts. Games were on Tuesday and Thursday nights, and the boys contributed twenty-five cents each to help pay for the lighting. But many were so poor they couldn't afford hockey sticks; Crawford remembers buying a dozen sticks and distributing them to the players in need.

"Gordie played four years with us," he recalls. "The first year he had no skates, so he played goal. The next year he got hold of a pair of skates someplace, and we had him on defense."

To Crawford, Gordie was "quiet, a little backward, never troublesome—a sincere sort of kid." Crawford refereed the games and left the coaching to his wife, who was called "Dot" for short. In those early years, Dot helped Gordie get his skates on the right feet; eventually, says her husband, she became "sort of like a mother to him. He had a lot of faith in my wife, and she worried about him like he was her own son. She'd listen to him, and he'd tell her everything, things he wouldn't tell me."

The friendship between Gordie and Mrs. Crawford continued long after he'd left home and was playing in Detroit. In the off-season he'd come home and visit the Crawfords' house: "He'd tell the wife everything that had happened to him. He was still a kid. He kept coming a few times after he first got married, then not at all for years."

On his King George school team, young Howe followed the same pattern of starting out as a goalie before moving up to defense and forward. In fact, his school coach, King George vice-principal Robert Trickey, later acquired a modest notoriety for at first advising his famous pupil that he'd have to stay in nets if he ever wanted to play hockey beyond Saskatoon. But the late Mr. Trickey soon saw the virtue of playing Howe up front. The school won the league championship in 1941 and 1942 and then again in 1944, the year Gordie was captain and his team went undefeated, outscoring its opponents by 106 to 6 in eleven games.

For the boy who had formerly been the butt of jokes and insults, hockey prowess brought with it a new stature at school. But he still carried himself meekly and modestly, his mother's son. Years later, Robert Trickey would observe, a touch pompously: "One of the outstanding characteristics about Gordon, as far as a teacher is concerned, is his kindliness. I can honestly say that never at any time did he cause me any disquieting moments when he was a student. Gordon didn't need to make himself noticed in ways that were, from a teacher's point of view, unacceptable."

In the winter of 1942, as he was about to turn fourteen, Howe was playing bantam hockey for both the school team and the King George Athletic Club. For the club, Mrs. Hodges and Gordie himself, it was a banner year; he played on the team that made it all the way to the provincial finals.

In a two-game, total-points, home-and-home series against Regina's bantam champions, Saskatoon tied the first game away but lost the second at home, losing the round by a total score of 10 to 6. Howe scored five of Saskatoon's six goals, even though he was playing defense because the team needed his size on the blueline. He attracted the attention of a Saskatoon *StarPhoenix* sportswriter covering the series: "Howe was a standout both defensively and on attack. Big and fast, he scored his three goals [in the first game] unassisted and looks like a good prospect for the future."

Frances Hodges has another type of memory of that time. "Ab Howe was a great storyteller, all about how he promoted his son in hockey. But when it came down to it, it was Gordon's mom and older sisters who saw he had equipment. His five sisters were real nice girls, big boosters who used to come and watch him play. Now, when the team travelled to Regina, the parents paid the shot. But the old man just wasn't interested: 'If you want to take my son to Regina, fine, but don't ask me to pay for it.' So I went to King George school to see the principal. I told him I was having trouble getting paid for Gordon and he wrote out a cheque. Gordon's sister Vi helped out with pocket money."

As Mrs. Hodges sagely observed: "No one gets where he is without help."

A photograph of the King George A.C. bantams shows Gordie as the tallest player on the team. He's standing in the centre of the back row, right beside his coach and protector Mrs. Hodges. At fourteen, he's virtually reached his full adult height of just over six feet. His face is elongated and handsome, his features finely sculpted below a thick shock of light-brown hair. His eyes remain intently serious and watchful, his lips apart in uncertain anticipation.

By that time, Gordie had been entertaining daydreams of hockey glory for years, innocent enough fantasies shared by innumerable boys his age. Like the other kids, he listened to Foster Hewitt broadcasting Toronto games from Maple Leaf Gardens on winter Saturday nights. Like the other kids, he saved the labels from tins of Bee Hive corn syrup and mailed them faithfully off to Toronto in return for photographs of NHL players. "All of us kids would go up and down the alleys looking in the ash cans for the labels," he recalled; he pasted so many photos into his scrapbook that it came apart at the seams. And like the other kids, he fantasized about playing in the NHL himself when he was older. He even practised his signature over and over, the autograph that would be in such overwhelming demand one day, trying out different versions and asking his mother which version he ought to use when he became a star.

Young Gordie liked to hang around outside the Saskatoon Arena, waiting for the arrival of the Saskatoon Quakers and their opponents in the old senior Western Hockey League, so he could carry their equipment into the arena and watch the game for free. Sometimes he'd get a used stick out of it, as he did from one of his first hockey heroes, Quaker forward Ab Welsh.

Once, a player with the visiting Flin Flon Bombers gave him an old pair of elbow pads. Another time, a young Flin Flon centre named Sid Abel let Gordie carry his skates. A couple of years later, Abel was playing in the NHL with Detroit; when the Red Wings came to town for an exhibition game, young Howe went to Abel's hotel room and once again asked if he could carry his equipment. And much later still, having acted on his fantasies, Howe would find himself playing alongside Abel, by then a veteran of both the NHL and the war, when they comprised two-thirds of the legendary Production Line.

Another local hero in the early 1940s was the Boston Bruin, later Toronto Maple Leaf, forward Mel (Sudden Death) Hill, who used to return to Saskatoon after the hockey season and cruise around town in his fancy convertible. Staring at Hill in admiration and envy, young Gordie began getting ideas—*that's* what he wanted to be. At home, he'd sit at the kitchen table, leafing through the merchandise displayed in the Eaton's catalogue and circling items he was going to buy for his mom someday when he was earning big money in the NHL.

At fourteen, Howe was still a gawky dreamer. But the condition wouldn't last much longer. He had no idea how quickly he'd be called upon to turn his rosy, adolescent fancies into gritty reality, or how challenging, difficult and painful the transition would be for him.

CHAPTER THREE

Leaving Home

"When initiation is in place, the old men help the boys
to move from the mother's world to the father's world."
—Robert Bly, *Iron John: A Book about Men*

A YEAR OR SO CAN MAKE an enormous difference to a young
man's maturity. If Gordie Howe hadn't been such a mother's boy at
fifteen, NHL history might be written very differently today. Or, to
be kinder about it, if the fifteen-year-old had already developed
the strength and independence he would exhibit even one or two
years later, the toughness to match his ambition, he'd probably
have become a New York Ranger. But he hadn't—and therefore
he'd wear a New York uniform for only a few days, and the
Rangers would spend most of the 1950s and '60s in or near the
NHL basement. And the Detroit Red Wings and their fans could
thank their lucky stars.

In 1943, the war still showed no sign of ending after four grim
years. Although many professional hockey players had signed up to
fight overseas, the NHL continued to ice six teams playing a full
schedule of fifty games. The Red Wings won the Stanley Cup that
year, the third in the team's history, led by their top scorer, Syd
Howe. Syd was from Ottawa and no relation to the Saskatoon
Howes; but earlier, when Gordie had played in the Kinsmen's
peewee league, his team had been the Red Wings, and his borrowed identity—it was the peewees' custom to assume the sweater
of an NHL star—had been that of his famous namesake.

As NHL clubs lost more players to the war effort, their scouts
became more active than ever in communities across Canada,

sniffing out new young prospects to replace the veterans. Saskat-chewan and the rest of the prairies were always a hotbed of minor-hockey talent. Inevitably, the local scouts began sniffing out Gordie Howe.

He had now completed a season of midget hockey in the Saskatoon Lions Club league, and his abilities were increasingly attracting attention. He was already a strong skater, with lots of moves and unusually deft puck control. Although he skated more often now on the smooth ice surface of the Saskatoon Arena, hanging around the place as much as he could while still attending King George, he'd later say he benefited from all those years out on frozen sloughs and natural rinks. Negotiating the bumpy, unpredictable ice outdoors meant your grip on the stick had to stay loose and light, so you could feather the puck delicately enough to keep control; if you had "cement hands" and held the stick too tightly, the puck would get away from you.

Howe's puck control made him an excellent playmaker and, combined with his fast and accurate wrist shot, a high scorer. One night in the midget league, after he'd scored nine points—three goals and six assists—a local merchant was so impressed that he gave Gordie his first pairs of new hockey gloves and shin pads.

Although still not in high school, Gordie knew he was nearing the age when he'd have to leave school and start earning a living. All the Howe kids worked by the age of sixteen. As his sister, Joan Clark, explained, this was necessary to ease the family's financial burden: "In those days, when you turned sixteen you went to work and started paying for your room and board."

So far, Gordie's work experience had been confined to manual labour. Ab Howe hired him for two summers to help out on construction jobs where Ab was foreman. Any suggestion that this amounted to favouritism could have been countered by the fact that Gordie was a willing worker and exceptionally strong, able to do the work of two men.

"Best man I ever had," Ab remembered. "Had him on the mixer with his brother Vern. He could pick up a cement bag in either hand—ninety pounds. Weren't the weight so much as you couldn't get a grip on them, the sacks were packed so tight. He'd pick them right up by the middle. His brother played out in two days, but Gordon, he liked that mixer."

This was one time when Ab didn't dilute his admiration with faint praise or backhanded compliments. "He was strong, all right. Fella came with some counterweights for a dragline in the back of his truck, and Gordon says, 'Mr. Driscoll, you want these off?' Well, it weren't a one-man job, but Driscoll, he winks at me and says, 'Sure, Gord, right over there.' Lifted 'em out of there like it was nothing. Driscoll like to fall over."

Ab was big and powerfully built himself, and Gordie had inherited his physique. Ab liked that, seeing himself reflected in his son. One time, the two of them were together on a job when three other men vainly tried to manhandle a large boulder into the back of a truck. Ab waved them off, summoned Gordie to his side and whispered, "Now, don't let me down." The two Howes shouldered the rock into the truck with ease.

Lacking body-building equipment or a weight-training program, Howe built his spectacular shoulder, chest and arm muscles that way. The Adams brothers of Saskatoon, who used to play hockey with him at their farm, remember him working for their father's cement company and "throwing cement bags around as if they were nothing." Later, Howe termed this work "a kind of weight-lifting program I didn't know I had." Instinctively, he knew the rugged labour would be good for his hockey career; in a very few years, he'd be known as one of the NHL's most physical competitors.

The first serious call from the NHL came in the person of a New York Rangers scout named Russ McCrory. McCrory visited the Howe home and propositioned Ab, Katherine and their son on behalf of his organization, outlining what the Rangers could offer in the way of training, minor-league experience, education and, eventually, money. He must have been persuasive: the Howes agreed that Gordie should attend the Rangers' tryout camp in Winnipeg later that summer. Gordie was heading, if not to the big time, at least a big step closer in that direction, and a step away from some labouring job that would use his muscles but little else. Physically, he was ready to answer the call—but not, as it turned out, emotionally.

When Howe stepped off the train in Winnipeg, it was the first time he'd been away from Saskatoon or his parents for any length of time, apart from the brief visit to Regina with the bantams the year before. This time he made the trip alone. Winnipeg seemed huge compared to either Saskatchewan city, its streets and buildings strange and imposing. He asked directions to the Marlborough Hotel, and once he'd found it, discovered he'd be rooming with another young lad, a would-be Ranger goaltender from the Lakehead.

"I was terribly lonely when I hit Winnipeg," Howe recalled. "The unfortunate part was that I was the only one out of the Saskatoon area."

A familiar face or two might have helped. But he saw only strangers when he joined the other rookies from all over western Canada in the old Amphitheatre, where the tryouts were being held. They signed in and were issued their equipment by the trainer, then sent to the dressing room to get ready. This presented Howe with a serious dilemma: he'd never worn some of the equipment before, such as the shoulder pads and jockstrap, and wasn't sure how to put them on.

Embarrassed by his ignorance, playing for time, he dumped the equipment at his feet and looked around. "I didn't say much, but I observed what was going on and dressed according to the fellow across from me. Don't know who he was, but every piece he put on, I put on the same way. I've been dressing the same way ever since."

His hesitation didn't go unnoticed by the other young men. They laughed and hooted and teased him, just as the kids had in the old days during reading in grade three. He was ready to throw in the towel and run back to Saskatoon then and there.

Out on the ice for the first practice, Howe encountered some of the veterans who had helped the Rangers win the Stanley Cup in 1940, such as Ott Heller and Alf Pike; there were also the Warwick brothers, Grant and Bill, who much later would lead Canada to a world hockey championship with the Penticton Vees. But Howe's next problem was even more disastrous for his roommate, the goalie: "On the first day of practice, he took a puck right in the mouth from one of the Warwicks, which ended his career, as a matter of fact, in a hurry. That left me rooming alone, which was worse yet."

To that point, the whole experience had been a little like going to the war that he was still too young to fight in.

Then there was the challenge of feeding himself. The Rangers had a training table set up for the players in the hotel. "We'd walk down the training table, and I was looking in awe at all the players, all these big fellows lined up to eat. They weren't pushing me out of the way, but it was just my backwardness, I think, that I stood back watching them. Then I found that time was so short, I couldn't get in to eat. So Alf Pike [a player who would later coach the Rangers] stepped in and took me by the hand and pushed a few fellows out of the way and said, 'Let the kid eat.' Then he drove me over to the rink in his big car—and it *was* big, because I remember my Dad pushing an old Model T around."

Despite Pike's kindness, the camp didn't get much better for Howe: he continued feeling miserably lonely and homesick the whole week. Even so, his playing ability impressed the famed Ranger bosses, manager Lester Patrick and coach Frank Boucher, enough that they wanted to make him New York property. But when they called him to their suite in the hotel to sign him to what was known as a C-form, Howe told them no, thank you. If they didn't mind, he just wanted to return home to his family.

It's said that Patrick kicked himself for years afterward for letting Howe slip away. But the shy, fearful teen-ager hadn't really given him much choice, not even when the Rangers offered him a scholarship to attend high school at Notre Dame College in Wilcox, Saskatchewan, home of Father Athol Murray's cele-brated hockey program: "The Rangers wanted me to go to Notre Dame school, and I thought it might be a pretty good idea. But I wanted to go back home and be with my friends, so I didn't sign any card."

Much later, Howe would say he regretted not having seized that opportunity to further his education. But for the time being, he just felt relieved to get safely back to Saskatoon. He reentered the familiar, comfortable confines of his old life, playing minor hockey, practising at the Arena whenever possible, helping out Mom and Dad, trying to finish grade eight. Meanwhile, as the year progressed, another NHL scout was nosing around, one who would have considerably more luck with the "backward" hot prospect.

When Fred Pinkney wasn't acting as timekeeper for the Saskatoon Quakers, he worked as a scout for the Detroit Red Wings. Buck Crawford, from Howe's King George Athletic Club days, relates that Pinkney had been observing young Gordie for some time, going back to his bantam period: "Fred asked me once if we had any good players. I said, 'I've got one that'll be in the NHL before he's eighteen. Come to a game and see for yourself. And if you don't want him, I'll tell Johnny Walker about him.' " [Walker was a Saskatoon railroad engineer who scouted for New York on the side.]

Pinkney visited the Athletic Club rink and asked Crawford to point Howe out to him.

"I said, 'I'll point him out all right—he'll score a goal in a couple of minutes,' " Crawford remembers.

"So I told Gordie, 'You get busy and score a goal fast, there's someone watching you.' And Gordie took the puck from the face-off and skated down the ice and put it in the net.

"I told Fred, 'That's the one. He's a natural.' "

Eventually Pinkney visited the Howes at home, just as Russ McCrory had. According to Crawford, "He made a deal with the old man. Pinkney wanted to sign Gordie to a C-form, which was all you needed to obtain the NHL rights to a player. But Gordie had to be sixteen first, so Pinkney gave Ab $100 to phone him the night before Gordie turned sixteen."

Other scouts were also interested in Gordie's rights. In late 1943 and early 1944, they kept sending the Howes letters and telegrams seeking permission to talk contract. But every time a telegram arrived, Mrs. Howe was terrified the worst had happened to one of her sons, Vern or Norm, who were both serving overseas. Ab didn't want his wife upset. "This was wartime, y'know," he explained in an interview. "So I sat down and wrote each one, 'Please refrain from sending telegrams.' If they wanted to see us about Gordon, come to the house. Which they did."

The story of Gordie's initial reluctance to commit himself to the

Wings reveals a striking, even poignant ambivalence in his ambition to become a hockey star, an echo of his misgivings at the Rangers' camp the previous year.

When Fred Pinkney came to the house with a C-form in his pocket, Ab was in the process of hanging a door. "I was hangin' a door that day, and he said, 'Is Gordie home?' And I said, 'Yes, he is. Well,' I said, 'just a minute now. This kid's good—I know he's good, you know he's good. But don't burn him out.'

" 'Oh no,' [Pinkney] said, and he gave me the rundown of the Detroit farm teams. And it suited me all right, so I said, 'Okay, go in and see him.'

"I'll bet you [Gordie] was half an hour before he put his name on that paper."

The Red Wings' 1944 tryout camp would be taking place in Windsor, Ontario, much farther away than even Winnipeg. Howe would say wistfully years later, "It was a million miles between Saskatoon and the Red Wings." The first thing he wanted to know from Fred Pinkney that day was whether any other Saskatoon players would be attending the camp; he remembered too vividly how alone and isolated he'd felt the year before. Pinkney assured him he'd have lots of company on the train trip east, including Gerry Couture and Pat Lundy from Saskatoon (both of whom would eventually play for Detroit).

But Ab was impatient with young Gordon. "He wasn't too swift about making up his mind, and I had work to do."

On that point, Howe later commented: "I didn't know what the heck was going on, to tell you the truth. I had two outfits around me, the New York Rangers and the Red Wings." It bothered him to think that by choosing one, he'd have to let the other down.

In the end, Ab decided to give his son a little push to help him resolve his uncertainty. He recalled asking Gordie:

" 'Do you want to play hockey?'

"And he said, 'Yes.'

" 'Well,' I said, 'then I think here's your opportunity. If you don't want to, say so. But I gotta hang that door!' "

It was Ab's shining moment as a father: he left the final decision up to his son.

"I liked the idea of going all the way down to Windsor with the fellows," Howe said later.

There were nearly two dozen of them in the sleeping car that rolled across the country in early September 1944, prairie boys going east, most of them for the first time. The trip took two full days and two nights, so there was time to make friends, time to watch the landscape change from the familiar yellow wheat fields to the green, dark forest to the rocky-shored vastness of Lake Superior and back to farmland in Ontario, time to prepare for the biggest adventure yet—a real shot at professional hockey. If it all seemed more real to Howe than the Winnipeg tryout, it was because he was a year older and that much readier.

Wanting him to make the best of the opportunity, Fred Pinkney had bought his discovery a brand-new suit and a pair of shoes. He knew Gordie had no spending money, so he'd stuck a five-dollar bill into the suit pocket, along with the train ticket to Windsor. This small investment was a statement of Pinkney's faith, not only in his young NHL prospect but in his own professional judgement. He had a strong hunch Howe could make the big time, but at sixteen a lot of things still had to jell.

Once in Windsor, Howe was practically within sight of the Red Wings' home building, Olympia Stadium, standing just to the north across the Detroit River. It was just after Labour Day. The Allies were pushing the German forces back across Europe, and the automotive economies of Windsor and Detroit, after languishing through the Depression, were pulsating with wartime production. In the old Windsor Arena, a different war was being waged as Red Wing veterans fought to keep their jobs safe from hungry minor-league upstarts and raw prairie teen-agers.

At the first practice, Howe and the other youngsters found themselves circling the ice with stars whose photographs and cards they'd only recently been collecting: forwards Syd Howe, Joe Carveth, Carl Liscombe and Mud Bruneteau; defensemen Bill Quackenbush and Flash Hollett. The Red Wings had finished second the previous season behind Montreal but had been eliminated by Chicago in the semifinals. Liscombe had been their top scorer that year, followed by Syd Howe, who had scored an extraordinary six goals in one game against the Rangers.

The man who had built the Detroit franchise over the years, jowly Jack Adams, was still coach as well as general manager. Adams hated losing. The previous season's outcome hadn't pleased him, and he was seeking new blood to revitalize his line-up, especially since three of his star players, Sid Abel, "Black Jack" Stewart and Harry Watson, were still away at war. Adams used to joke that, during the war years, he'd take a look at anybody to plug the holes in his team: "Anybody who had a pair of skates and a 4-F card and wasn't in the army, we used him."

Adams's scouts were under orders to send him all the promising young players they could unearth from small towns across Canada. Like a prospector panning for gold, he'd check them out at training camp, keeping only the nuggets. The rest he'd send home, but not before letting them play for a few shifts on a line with some of his famous pros, giving the lads a taste of the NHL and a reason to spread the good word about the Red Wings to other potential recruits: "I figured they'd go back home and sell your club. They'd say, 'Well, they gave me a great chance.'" Adams had many less appealing characteristics, but he was a canny promoter of his team.

One recruit who would impress Adams enough to make the big time that year was a nineteen-year-old rookie left wing from northern Ontario named Ted Lindsay. Today, Lindsay recalls that training camp with a freshness that belies the half-century since then.

"It was a really hot September toward the tail end of the war. A lot of the Wings had wartime jobs in the Ford plants in Detroit. At camp, there wasn't enough equipment to go around—you had to wear the same stuff other guys had been wearing in the previous shift. So by the time you put it on, it was all wet and cold, and everything was made of wool and leather in those days."

Although Lindsay had a year of junior hockey left at St. Michael's College School in Toronto, Adams offered him a chance to turn pro right away. To Adams's surprise, Lindsay didn't fall all over himself with gratitude, but said that he would rather go back to St. Mike's. "I wanted to play hockey and figured I had no reason to sit on the bench. Being in the NHL didn't excite me if I wasn't going to play." Lindsay agreed to sign only after he had wangled a two-year contract out of Adams, with assurances that he'd get a regular shift and wouldn't be relegated to the minors. Adams even threw in a signing bonus.

As he sat in the stands watching the players work out under his assistant, Tommy Ivan, Adams thought he also saw something special in another youngster, a rangy, six-foot kid with a long, well-balanced stride. He watched the kid pick up the puck, skate down to the blueline, split a couple of old pros on defense, shoot and score. Later the kid drove in on net and shot right-handed, then came right back and shot again, but left-handed. Adams told him to repeat the manoeuvre. He did.

"He did so many things with the puck," Adams would recall, "and did them so easily, that he stood out. He was doing things that the other kids couldn't do. So I called him over to the boards and I said, 'What's your name, son?'

"He said, 'My name is Gordon Howe. But I'm no relation to that guy over there,' meaning Syd.

"And I said, 'Would you go to Galt to play junior?'

"He said, 'I'll go any place you want me to go.'"

Speaking after his protégé had become a star of stars, Adams was, of course, blessed with 20/20 hindsight. It enabled him to say things like, "He was one of those players who come along every fifty years, or every century," and to praise Fred Pinkney as "a real good judge of hockey talent." But even at the time, to give Adams his due, he wasn't about to let this precocious teen-ager get away and end up with some other team. At the end of the two-week camp in Windsor, Adams signed Howe for the Detroit organization, locking up his rights for what would turn out to be a twenty-nine-year association with the club.

Interestingly, in Howe's own version of the signing, he wasn't quite so quick to jump at Adams's offer. First, he wanted to know which other players were being sent to the Red Wings' junior team in Galt. He didn't want to go on his own to some unfamiliar destination where he'd be surrounded by total strangers. Adams and Ivan assured him there would be other guys there who'd been at the training camp.

Howe listened and nodded. Then, as Tommy Ivan remembered it, Gordie asked about one of his buddies from Saskatoon, Terry Cavanagh: "What about Terry? What's he going to do?"

Told by Ivan that Cavanagh would be in Galt also, Howe seemed satisfied. He said he thought it would be nice to go along to Galt with the others, but first, would it be okay if he went back home to talk it over with his folks?

"That's fine," Adams said. "You go home and talk to your parents and then come back. Bring all your clothes with you."

"I haven't got any," Howe replied.

We can assume he didn't mean that literally. But it does sound as if his wardrobe wasn't exactly extensive. In fact, Howe's only other request on signing was a Red Wings windbreaker like the ones worn by the men on the big team. Adams promised him he'd get one.

Galt, Ontario, is now incorporated into the larger municipality of Cambridge, ninety kilometres west of Toronto. Its outskirts resemble those of any other North American community today, homogenized by the chain stores and fast-food franchises of the shopping-mall culture and patrolled by teen-agers wearing Chicago Bulls jackets. But when Gordie Howe went to live in Galt in the fall of 1944, the town must have reminded him a little of Saskatoon.

Galt was somewhat smaller and older, but like Howe's hometown, it was built along both banks of a river—the Grand—and it contained a similar mixture of modest bungalows, where the working class lived, and spacious brick residences with white verandahs, for the well-to-do, up on the high ground overlooking the river. Galt also had a strong community spirit and tradition of neighbourliness. Its settlement by Scottish colonists was remembered in its street names—Bruce, Ainslie, St. Andrews, Glebe—and in its towering, steepled Presbyterian churches. Its importance as an early industrial centre of Upper Canada, powered by the surging waters of the Grand, could be seen in its window-lined stone factories, still busily engaged in manufacturing everything from shoes to farm implements and weapons of war.

After visiting with his family and friends back in Saskatoon for a few days, Gordie returned east on the train by himself. He found it a much longer and lonelier journey than the previous trip to Windsor. As he described it, he felt echoes of Winnipeg a year earlier: "I came back all alone, didn't know what to do, didn't even know where I was going to stay in Galt."

The train pulled into Galt's old-fashioned brick railway station, and to Howe's surprise, his new coach, Al Murray, intercepted him and told him to stay on board. The team was in a car up ahead, about to depart for an exhibition game in Windsor. So at least he'd get into playing hockey right away.

The only trouble was, exhibition games were all that Howe would be playing for the rest of the season. Murray, an NHL defenseman with the old New York Americans in the 1930s, explained that only a limited number of junior players could be transferred from the west to play in the Ontario Hockey Association; Detroit had been unable to arrange for Howe's transfer to play with the Galt Junior Red Wings. This meant he couldn't compete in league games, but Jack Adams still wanted him to practise with the team and get experience by playing in exhibition games. (Another version of the story, as related by Adams himself, was that the Wings couldn't obtain Howe's transfer because he was too young.)

Howe wasn't one to object. He accepted the arrangement, figuring that the best thing for his hockey career was to stay put. "I was stubborn enough to realize, and I guess smart enough," he rationalized recently, "that I'd get more out of practising [with the Galt juniors] than out of the twelve or fifteen games I'd have played out west."

It didn't hurt him, either, that Galt had a good team. A few of his new teammates would become familiar names in the NHL in the coming years: Marty Pavelich, Fred Glover, Lee Fogolin. (A year or so later, Terry Sawchuk would also be on the Galt team.) In the OHA they played against future Red Wing teammate Red Kelly of Toronto St. Mike's.

Pavelich says today that Howe's teammates in Galt recognized and appreciated his talents. "Gordie stayed all winter with us. If we'd had him playing regular-season games, we'd have had a good chance to win the Memorial Cup that year."

Like Howe, Pavelich was sixteen and had left home—Sault Ste. Marie, Ontario—to try his chances at becoming a pro hockey player. Even if it didn't work out, Pavelich was bound to have a good time. Unlike Howe, he was extroverted and sociable, and he took quickly to life in Galt. "It was a nice-sized community, and the people were nice and welcoming. You'd stay in a rooming house with a family for around $8 a week. I had three great years there—I liked it so much, I stayed on in the summer and played baseball."

The team arranged for Howe to room in another home, where his Saskatoon friend Terry Cavanagh was also living. Despite what Pavelich terms "the nice family atmosphere," Howe continued feeling homesick and out of place. Those feelings got to him particularly on the morning he was supposed to begin his high-school education.

The team had enrolled Gordie in grade nine in the venerable Galt Collegiate Institute and Vocational School. As instructed, he walked along Water Street to the school, planning to present himself at the office to register for classes. He hesitated on the sidewalk underneath a large tree. On the far side of a football field, the massive granite bulk of GCIVS reared up. The building had the castlelike quality of King George back in Saskatoon, but unlike King George's familiar red-brick warmth, this structure seemed immense and grey and cold. Its square, medieval-style towers were reminiscent of a fortress, or perhaps a prison. On the grass of the field and around the school's rounded, ornate portals, teen-aged boys and girls were gathered in groups, talking and laughing, waiting to go inside. Gordie could see how close they were; they'd probably all grown up together.

After contemplating the scene, turning over in his mind the idea of consigning himself to that alien institution with his shaky grasp of academics, Howe crossed the street instead. He headed along the railway tracks, walking until he spotted a series of factories. One of them had a "Men Wanted" sign posted. He went inside and signed up for paying work with Galt Metal Industries, which had contracts for wartime production: "I got a job at Galt Metal Industries, spot welding and grinding parts for the cooling system of Mosquito bombers. I think someone on the club must have talked to someone at the company, as they kept me away from the big presses. I guess they were worried about something happening to my hands. Jack Adams sent me some money and I got a new job at the factory. They made me sort of an inspector working on three-inch mortar shells."

GORDIE: A HOCKEY LEGEND

Howe has called his decision that morning "the biggest mistake of my life." It put a permanent end to his formal education, and today he blames his lack of schooling for an inability to express himself as well as he'd like. He also asserts that the Galt hockey management should have taken more responsibility for keeping their players in school. "I blame myself, yes. But when they [Galt Metal Industries] phoned the gentleman in charge [of the hockey team] to document who I was, he said, 'If he wants to work, let him work.' They should have thrown me back in school where I belonged."

But if he'd stayed in school, would he ever have become Gordie Howe? The only two superstars to be universally mentioned in the same breath today—Wayne Gretzky and Mario Lemieux—also dropped out of high school. Being a great hockey player often seems to be a specialized calling all on its own.

Marty Pavelich resembled Howe in being a working-class kid who preferred having a job to studying. But today Pavelich has a more forgiving attitude about the decision they both made in Galt. "You have to remember, we'd come out of a Depression, and a lot of our families didn't have much money. So we didn't think of education—we would rather work. I got my education through hockey, and it's been wonderful to me. We were looking to make some money and looking to get on."

To Pavelich, those far-off days in Galt have an almost romantic aura about them. It's a feeling reflected in a comment by his old Detroit teammate and business partner, Ted Lindsay, who says Pavelich was so personable and popular and made so many friends there that "he could have been elected mayor of Galt."

"Life was different in those days," Pavelich says. "It was a more innocent time, an exciting time. You were young and away from home, there was the excitement of the war, then the excitement of celebrating the peace."

By the time Howe, Pavelich and the rest of the Galt Red Wings celebrated the peace, it was the following August, and they were back at training camp. Pavelich would return to Galt for two more years, but Howe would move on, climbing more quickly up the professional ladder of the Detroit organization, one giant step closer to the National Hockey League. He would never play for a Canadian city again.

Breaking In

"Away from the ice he is a typical teen-age youngster.
He enjoys swing music and malted milks. He is shy and
afraid of the opposite sex."

—Detroit Red Wings' press guide on Gordie Howe, 1946

GORDIE HOWE WAS SEVENTEEN when he turned professional in
the only profession he would ever really practise. Under today's
rules, he'd have been too young even to sign with an NHL team; in
addition, he'd have been subject to the amateur draft eventually,
and so might have played anywhere in the league, depending on
the vagaries of the drafting process. But things were a lot cozier in
the 1940s. The Detroit Red Wings had held the inside track on
Gordie Howe ever since Fred Pinkney had slipped Ab Howe $100.

At just over six feet, and still 18 pounds below his eventual
playing weight of 205, young Howe was already exceptionally big
for a hockey player in that era. He was unquestionably an adult on
the ice, a man to be reckoned with. Off the ice, he was a nice,
gullible, socially unsophisticated kid. It was a contrast that would
persist for a considerable time to come.

At the Wings' 1945 training camp in Windsor, Jack Adams and
Tommy Ivan studied the improvements their promising recruit
had made during his low-key season of practices and exhibition
games in Galt. Despite Gordie's lack of game experience, they saw
he'd worked hard at developing his natural talents, and after
watching him score two goals in an exhibition game in Akron,
Ohio, they decided he was ready—if not for the big team, at least
for tougher challenges than he'd face playing in the junior ranks.
They summoned him to Adams's suite in Windsor's Norton

Palmer Hotel to give him a contract and settle the formalities of turning him pro with their number-two farm club, the Omaha Knights of the old United States Hockey League.

Adams's opening offer to the prodigy who would become hockey's greatest star was $2,200 for the season, plus $500 as a signing bonus. As an incentive, the bonus fell a little short of the $2 million that the Ottawa Senators would pay eighteen-year-old Alexandre Daigle as part of a five-year, $12-million deal in 1993. There couldn't be a better illustration of the grotesque disparity in the NHL pay scale between then and now. Still, the world was a different place in 1945, and Howe (like Daigle) had yet to prove how much he could do.

The Red Wings' offer was pretty standard for a rookie in those days. Although Jack Adams would later claim that "Howe was beginning to show signs of greatness, even at seventeen," the offer certainly represented no particular risk-taking or clairvoyance on Adams's part, no prophetic leap of faith.

But to Gordie, $2,700 was a lot of money to mention all in one breath. It promised, at least in the short term—which is long enough for most teen-agers—more financial security than Ab Howe had known back in Floral or during the early years in Saskatoon.

There was just one outstanding matter Howe wanted to clear up with "Mr. Adams," as he'd always call his boss in public (and does to this day), before he put ink on the contract. Adams recalled it years later:

"He looked at [the contract] but didn't sign it. So I asked him what was wrong, wasn't it enough money? He just looked at me and said, 'I'm not sure I want to sign with your organization, Mr. Adams. You don't keep your word.'

"Naturally, I was flabbergasted, and I asked him what he meant. 'Well,' he said, 'you promised me a windbreaker and you never gave it to me.' You can imagine how quickly I got that windbreaker. But that's how close I came to losing him."

Adams was exaggerating his anxiety for dramatic effect. Howe was no shrewd, hard-headed negotiator, then or later, as he's the first to admit; and he'd come too far up the ladder this time to bolt, as he had from the Rangers' camp in Winnipeg. It was simply an incredibly cheap price for the Detroit coach and G.M. to pay for the player he'd go on to build his franchise around.

In fact, this first bargain-basement deal would set the tone for two decades of Howe's salary negotiations. The Red Wings would grow into one of North America's wealthiest sports franchises, at least in part from Howe's playing, while he himself earned only modest increases every year. As David Cruise and Alison Griffiths observed about the windbreaker incident in their book *Net Worth*, "That one act of defiance was to last Howe 20 years."

That season, the Wings moved into the Olympia to finish their training. Howe recalls that Adams, who had served in the Canadian Army during the First World War, ran the show like a boot camp. The arena was turned into one big dormitory, with camp cots in the corridors below the stands. Adams gave the excuse that accommodation for the players was scarce in Detroit, which was booming and overcrowded because of the war, but the military-style setup perfectly suited his tightfisted and controlling style. The players were locked in at night; there were curfews and bed checks. There were also rats—not rink rats, in the old Canadian sense, but rodents.

The Olympia wasn't even twenty years old at that time, but since management wouldn't spend the money to maintain it properly, the rats proliferated. They lived on the popcorn that the fans dropped under the seats. At night, while Howe and his teammates slept, the rats came out on the prowl, so the players kept their hockey sticks handy beside their cots, just in case. "We were always killing them," Howe said later. "Sometimes we used them for pucks." It was a novel variation on the frozen horse droppings of his boyhood.

Opened in 1927 at the corner of Grand River Avenue and McGraw, the Olympia was one of a generation of big-city arenas constructed during the 1920s. Others were New York's Madison Square Garden, Chicago Stadium and Boston Garden, all built to present boxing and wrestling when those sports were at the height of their popularity. The seating rose in steep tiers—two tiers in the Olympia, three in Chicago Stadium—as perpendicularly as possible, allowing spectators a good clear view down onto the ring or rink. So even though the arenas weren't built primarily for hockey, their sight lines were excellent for hockey fans, too. If you tripped in the aisle at the Olympia, it felt as if you were going to land down at centre ice.

Although its official seating capacity was 14,200, the Olympia was often filled to bursting with standing-room spectators and fans hunkering down in the aisles, swelling attendance to well over 15,000. The place was routinely condemned by the Detroit fire marshalls as a hazard to public safety, but somehow nothing was ever done to close it; some whispered of payoffs in high places.

One who remembers the Olympia well is a man who toiled in its dank bowels for over thirty years, the Red Wings' former trainer and back-up goalie Ross (Lefty) Wilson. "Left" to his friends, Wilson was a colourful hockey character from the Original Six era to the early 1980s. He was a notorious heckler of opposition stars and referees from behind the Detroit bench, and for three decades his blaring cries could be heard throughout NHL arenas around the continent.

Now seventy-five, Lefty lives in retirement in the Detroit suburb of West Bloomfield with Lil, his live-wire wife of fifty-three years. On the floor of the Wilsons' rec room, surrounded by hockey trophies and live-action photographs and surmounted by a coat rack constructed entirely of hockey sticks autographed by NHL stars, lies an unusual souvenir: a big, circular, thick-piled red carpet emblazoned with a huge white number nine. It's the carpet that was rolled out onto the Olympia ice for Gordie Howe's retirement ceremonies in 1972, a gift Lefty later received from Number Nine himself.

But back when Lefty Wilson first met Howe, both were rookies at that 1945 training camp, battling rats and trying to impress their coaches. One day, Wilson was in the Olympia's carpentry shop when he felt something large hit his ankle. "It ran up inside my pant leg," he recounts. "For a second I didn't know what the hell it was, but I undid my belt and covered my privates. Well, it scratched me on the ass. Of course it was a rat, so I knocked it back down my leg and killed it with a broom handle."

Wilson got on the phone to the team doctor: " 'Doc, I've been either scratched or bitten by a rat,' and I gave him the story. He started laughing, then two seconds later he said, 'You get your bucket up here in a hurry for a rabies shot.' "

Wilson was nine years older than Howe, but unlike the seventeen-year-old he was struggling desperately at training camp; he began to despair of ever making it as a pro goaltender. He'd played minor-league baseball in Roanoke, Virginia, and Savannah, Georgia, done war work for General Motors in St. Catharines, Ontario, and served in the Royal Canadian Navy, but at the Wings' camp, "I couldn't stop a balloon."

He was about to quit when Adams said, "Kid, I'll tell you what I'm going to do—I'm going to send you to Omaha, Nebraska, as spare goaltender and trainer."

"I knew little about either job," Wilson recalls, "except that I'd be making more money than I'd made at General Motors. So Howe signed for $2,200 and I signed for $2,100, and we both went down to Omaha."

Arriving there with young Howe, team captain Jimmy Skinner (later a Detroit coach and scout) and the rest of the team, the Wilsons liked Omaha, a manufacturing and railway centre on the Missouri River. Lil Wilson remembers it then as "a clean, beautiful city, with very little crime." The Knights were starting their first season as a Detroit farm club, competing in the United States Hockey League against such cities as Dallas, Fort Worth, Tulsa, Minneapolis and St. Paul. They played their home games in the Aksarben (Nebraska spelled backwards) Arena and were known locally as the Omaha Aksarben Knights—hence the logo on the team sweaters, the letters AK inside the letter O.

Jack Adams also sent Tommy Ivan down to Omaha as coach. Ivan told Lefty Wilson he now had a third responsibility as well: to be a big brother watching over the younger players, especially the youngest, greenest and least worldly rookie on the team. It turned out to be a more time-consuming job than Wilson had expected.

"Gordie was a big, shy kid," he remembers, "and in Omaha they wouldn't let him into the bars. After the games Lil and I wanted to go for a beer with the boys, but we always had to take him home first."

"Somebody had to be with him," Lil chimes in. "You didn't want him to go home by himself. We had to baby-sit him."

51

"Yeah, but first he had to eat."

"And boy, could he eat! We coulda killed him! We'd take him to a coffee shop and he'd have a great big hamburger and a shake, then he'd say, 'I think I'll have another hamburger,' and I'd be kicking Lefty under the table, thinking, 'There goes our night out. I'm gonna kill this kid!'"

On the ice, Howe was a different story; he had no trouble looking after himself. Tommy Ivan discovered this early in the season, when he participated in an intra-squad game. The coach divided his players into two sides, East and West, with Winnipeg as the dividing line, and filled in personally for an injured player on the East side. Determined to show what he could do, Howe gave no quarter to his teammates *or* his coach: he rode Ivan, a diminutive man who stood only five-foot-five and hadn't played beyond the senior amateur level, out of the play and into the boards, inflicting a cut under his chin that required eight stitches. "I never knew whether it was a stick or an elbow!" Ivan said later.

Ivan had been brought into the organization as a scout in 1938. After coaching the Wings' junior teams in Galt and Guelph and serving in the Canadian Army, he was promoted quickly by Jack Adams and would eventually become his successor behind the bench. As Howe's first professional coach, who would also coach him later for seven seasons in Detroit, Ivan had more influence on Howe's playing than any other coach, including Adams—although most who filled that role later said Howe required no coaching at all.

In Omaha, Ivan paced young Howe, waiting until he'd adjusted to the rugged, competitive level of the USHL before playing him regularly. Soon Ivan decided Howe was up for it: "Gordie was a hard-nosed kid. He used to get some foolish penalties, but appeared determined to prove early he was no patsy."

Howe recalls the game in Dallas when he made that point for keeps. It was more than twenty games into the season, and Ivan still hadn't been playing him very much. A big fight broke out while Gordie was sitting on the bench, and he decided to get involved: "Somebody was beating up my roommate. I didn't like it, so I jumped over the boards and nailed him." The victim was a player Howe knew from Saskatoon: "He was big, but he wasn't the toughest guy in the world."

When Howe returned to the bench after serving a penalty for fighting, Ivan asked him, "What's the matter with you, young man? Don't you like that guy?"

Howe replied, "I don't like anyone out there." He didn't miss another shift for the rest of the season.

As far as the seventeen-year-old could see, it was his father's dictum—"Never take any dirt from nobody"—proving itself. Like any lesson he learned, Howe learned it well, taking it deeply to heart. People used to ask why he fought so much during his early years in pro hockey: "It's because that's how I thought I'd made the league."

But his offensive skills were also attracting notice. Jack Adams used to relate the story of an encounter between Howe and Ott Heller, the veteran New York Rangers defenseman of the 1930s and '40s, who by then was a playing coach for St. Paul in the USHL. In one game, Howe came straight at Heller with the puck; he deked him and skated by him but didn't score. Heller made a mental note of Howe's manoeuvre and thought, "He won't get away with that next time." But next time, the ambidextrous Howe switched hands on Heller, gave him a head shift and skated around him again. "When I looked around," Heller said, "the red light was on."

Pretty soon, other NHL teams were checking out the big kid. Toronto coach Hap Day and his chief scout, Squib Walker, visited Omaha and tried to make a deal for Howe's rights. But their interest only made Ivan and Adams more intent on keeping the young player. By the season's end, he'd collected 22 goals and 26 assists, not bad against professional competition for a teen-ager who could have been playing junior.

On the road, Howe still acted "backward," as if he didn't really belong or didn't deserve the privileges that older players took for granted. During one swing around the league, the team was installed in a Minneapolis hotel before a night game. In the late afternoon, Howe went downstairs to eat dinner in the hotel restaurant. "Several of the guys were there," he recalled, "but I looked at that big dining room and it looked so nice that I didn't want to go in. So I went around the corner and had a milkshake." Somehow the low-calorie dinner was enough for him: "I scored two goals on that milkshake and we beat them 3-1."

Like the other Omaha players, Howe spent the season living in the home of a local family. His first roommate was another young westerner, George Homoniuk, with whom he got along well. Later he roomed with an older player, a defenseman named Gunner Malone—so-called because of his hard shot, not his wartime occupation—who was inordinately fond of both clothes and booze. According to then-captain Jimmy Skinner, "Malone would check into camp with a new wardrobe. But as his thirst increased and his money decreased, he would sell his suits to Gordie at cut-rate prices."

While Howe was improving his standard of dress, Lefty and Lil Wilson worried more and more about Gunner's drinking. Lefty used to tell the rookies not to try to prove their manhood by keeping up with the veterans' capacity for alcohol. "You'll kill yourselves," he warned them. But Malone was too old to be lectured, and probably beyond redemption already. He resisted Lefty's attempts to help him, dying only a few years later of alcohol-related causes.

As the only Knight who couldn't get served in a bar, Howe was able to save his money. By the end of the season in Omaha, he still held onto $1,700 out of his $2,700 total earnings. But he was a frugal lad by upbringing and would never become much of a drinker anyway. Certainly he hadn't inherited his father's taste for a pint; the night he'd gone out on the town to celebrate turning pro, he'd drunk exactly one beer—his first. Religiously looking after himself, physically and mentally, would become the main secret of Howe's longevity as a player.

Between seasons in the summer of 1946, Ivan sat down with Adams to assess the current prospects in their richly endowed farm system. The last stop for a rising player before making the Red Wings, or the first stop on the way back down, was the farm team in Indianapolis: the Capitals of the American Hockey League.

When Ivan jotted down the players he felt should make the jump from Omaha to Indianapolis, Adams was surprised not to see Howe's name on the list: "What about that big kid? You've been talking about him all winter."

"I don't think Howe should play in Indianapolis."

"Why not?"

"He should play with the Wings."

Adams agreed. They signed Howe to a one-year contract with Detroit, doubling his salary to around $5,000. The contract contained the usual minor-league clause, stipulating that if he didn't make the club, he'd be sent down to Indianapolis and earn only $3,500.

Howe said years later he was "terrified" when he saw that clause: "That alone was enough to make me determined to stay up with the Wings."

Detroit has changed considerably from the city where Gordie Howe arrived in the autumn of 1946 to spend the next twenty-seven years of his life. Today, the megalopolis of nearly five million sprawls over five thousand square miles. Its endless suburbs and satellite cities are the logical extension of the automobile culture that Detroit spawned and that in turn reshaped Detroit.

Most residents of the metropolitan area live in one of those outlying communities and not in the City of Detroit at all. They spend large portions of their lives driving from one suburb to another along the ubiquitous freeways, so that the place resembles Los Angeles without the Pacific or the palm trees—but with similar levels of crime and racial tension. Visitors are warned by cabbies and other locals to stay out of the "armed camp" downtown.

Islands of affluence do exist downtown—Renaissance Centre, Civic Centre, Greek Town—but their patrons are loath to wander the streets beyond into the poverty-ridden surrounding areas, with their high incidence of violent crime. The Red Wings now play in the modern Joe Louis Sports Arena, down by the harbour; fans drive to the games, park in the big, secure parking garage and drive home again. The old Olympia has been demolished, commemorated only by a plaque erected in 1993.

When Howe started playing for Detroit, the city had just two million people but had already experienced serious outbreaks of racial violence. It was an enormous, bewildering place to the Saskatoon teen-ager, even after Omaha. Accordingly, he devised a simple strategy for finding his way around: no matter where he had to go in Detroit, he'd always start out from the Olympia. That way, he was sure to find his way back, keeping his bearings in the forbidding urban landscape.

This was unfamiliar soil for hockey to take root in. Yet it did take root, and today Detroit is perhaps the most committed and knowledgeable hockey city in the U.S., although Bostonians might argue the point. For many years the Detroit area has had a vigorous minor-hockey program, as well as its own junior A team, currently competing in the Ontario Hockey League. Much of the credit for all this must go to the success of the Red Wings franchise and especially to its prime builder, Jack Adams.

Adams was an irascible, conniving, narrow-minded, paternalistic, hysterical old tyrant; he was also one of the most authentic and experienced all-round hockey men of his era. He did as much as any Canadian to win the sport an American audience and thereby to skew the NHL's future development irrevocably towards the U.S. market. Adams once declared, "I think the smartest thing I've done in my life is to take out American papers. This country has been good to me and I've never missed voting in any election . . . I am proud of my citizenship."

And, as we've already seen, Adams played a decisive role—partly through good judgement, partly through luck—in introducing Gordie Howe to the NHL. Howe would eventually call Adams "my second father": sincerely meant, no doubt, but with a certain undertone, given Ab Howe's prickly nature.

Adams came by his position in Detroit honestly. As a young hockey player out of Fort William, Ontario (now Thunder Bay), he began playing with the Toronto Arenas in the NHL's very first season, 1917-18, when the Arenas won the Stanley Cup. He went on to star with the Vancouver Millionaires of the Pacific Coast Hockey Association, where they played the old seven-man game. In Vancouver, Adams was a teammate of the legendary Fred (Cyclone) Taylor and was no slouch himself: gutsy, pugnacious and fiercely competitive, he led the league in both penalty minutes and goals (twenty-five in twenty-four games during 1921-22), was named an all-star and competed twice for the Stanley Cup. One man who played against him for many years termed Adams "an awful slasher." Hired back by the NHL, Adams spent four seasons with the Toronto St. Pats and one more as assistant playing coach with the Ottawa Senators the year they won their last Stanley Cup in 1927.

Thus Adams was a battle-scarred, ten-year veteran of pro hockey's earliest wars when he moved to Detroit to coach a new franchise during its second season, 1927-28, in a new building, the Olympia. The team was called the Cougars then; the Detroit owners had bought the Victoria Cougars the year before, when the Pacific Coast league folded.

Adams and the team both struggled for several seasons. After the Depression hit, the Cougars went into receivership and became the Detroit Falcons, and Adams found himself putting his own money down to help meet the payroll: "I hope we don't break any more of our sticks," he once wisecracked, "because we can't afford to buy new ones." He also said that if Howie Morenz had been put on the block for $1.98, he couldn't have afforded him.

Adams's fortunes rose rapidly after another Canadian-turned-American, Chicago-based grain and shipping magnate James Norris Sr., bought the Detroit team in 1932. Remembering his long-ago playing days with the Winged Wheelers of the Montreal Amateur Athletic Association, Norris gave his hockey team a new logo—a winged automobile tire, based on the old Montreal A.A.A. symbol—and a new name, the Red Wings. And he gave Jack Adams a decent salary budget and one year in which to produce a winning team.

The Norris-Adams collaboration succeeded. Adams kept his job by making the playoffs that season, boosting fan interest and filling the Olympia. Noted for their roughhouse style, the Red Wings won their first Stanley Cup in 1936, repeating the following year and in 1943. Adams not only served as both coach and general manager but also handled the club's promotion and publicity and even wrote a regular newspaper column, "Following the Puck," to educate Detroit sports fans about hockey.

Initially, the team's biggest spectator interest came from the other side of the river. But the Windsor fans infuriated Adams by insisting on being Canadians and cheering for Toronto and Montreal, so he became bent on indoctrinating Detroit citizens about the delights of having their very own team playing this wild, violent, alien sport. In the course of selling hockey in Detroit over the years, his relationship with the local media became so cozy that he could plant stories at will, in the process manipulating his players and stifling criticism of his own actions. His news-management tactics reached the point where the hockey writers for the Detroit dailies, John Walter at the *Detroit News* and his brother Lew Walter at the *Detroit Times*, would actually write a story on the Red Wings, punch it up by inventing some colourful Adams quotes, then show it to Adams for approval before publication.

Howe's first season with the Wings was Adams's last as coach. By that time, Adams was fifty-one and courting heart trouble. He'd ballooned far beyond his playing weight to become a porker in a three-piece suit, his vest buttons popping over his broad paunch, his bow tie engulfed by a bulging bull neck. His trademark look featured little spectacles perched on a pug nose and a wide-brimmed fedora pulled low over his sweating forehead. Red-faced, his lower lip protruding moistly from his jowls, Adams threw tantrums when his team lost. He'd kick the team oranges across the dressing room and hurl anything he could lay his hands on at the players, reaming them out with withering insults and threats as if they were ten-year-olds.

In the 1946-47 season, Adams was rebuilding the Red Wings, moulding a team with the legs and spirit of youth around a small nucleus of veterans. He always sought a judicious balance of experience and inexperience; his maxim was to juggle his line-up every season, even after winning a Stanley Cup.

Adams liked to say he'd learned the hard way about the necessity of doing this: after winning the Cup twice in the 1930s, he'd kept his team intact, and it had immediately fallen to last place. "I decided," he later declared, "we'd never stand pat again."

The year before Howe's arrival, the Wings had finished fourth and been eliminated by Boston in the semifinals, so there was plenty of room for improvement. Their top scorer had been Joe Carveth, who had finished eighteenth in the league; characteristically, Adams traded him to Boston for Roy Conacher, the younger brother of the renowned Charlie and Lionel. Happily for Adams, two outstanding players had returned from the war during the previous season: centre Sid Abel and defenseman Black Jack

Stewart. He also had a star defenseman in Bill Quackenbush and two strong young performers, both beginning their third seasons, in goaltender Harry Lumley and bellicose left wing Ted Lindsay. Adams added high-scoring Billy Taylor, obtained from Toronto in a trade for veteran Harry Watson, and had three young hopefuls from Saskatoon: Gerry (Doc) Couture, Pat Lundy and Gordie Howe.

In the home opener against Toronto on October 16, 1946, Adams started the game with a new line. He put Abel at centre; Adam Brown, a 20-goal scorer the previous year, at left wing; and the total unknown, Gordie Howe, at right wing. That night at least, the line distinguished itself.

Brown scored the first goal from Abel. Then, in the fourteenth minute of the second period, forty seconds after the Maple Leafs had tied the score 1-1, Abel passed the puck to Brown. Brown head-manned it to Howe at the Leaf blueline, and the rookie broke through the defense and found himself alone in front of Toronto's famed goalie, Turk Broda. "The puck was lying loose, ten feet from the net," Howe remembered. "And I just slapped it in." Broda went sprawling, the first of Howe's 801 regular-season victims in the NHL.

(Eons later, Broda commented, "You know, I'm damn proud of that goal. Think of it, I was the first guy he scored on.")

Howe also threw his big body around with abandon. In the third period, he checked Toronto captain Syl Apps so hard that Apps had to leave the game with a twisted knee. With only eleven seconds left, Toronto now leading 3-2 and Lumley pulled for a sixth attacker, Abel—a clutch player if ever there was one—beat Broda for a tie. The Detroit fans went home happy, and Gordie Howe had made an auspicious debut. The next day, the *Detroit News* said, "Gordon Howe is the squad's baby, 18 years old. But he was one of Detroit's most valuable men last night. In his first major-league game, he scored a goal, skated tirelessly and had perfect poise."

Unfortunately, the rest of the season didn't follow that pattern. It would be nine games before Howe scored his second goal, another eleven before his third. Far from burning up the league in his rookie year, as Gretzky, Mario Lemieux, Pavel Bure or Teemu Selanne would in theirs, Howe still suffered from on-ice awkwardness, inexperience and self-doubt. One NHL trophy he'd never win was the Calder; the rookie of the year for 1946-47 would be the Maple Leafs' hustling Howie Meeker, with 27 goals.

Young Howe's chosen remedy for shoring up his flagging confidence was fighting. That year, he logged a lot of bench time in the fifty-eight games he dressed for, often seeing no action at all; but in the early part of the season, he fought with somebody in almost every game in which he got on the ice.

He didn't pick the easy marks, either. One night in Toronto, it was Maple Leaf tough guy Bill Ezinicki. Another night in Montreal, it was none other than Maurice Richard. Howe managed to knock the Rocket, who was nearly as big as he was, to the ice. The linesmen were separating the two when Abel skated up to Richard and foolishly taunted him, "That'll teach you, Frenchie—" but got no further; Richard broke Abel's nose with a solid right.

Howe's teammate and fellow Saskatonian Gerry Couture, who had made the team in 1945, remembers Howe's early belligerence: "He loved to play hockey, and he loved to fight. In fact we weren't sure, in the first year or two, whether he was going to stay with hockey or whether Nick Lund, who was the fight promoter in Detroit at the time, was going to sign him up for a bout at the Olympia."

Howe's conviction that he had to fight to prove he belonged in the NHL—indeed, that fighting was expected of him, after his experience in Omaha—finally landed him in trouble with the boss. Adams called him upstairs to his office at the Olympia and read the riot act: "What are you trying to do, my boy? Beat up the entire league one man at a time? You've proved you can fight, now prove you can play hockey! From here in, the handcuffs are on."

Adams's reprimand gave Howe permission to concentrate on his game. He had some good teachers in Detroit, if only by example, and he was a careful study, if not a quick one. He acted all his life on some advice he received from the team's chief scout, Carson (Shovelshot) Cooper, who had starred for Detroit in the late 1920s and early 1930s. As Howe recounted it, Cooper told him, "Kid, draw an imaginary line, twenty feet out from the side boards, and stay there. That's your territory."

"I've never forgotten that," Howe said.

He also remembered some encouraging words a year earlier from the departed Joe Carveth, who had warned him not to be too surprised if the first half of his rookie season didn't go well, because things would settle down in the second half. That proved true in Omaha, and to some extent in Howe's rookie year in Detroit also. Although he scored only 7 goals all season, he eventually collected a respectable 15 assists, for 22 points—a total he'd double the following year.

During that first season, Howe also received the Adams treatment on occasion. Perhaps because he played him so little, Adams would forget Howe's name in the heat of battle.

"Get out there, Syd!" he bellowed at Howe once, confusing him with the star of old, now retired. "Go on, Syd!" Adams roared impatiently, and Howe looked around, up and down the bench, wondering what was taking Abel so long. "It's you, Syd, it's *you*!" Adams screamed, running over behind Howe, utterly beside himself.

"Oh, but sir," Howe began earnestly, "my name isn't . . ."

Indignantly Adams cut him off, cuffing him across the back of the head: "For the love of God, never mind that! Get out there!"

One man who did remember Howe, and taught him a lesson in NHL etiquette, was the Maple Leafs' forward, former Red Wing Harry Watson. A few years earlier, back in Saskatoon, Howe had played against Watson, who had been stationed at RCAF No. 4 airbase. "He must have seen something in me, because he talked to me a lot," Howe remembered. "So when the Wings played Toronto, who was I checking? Big Harry. We were down at the far end together, and he yelled, 'Look out, kid!' And I thought, gee, that's very nice of him, because I hadn't seen him coming and he could have nailed me pretty good. So we came down to the other end and he had his back to the play too, and I yelled, 'Look out, Mr. Watson!' He looked at me and said, 'We're going to get along just fine.'"

Later in his long career, Howe would develop a well-deserved reputation for not giving an easy ride to obnoxious rookies out to make a name for themselves by nailing Number Nine. But he always reserved his most generous and gentle treatment for any kid from Saskatoon.

That season, Detroit failed to improve on its fourth-place finish of the year before, losing this time to second-place Toronto—the eventual Cup winners—in the semifinals. In Howe's first playoff experience, he distinguished himself chiefly by getting into a brawl. He and the Maple Leafs' Gus Mortson began fighting while sharing the penalty box at the Olympia. Their squabble spilled over into the aisle and almost started a riot involving some Detroit fans, one of whom threw a chair at Mortson. Finally, the police had to step in to restore order.

In fact, Howe had simply been responding to Mortson in typical fashion by loyally rallying to the defence of a friend. Moments earlier, Mortson had been mixing it up with Ted Lindsay. During the course of that season, Howe had become fast friends with Lindsay, forging an alliance that would make an enduring impact on both his hockey career and his life.

CHAPTER FIVE

Working on the Production Line

"I guess I held everybody in awe."
—Gordie Howe, on his first seasons in the NHL

ASK TED LINDSAY ABOUT MEETING HOWE at their first training camp in Windsor, and he remembers it all, right down to the heat, the crowded, steamy dressing room, the itchy feel of the soggy wool sweaters, and the precise date.

"This coming September," Lindsay recalled early in 1994, "it'll be fifty years since Gordie and Marty Pavelich and I met: September 8, 1944. The year I turned pro with the Wings."

Only nineteen at the time, Lindsay had already given Jack Adams notice that he'd be difficult to control. It was a trait that made him highly exceptional among players of that era, even veterans. But then Lindsay was an exceptional young man, an extrovert who packed equal parts talent and aggression into his small (five-foot-eight, 160 pounds) but explosive frame. For Adams, Howe and Lindsay would be completely different players to handle: the one deferential and malleable, submitting to authority; the other assertive and rebellious, daring to challenge his elders. And yet in their opposite ways, Lindsay and Howe would be as indispensable to Adams's success as to each other's.

Growing up in the northern Ontario gold-mining town of Kirkland Lake, Lindsay had four older brothers who had gone away to war. Too young to enlist, he'd sought the moral equivalent of war in hockey. After excelling at the juvenile level, he had just one problem: there was no junior team in Kirkland Lake to move up to. His solution was to look for a school in the south that would give him a playing scholarship. After finding a priest in Kirkland Lake to make the necessary arrangements, Lindsay and his hometown teammate, Gus Mortson, would so impress St. Michael's College that the school started sending scouts to Northern Ontario on a regular basis.

The initiative was vintage Lindsay, a vote of confidence in himself: it didn't matter to *him* if he was from Nowhereville, Ontario. Soon he was starring for St. Mike's, and two years later he and Mortson helped their team win the Memorial Cup as Canada's junior champions.

Toronto signed Mortson but passed on Lindsay while he was available in their own backyard—an error that would rankle the Maple Leafs' owner, Conn Smythe, forever. Carson Cooper quickly snapped Lindsay up for the Red Wings.

As we've seen earlier, Lindsay was in no hurry to turn pro at the Wings' 1944 camp. This had made him a puzzle to Jack Adams, who phoned St. Mike's and demanded to know, "What are you offering this kid to stay there?" Told "Nothing," Adams was forced to realize Lindsay simply had a passion for playing hockey and wouldn't be content to sit on anybody's bench.

During his rookie season in 1944-45, armed with his contractual guarantee of a regular shift, Lindsay made an immediate impact on the league: he scored 17 goals in forty-five games for Detroit, and 2 more in the playoffs. When the war ended and the Lindsay boys came home from overseas, their little brother was already a rising star in the NHL.

With unnecessary modesty, Lindsay says today, "I got into the league because so many good players were in the service." He gives credit to his first Red Wing linemates, Joe Carveth and Murray Armstrong—"the two finest guys I ever met"—for settling him down, feeding him passes and helping him look good. But Lindsay would soon be a bona fide star in his own right. One of the great ones of the Original Six, he would go on to become a nine-time all-star (eight times on the first team) who would score more regular-season goals (379) than any left wing until Bobby Hull, serve more penalty minutes (1,808) during his era than anyone at any position and be inextricably linked with Gordie Howe's first decade in the NHL.

The difference between Lindsay's personality and Howe's is the contrast between their rookie seasons. Whereas Howe began slowly and hesitantly, Lindsay started with a bang. Whereas Howe was grateful for whatever he was given, Lindsay was arrogant and demanding from the word go. Whereas Howe saw himself as an underdog, Lindsay saw himself as a winner.

Their hockey backgrounds too had been different. Lindsay had two solid seasons of fierce junior A competition behind him, including two Memorial Cup finals; Howe's experience had been relatively limited, especially during his year in Galt. And by the time Howe broke into the NHL, many established players had returned from wartime service, stiffening the competition in comparison with Lindsay's rookie season.

Nonetheless, Howe at eighteen and Lindsay at twenty-one were inexorably drawn to each other. In those days, and for years afterwards, all the Red Wing bachelors roomed together at various houses maintained by arrangement with the team. One such rooming house was run by two French-Canadian brothers named Michaud; another was operated by a woman known as Ma Tannahill. But the most celebrated was the one where Lindsay lived, the home belonging to Minnie (Ma) Shaw, located just a block and a half from the Olympia, and generally remembered by Red Wing vets of the 1950s as "the last white home on McGraw Avenue."

Ma Shaw was a formidable, grey-haired widow who liked playing the piano, dealing cards and watching her "boys" in action at the Olympia. She combined the roles of den mother to the unmarried players and watchdog for Jack Adams, to whom she reported on her charges' conduct. Between the late 1930s and 1959, an estimated 175 players passed through the two-storey brick house she had inherited from her parents, where at any given time four Red Wing bachelors were billeted in the four bedrooms upstairs.

After Lindsay broke in with the Wings, he roomed at Ma Shaw's with Bill Quackenbush, Black Jack Stewart and Harry Lumley. This living arrangement suited the players' income level (no penthouse apartments back then), but it also provided them with comradeship in a strange city, kept their morale up and cemented team solidarity. The players not only played as a team but lived, partied and hung out as a team. It helped them concentrate on hockey, keeping it their central focus. Adams didn't want them thinking about anything else, especially women, which he considered the most ruinous distraction of all. In the unfortunate event that a player got married, or was traded, he'd move out of the house and another Red Wing bachelor would move in.

Early on, Howe joined the gang at Ma Shaw's, replacing Quackenbush. He and Lindsay soon became inseparable. Leonard (Red) Kelly moved into Ma Shaw's the following season. "You never saw Ted without Gordie," he says now. "They were like *that.*"

The Lindsay-Howe friendship reached the point where Gordie spent so much of his spare time with Ted, he scarcely got to know some of the other players. As Colleen Howe would remark, "Ted was 'family' to Gordie, really the only family he had outside of Saskatoon."

Howe and Lindsay were the original Odd Couple: the self-effacing, easygoing, proverbial good boy—not only "the squad's baby," as the *Detroit News* had called him, but its ultimate boy scout—teaming up with the high-strung, cocky, smart-mouthed bad boy. But in fact, they needed each other. Their friendship was based on a symbiosis; each counterbalanced the extremes of the other's personality. Together, they both felt more rounded and complete, comfortable. "We were good for each other," Lindsay says. "Off the ice and on."

On the face of it, Howe would appear to have needed Lindsay more than the other way around. Still feeling insecure about his place on the team, awed by the pressures of playing in the NHL and overwhelmed by the confusion of the big city, Howe benefited from his older teammate's experience and example. Whatever they did together, whether eating out (Ma Shaw didn't provide meals), bowling, playing hearts or cribbage (a game Howe learned during his first season), entertaining themselves on road trips or just practising at the Olympia, it was Lindsay who had the ideas, set the tone, took the lead. By showing Howe the ropes, Lindsay provided him with encouragement and security. Howe followed gratefully, as he'd learned to do by following his strong-willed father—and as he'd later follow in his marriage.

Long after they'd both retired from hockey, Howe would recall early lessons in self-preservation he learned from Lindsay: lessons such as, "It takes two seconds after you jump on the ice to see where trouble's coming from and where help's coming from," and "Never drop your stick until the other guy does."

Howe even learned to sass Adams behind his back (although he'd never dare do it to his face). Harry Lumley, who later starred in goal for Toronto, recalls the time when Howe, with his effortless skating style and apparently easygoing manner, exasperated Adams enough to draw a dressing-room putdown.

"Gordie looked so lackadaisical out on the ice," says Lumley, "that Adams gave him hell. He said, 'You! You take it so easy out there, you should *pay* to get in!' Next day, Gordie came in with a game ticket and told us, 'Look, I paid my way in.'"

But since a leader needs followers, Lindsay needed Howe, too. And Ted, being a perceptive judge of character, could see Gordie's enormous potential lying just underneath the surface of his "backwardness": his potential not only as an athlete but also as a human being who was just beginning to emerge from adolescence. Lindsay liked being around somebody with talent, with gifts, however underdeveloped as yet.

Reflecting on the way Howe was back then, Lindsay calls him, with characteristic bluntness, "a hick, a real farm boy." But he was already noticing some changes in the Howe he'd first met at training camp two years earlier: "He'd matured a little in Galt and Omaha. He was shy and introverted, and still is, but not as shy as he gives the appearance of being. He was introverted to a point, but with a good wit. When he was comfortable, he could come up with some good lines and good conversation."

Their friendship shines through a wonderful late-1940s photograph of the pair standing together in the dressing room in their Red Wing jackets, that elusive prize that Howe had signed his contract to get. Their unabashedly delighted grins—Gordie's boyish, Ted's manly—tell much about the pleasure they took in each other.

There was a similarity between Lindsay and Howe. Both were rugged risk-takers, fearless and even mean, on the ice. But Lindsay could be that way off the ice, too—in fact, he was that way whenever he bloody well felt like it—whereas Howe always acted reserved, courteous, modest, *nice*, never rising above his station. Only when he played hockey could Howe release the bitter pride and anger buried deeply within him, the need to even the score with a world that had belittled and shamed him ever since he was a kid. Only then could he revenge himself, taking it all out on the slashers and hookers and spear-carriers of the NHL.

Howe worried about people's good opinion of him. But Lindsay always felt free not to give a damn what people thought. Lindsay acted out Howe's dark side. And Gordie would watch with glee and cheer him on, participating vicariously in Ted's defiant displays of power.

Howe and Lindsay's off-ice friendship wasn't visible to spectators at Red Wings games, of course, but their compatibility as wing-mates definitely was. The line they played on for ten seasons, centred first by Sid Abel and later by Alex Delvecchio, Dutch Reibel and others, was the most successful, exciting and dominant of its era—perhaps the greatest attacking line of any era in the NHL.

"Tommy Ivan was the one who put us together," Lindsay says. Ivan assembled the original Production Line of Howe, Lindsay and Abel in fall 1947, the beginning of Howe's second season.

After a year of coaching Indianapolis, Ivan had moved up to Detroit to take over the coaching duties from Jack Adams, who had brought himself near physical and mental collapse from trying to control every aspect of the organization. Relinquishing the job to Ivan, Adams would say, added ten years to his life. He continued running the club as general manager, making Ivan's life miserable by trying to coach over his shoulder—literally, since Adams always sat just one row behind the Detroit bench—but Ivan would earn his players' undying gratitude and loyalty for acting as a buffer between them and the old tyrant. For seven years, he'd fend off Adams's chronic meddling, erratic judgements and irrational temper, and the Wings would respond by performing with greater enthusiasm than they had ever shown under Adams, and with even greater success.

One of Ivan's first and most crucial decisions was a brilliant stroke of casting. Between the Odd Couple, he inserted the ideal centreman for bringing out the best in both of them.

Sid Abel, from Melville, Saskatchewan, had broken into the NHL with the Red Wings in 1938. He'd played five seasons before serving in the war, becoming the team's number-two scorer after Syd Howe, and had starred on the 1943 Detroit team that won the Stanley Cup. Abel brought savvy and seasoned maturity to his two new linemates, whose youthful ebullience, in turn, provided him with a fresh lease on life over the next five seasons. The best part of Abel's playing career was now to come.

For Howe, the chance to play not only with his pal Lindsay but with his hero Abel was the major break of his career. At one time, he'd felt honoured just to carry Abel's skates into the Saskatoon Arena. Even one season earlier, he'd still held Abel in awe, thrilled just to be a member of the team he captained.

Gordie had kept a scrapbook of all the news stories that mentioned his name, so that he could take it home in the summer and prove to his buddies he'd actually played in the NHL. He was still getting over his sense of awe. "I guess I held everybody in awe," he said. "All I wanted desperately to do was hang on for a full season, so I could go back to Saskatoon and brag about it."

Now he'd not only hung on for a full season but would be playing on the same line as Abel—and even better, under the familiar, sympathetic eye of his old coach from Omaha. Tommy Ivan was continuing the rebuilding job Adams had begun the previous season. With his first-hand knowledge of Howe's capabilities, Ivan was ready to give him a regular shift on the team's first line—and hence the experience Howe needed to release the potential Ivan sensed lay within him.

Ivan liked to present himself as a simple, old-fashioned, physically minded coach, and as Jack Adams's man. He once said, "Fundamentally, there are only two basic manoeuvres in hockey. Either you knock the puck away from the man, or you knock the man away from the puck." In this, he claimed to be dutifully following Adams's methods.

But Ivan also used other, subtler methods of his own to mould and motivate one of the most successful teams in NHL history. He believed most athletes respond better to encouragement than to Adams-style bluster and ridicule. During the seven seasons he coached the Red Wings, Ivan's teams would win the league championship an extraordinary six times straight, from 1949 through 1954, and the Stanley Cup three times. In 1955, the season after Ivan moved on to Chicago, the team he'd built would add a seventh consecutive championship—still a record today—and a fourth Stanley Cup.

From the start, a large part of Ivan's growing success was the high scoring of the Production Line. The three linemates worked at further developing the instinctive rapport that would become their hallmark. After practice, they'd stay behind on the ice; Howe and Lindsay fired puck after puck from different angles and Abel, stationed in front of the crease, practised tipping them in. Over the years, they'd score a lot of goals that way.

But they had many other ways of scoring, including a patented play that worked particularly well in the familiar confines of the Olympia: Howe or Lindsay would fire the puck into the opposite corner, banking it off the boards at just the right angle for the other to intercept the rebound on his way into the net. Former teammate Murray Costello remembers them marking their spot in the corner every time the boards got painted. They worked that play for years.

"Gordie would lead the charge down the right wing," Costello recalls, "and just after he crossed centre ice he'd fire the puck between the defensemen. If he hit that spot just right, and he was uncanny about hitting it, the puck came right out to the top of the left circle, and Lindsay would scoot in behind the defensemen and get a point-blank shot on goal."

In its first season, 1947-48, the Production Line powered the Red Wings to a second-place finish, just five points behind Toronto—a major improvement over the previous year. The three linemates were Detroit's top scorers, as they would remain for several seasons. Lindsay led with 33 goals and 19 assists for 52 points, which placed him ninth in the league (the NHL played sixty games then). Howe and Abel weren't far behind, tied at 44 points, both of them with considerably fewer goals (16 and 14 respectively) than assists. But at that point, the Production Line was just warming up.

In the semifinals, the Wings eliminated New York in six games, and Howe scored his first playoff goal. Detroit moved on to the finals against powerful Toronto, Stanley Cup champions in the previous year. Two rookies who had arrived in Detroit that season, Red Kelly from St. Mike's and Marty Pavelich from Galt, performed impressively on defense and left wing respectively. But led by three veteran centremen—Syl Apps, Ted Kennedy and Max Bentley—and with a powerful defense and goalie Turk Broda excelling as usual at playoff time, the Maple Leafs simply had too much depth and experience for the Red Wings; they rolled over Detroit in four games straight to capture the Cup again.

In one game, little Howie Meeker made the error of mixing it up with big Howe. As described by the *Toronto Star*, "Howie swung once and buried his head in Howe's midriff. Gord promptly hit him three on top of the noggin, raising a set of goose eggs."

That was also the season when Howe began wearing number nine. Previously, the sweater had been worn by veteran Roy Conacher, who was traded at the beginning of the year. Far from trying to match Maurice Richard, Howe had simply acquired the number for a very practical reason—and, typically, not by his own initiative but at someone else's suggestion. In those days, NHL teams often travelled by overnight train, and the lower twelve berths in the Red Wings' twenty-four-berth sleeping car were assigned to players with the lowest numbers. Howe, wearing number seventeen, had occupied an uncomfortable upper berth during his rookie year. So when Conacher was traded, trainer Carl Mattson helpfully pointed out to Howe that he'd sleep more soundly if he grabbed a lower sweater number, and hence a lower berth.

The following season, 1948-49, Ivan's team made further progress; Detroit began showing signs of becoming the powerhouse of the future. As the younger players matured, approaching the skill level of the veterans, the Red Wings developed greater balance and poise. They occupied first place throughout much of the season, in spite of injuries to both Lindsay and Howe.

Lindsay broke a bone in his foot after taking a nasty chop from Boston's Milt Schmidt, who received his comeuppance two weeks later from Marty Pavelich. Howe, meanwhile, had been suffering from knee trouble; in December, the team doctors decided he needed surgery to repair torn cartilages. After the operation, Howe sustained his longest absence from active service with the Wings—twenty games. It's part of the miracle of his longevity that his worst and most debilitating injuries occurred at the early stages of his career. Howe just seemed to grow a tougher and more durable hide as he advanced in age.

Then, as always, he was a quick healer. On returning to action six weeks after his knee operation, he wasted no time getting back into the fray: in a game at the Forum, he and Abel renewed their old enmity with Maurice Richard. Both fought the Rocket in turn, goading him into losing it so completely that he was slapped with a game misconduct by King Clancy, then a referee. The Rocket was having a bad year.

At the end of the 1948-49 regular season, the Red Wings finished first. It was the beginning of their record seven straight championships. Abel won the Hart trophy as the league's most valuable player, and he and Lindsay tied for third in scoring, even though Lindsay had missed ten games.

Howe was the team's next-best scorer (apart from Bud Poile, who played for Detroit that year after a trade and was gone the next season). Howe's 12 goals and 25 assists, scored in only forty games because of his operation, put him just a single point behind Richard, who had played fifty-nine games. To his delight, Howe was named along with Lindsay to the second all-star team—the beginning of Howe's record twenty-one all-star selections.

The first-team all-stars included Richard at right wing, Abel at centre and the Red Wings' defense pair, Quackenbush and Stewart. Quackenbush also won the Lady Byng trophy, having drawn not a single penalty minute all season—a distinction that didn't endear him to Jack Adams, who, in the spirit of Don Cherry, would soon show what he thought of gentlemanly conduct by trading Quackenbush to Boston. But Adams enthused shamelessly to the press about the progress of his favourite young protégé:

"Gordie Howe is the greatest young player I've ever seen," he proclaimed. "There is not enough money in the NHL to buy him. I just love the kid."

Whatever his teammates may have thought of this effusion, it was a public vote of confidence in Howe, and it made a highly positive impact on him. From that point, late in the '49 season, his star took off on a trajectory that would never falter. He shot to prominence in the playoffs that year, leading the post-season scoring with 8 goals—all of them coming in the seven-game semifinals against Montreal—and 3 assists.

But the league champions couldn't break their Maple Leaf jinx. After the Red Wings eliminated the Canadiens in a tough, seesawing series dominated by the Production Line's scoring, their fire was spent; they just didn't have enough left for the finals. Young Howe in particular was stymied by Toronto's close checking. The Maple Leafs may have finished a distant fourth in the regular season, but for the second year in a row they had too much balance and poise for Detroit, whose offense was clearly lopsided—there was the Production Line, and then not much else. Toronto swept the Red Wings four games to none, becoming the first team to win three consecutive Stanley Cups since the Ottawa Silver Seven forty-four years earlier.

It's instructive to compare the Detroit and Toronto teams of the late 1940s—the one a dynasty on the rise, the other a dynasty nearing its end. Probably no one is in a better position to make that comparison than Ted (Teeder) Kennedy, the Leafs' former captain and an exceedingly thoughtful analyst of the game, who played a lead role for Toronto on five Stanley Cup winners between 1945 and 1951. Now an official with the Fort Erie, Ontario, racetrack, Kennedy speaks of the crucial difference that coaching made to the two teams when Jack Adams was running the show in Detroit.

"Even though Detroit would finish ahead of us in the regular season," Kennedy says, "we were much better coached, especially in the playoffs. The most knowledgeable coach of that time was Hap Day. He and Conn Smythe worked closely together to design the Leaf system. Smythe was a hockey man, and he understood men—he'd address the team with fire in his eyes—while Day was a great analyst and tactician.

"Checking and positional play were so vital in those days, especially in a short playoff series. Games would usually be won by a goal or two. If you got two goals down in the third period, forget it. The Leafs were better schooled, and we executed better: we just checked, checked, checked, checked. I guess it wasn't pretty to watch, but it sure worked. We weren't the best team all year. We were only the best in the playoffs."

Kennedy believes Adams could sometimes be a liability for Detroit. "Adams was a tremendous competitor, there was no one who wanted to win more. But he'd become so emotional, he'd lose his perspective about what was going on on the ice. Eighty per cent of the game is motivation, and Adams certainly knew that. But I don't know how good he was at teaching the game."

After winning their third straight Cup in 1949, the Maple Leafs would triumph one more time, in 1951; Joe Primeau would be the coach then, still using the system Day and Smythe had devised. But whereas Toronto excelled at teamwork and military-style tactics, the Red Wings would eventually surpass them on the strength of sheer talent and individual brilliance.

Kennedy agrees that the Production Line was the fulcrum of the Detroit team, crucial to the Red Wings' gathering, glorious strength. "Abel was an excellent centreman for those two guys. They really complemented each other, Abel dealing out the passes to those two young fellows scooting in from the wings. Abel was much older and more experienced, and he could feed them, but he could also finish off, like Esposito. He got his share of goals. Lindsay was great, too. And Howe was a natural—an athlete pure and simple, who did things instinctively and could have been outstanding in any sport."

After a long summer to think about their second straight shellacking by Toronto—a summer Howe spent as usual back home in Saskatoon, staying with his mom and dad, and playing baseball to stay in shape and have fun—the Red Wings returned to the Olympia to prepare for the 1949-50 season. It would be the club's best season in many years: the true beginning of the powerful

Detroit machine that continued rolling over the opposition well into the middle of the new decade. It would also be a superb season for the Production Line, their finest ever. But it would be a year of near-tragedy for Gordie Howe, his family and his growing legion of admirers in Canada and the U.S.

CHAPTER SIX

Triumph and Near-Tragedy

"I like to earn things. To be on the ice, and sweat and bleed with the boys."
—Gordie Howe, 1992

AT THE TWENTIETH CENTURY'S MIDPOINT, Detroit proved it had become the most powerful club in the NHL. The Red Wings finished in first place by an even wider margin, 11 points, than the previous year. Utterly dominating the NHL, the Production Line terrorized opposing goalies. Lindsay, Abel and Howe finished the 1949-50 season in an extraordinary 1-2-3 position in the scoring race, which looked like this by the end of the schedule:

	GP	G	A	PTS	PIM
Ted Lindsay	69	23	55	78	141
Sid Abel	69	34	35	69	46
Gordie Howe	70	35	33	68	69
Maurice Richard	70	43	22	65	114

Howe and Abel had evened out their goal and assist production. And Lindsay had reversed his imbalance of two seasons earlier: he'd become much more the playmaker, while remaining as unrepentantly belligerent as ever.

It's problematic to compare the Production Line, on the basis of scoring alone, with other great NHL lines of all time: over the years, there has simply been too much variation in the length of the season (it was extended from sixty games to seventy in 1949-50), in the quality of hockey following expansion years and in the changing nature of the game itself. One attempt at a semiobjective ranking appears in Stephen Cole's *Slapshots: The Best and Worst of 100 Years of Hockey*. Cole's system compares lines on a mathematical basis: it gives points for all-star selections (10 points for first team, 5 for second); Hart trophies (10 points for winning, 5 for coming second); and Stanley Cup wins (10 points).

Admittedly, such a system contains its own built-in bias because of the subjectivity of all-star and Hart selections. Nevertheless, on the basis of that system, the Howe/Abel/Lindsay line ranks impressively far ahead of any other line in NHL history. They garner 245 points, compared to 200 for the second-place line—Gretzky, Jari Kurri and Esa Tikkanen of the Edmonton Oilers in the mid to late 1980s—and 190 for the third-place line, the Canadiens' Punch Line of Maurice Richard, Toe Blake and Elmer Lach.

Today, Lindsay sees the key to the Production Line's phenomenal success in Abel, a mentor who knew how to guide his radically different young linemates in the direction each had to go. "Sid was great for us. He was our father image. Remember, I was twenty-two at the start, and Gordie was only nineteen. I was the kind who had to be calmed down; Gordie had to be jacked up. Sid had our respect. We appreciated his guidance."

Abel and his wife, Gloria, would invite the two wingmates over to their house for a good spaghetti dinner and a little family atmosphere. Then the three men would go out and play dazzlingly together, tearing up the ice like reckless, inspired youngsters.

"We were good for Sid, too," Lindsay says, "because we had the legs and the talent, the instincts. Somehow we always knew where the other two were. Wherever the ice was open, you'd throw it and you'd know Gordie or Sid would be there. It was just great *chemistry*."

Abel, always inclined to kid around about his linemates, liked to play the graybeard annoyed by the rambunctious young pups. He complained tongue-in-cheek that Howe was too good a stick-handler—"Does he have to stick-handle around the same player three times?" he protested—and once remarked that centring Howe and Lindsay was such a cinch, he could do it in a rocking chair. So the boys arranged for Old Bootnose, as Abel was known after Richard's ruinous punch, to be interviewed and photographed at centre ice in a rocker.

Long after his retirement as an active player, when he'd become a team executive, Abel continued to downplay his contribution to the line. He told an interviewer, "Gordie was the puck carrier, Teddy was the spirit and the drive, and I was more or less the garbage man." It's hard to imagine any of today's millionaire superstars, even the earnest Gretzky, characterizing himself in quite such modest terms.

Howe used the same word as Lindsay to describe their intuitive interaction on the ice: "I think it was *chemistry*. I knew Ted, where he was, I didn't have to look. Some of my plays were started before I even picked him up, [or knew] where his direction was. I read him well and he read me well."

At the beginning of each season, Adams and Ivan would try to break up the Production Line, in an attempt to create three lines closer in strength. "They were always shuffling the lines," Howe remembered, "trying to get equal balance among them. But as soon as the team had a little trouble, they always put us back together again, and away we went. Why different players connect right off the bat, I really don't know. But in the case of Sid Abel, he showed his way of handling men back then by needling me to get me going. And the other guy, Lindsay, you had to feed him tranquillizers to calm him down."

In Howe's memory of those days, Lindsay remained the rogue while Howe was the choirboy. "Lindsay probably got me in more fights than I wanted to get in. Every time we took a face-off, he was picking a fight with the guy opposite me, telling me to run my stick through him. First thing I knew, I'd be getting hit in the head with the other guy's stick, which brought me right back into the fisticuffs."

Howe's depiction of Lindsay's devilry and his own sweet innocence certainly doesn't explain Howe's long history of fighting in the NHL, both before and after he and Lindsay were linemates. Nor does it shed light on one of the most famous incidents in Stanley Cup history: Howe's potentially horrendous accident involving fellow second-team all-star Teeder Kennedy in the first game of the 1950 semifinals against Toronto.

The incident has been described many times, in incomplete or conflicting versions. What follows is an attempt to record it based on a synthesis of the many accounts given to date, including a current one from Kennedy himself.

The semifinal series opened at the Olympia on March 28, 1950, just three days before Howe's twenty-second birthday. The Red Wings had once more led the league all year, and their fans were in an agony of hope and desperation to see them break their playoff jinx against the Maple Leafs. But in the second period, the Leafs were already leading 3-0. The Wings were straining badly, bamboozled once more by Toronto's defensive strategy.

Kennedy, the Toronto captain, circled back in his own zone to collect the puck from defenseman Jimmy Thomson. Seeing his teammates re-forming, Kennedy led the rush up the left boards—Howe's side of the rink. When he reached centre ice, Kennedy's peripheral vision picked up Howe's big frame hurtling towards him at an angle, coming at top speed from the right and slightly from behind. Referee Georges Gravel already had his arm up to signal a penalty when Kennedy, sensing he was about to take a crushing hit into the boards, simply released the puck and pulled up short.

As he was about to converge with Kennedy, Howe appeared to stumble, or trip, or get butt-ended by Kennedy's stick—the story differs depending on one's angle of vision and team bias. Propelled by his own terrific momentum, Howe glanced off the Leaf captain. Now completely out of control, he plunged head-first into the boards, the side of his face hitting the wooden moulding running along the top edge. His head twisted grotesquely as he sagged to the ice. Simultaneously, Red Wing defenseman Jack Stewart, who had also been gunning for Kennedy, sprawled over Howe's collapsed body.

Howe lay very still. The frenzied crowd quickly fell silent. Thick ribbons of blood began streaming across his forehead, nose and cheek, staining the ice.

The incident had occurred directly in front of the Detroit bench. The Red Wings' trainer, Carl Mattson, jumped over the boards and crouched beside Howe's unmoving form. The spectators began realizing this wasn't some ordinary collision, where the injured player eventually responds to smelling salts, is assisted to his feet and skates groggily back to his bench. Grey-faced, the trainer signalled to first-aid men. Two of them immediately arrived on the ice, carefully lifted the unconscious body onto a stretcher and carried Howe into the dressing room.

The Detroit players standing at the bench angrily began accusing Kennedy of injuring Howe. So Kennedy skated over to Tommy Ivan and tried to explain he hadn't been responsible. He was counting on Ivan to be his normally level-headed self and to react rationally. But the coach was as upset as his players and demanded referee Gravel give Kennedy a major penalty. Gravel did not.

"They accused me of butt-ending him," Kennedy says today, his memory and conscience both clear forty-four years after the incident. "But I was a right-handed shot, so the butt of my stick was away from Howe. If there was any contact between us, it was very slight. He'd been going full tilt. He'd been going to run me into the fence. He was the faster skater, he was gaining on me, and I knew he was going to get in a good shot. The only thing I was guilty of was getting out of his way. Gravel had his hand up because, I presume, he saw a deliberate attempt at charging or boarding."

Kennedy attributes the Red Wings' accusations to the heat of the moment—the shocking sight of Howe's inertness on the ice, the copious blood, the damaging loss of their rising young star, and the fact that "there was an awful lot of animosity between our team and theirs, because of the success we'd had against them."

Kennedy's version is corroborated by Harry Lumley. The then-Detroit goalie saw the whole thing from his vantage point in the net. "Gordie went to hit Kennedy but missed him," Lumley says now. "My opinion is that Kennedy simply avoided the check and Gordie hit the boards." And yet many Red Wings of the time, including Marty Pavelich and even Howe himself, still believe the butt of Kennedy's stick caught Howe in the eye, although without any intent to injure.

Later in the game, Kennedy suffered a severe charley horse from being vengefully checked into the Detroit net. The next game of the series would be even wilder, with bitter fighting and stick-swinging by both teams. Eventually, an official inquiry into the incident by the NHL would exonerate Kennedy of any wrongdoing.

Meanwhile, team doctor Dr. Charles Karibo ordered Howe to be rushed to nearby Harper Hospital in the ambulance that was always kept on standby at the rear of the Olympia. On examination by hospital physicians, Howe was found to have a fractured nose and cheekbone, a badly lacerated eyeball and—by far the most dangerous injury—apparent hemorrhaging of the brain. His blood pressure was falling, his pulse depressed.

The resident in charge telephoned Dr. Frederic Schreiber, an internationally known neurosurgeon, who hurried to the hospital to assess Howe's condition. Dr. Schreiber recommended immediate surgery to avert brain damage and possibly death. The person who gave permission for the surgery to proceed, the only person with authority to stand in for the family, was Jack Adams. Adams said later that Howe became semiconscious before entering the operating room and, characteristically, tried to apologize for not playing better.

At 1:00 A.M., Dr. Schreiber began an extremely delicate procedure. He drilled a small opening in Howe's skull just above his right eye and slowly drained a pocket of fluid to relieve mounting pressure on the brain. In all, the operation took ninety minutes. Howe was placed in an oxygen tent immediately after surgery.

Adams put in a call to Saskatoon. He informed the family of what had happened and offered to bring Mr. and Mrs. Howe to Detroit, telling them, "It's touch and go."

That night, radio stations in Detroit and across Canada carried updates on Howe's condition. In Saskatoon, the station stayed on the air all night to carry reports, instead of signing off at the usual hour. Howe's life-threatening accident became the top story in the news.

The Red Wings, staying in seclusion in Toledo during the playoffs, wouldn't go to bed until they heard the medical verdict about their teammate. Finally, Adams phoned Ivan to tell him the news: Howe had pulled through the surgery successfully. His condition was now listed as serious, but no longer critical.

Next morning, the hospital issued a detailed bulletin. Howe was recovering and had escaped a skull fracture. His eye would not be permanently damaged. The fluid was still draining from his brain, but he had regained full consciousness and had been removed from the oxygen tent. And incidentally, he'd probably be able to play hockey again next season.

When Katherine Howe and her eldest daughter, Gladys, arrived in Detroit by plane, her son was still on the serious list and not allowed to see visitors. Mrs. Howe went directly to Harper Hospital.

"I went to his door," she related some years later, "and the nurse came out and said, 'Shh, you can't come in here.' And I said, 'Oh yes I can, you're not keepin' me out.' She says [realizing it was Howe's mother], 'Oh, I'm sorry, but don't cry and make a fuss.' And I says, 'I don't think I will.'

"So I walked up to the bed, and his sore eye was all bandaged up, and his other one was, oh, so *black*. I said, 'Come on, Scout, it's time to get up. What are you doin' in bed here all day?'

"And he didn't move. And I looked at the nurse, and she said, 'Go ahead,' so I talked to him again. And all at once, up comes his hand and down goes the cloth on the eye, and he says, 'Oh, Mom, what are *you* doin' here?'

"And I says, 'I just come to see you. Everybody's concerned about you.' Oh, of course he grabbed me, and he was the one, really, who broke down, you know."

Mrs. Howe came to visit her son in the hospital every day and was present a few days later when his bandages were removed permanently. On one of her visits, Howe pressed a hundred dollars into her hand and told her to visit the Detroit shops and buy herself some nice clothes.

Mrs. Howe even attended the next playoff game as the Red Wings' guest, accompanied by Gladys, and came away appalled by the violence the players inflicted on each other. It was her first NHL game, and she cried. She wouldn't mind at all, she insisted tearfully, if Gordie had to quit this crazy game.

Howe's accident and miraculous recovery were the talk of Detroit. He received a steady stream of mail wishing him well, sometimes accompanied by small gifts. Today, as with all the other injuries he suffered or inflicted, Howe jokingly passes the incident off as just part of the game: "I tell everybody I used to be pretty at one time. But [the accident] took my nose and put it over here."

Meanwhile, the Red Wings finally proved they could lick the Leafs when it counted. They emerged victorious in the seventh game of the series by the slimmest of margins, 1-0, after a goal-tenders' duel between Lumley and Broda for three scoreless periods. Defenseman Leo Reise scored in overtime, his second game-winner of the series, to lift the Wings into the finals against the New York Rangers, who had eliminated Montreal in five.

Howe's teammates phoned him at the hospital to tell him the good news. He surprised them by saying he'd watched the whole thing: the television era had arrived for the NHL.

The finals turned out to be just as close and dramatic as the semifinals. Detroit and New York would take each other to seven games, three of them ending in overtime. With a strong offense led by Don Raleigh, Edgar Laprade, Buddy O'Connor and future Red Wing Tony Leswick, and with Hart trophy-winner Chuck Rayner superb in goal, the Rangers under coach Lynn Patrick threatened (as they would again in 1972 and 1979, finally succeeding in 1994) to win their first Stanley Cup since 1940.

For Detroit, the returned Joe Carveth and Saskatoon's Gerry Couture, who normally played on a line with George Gee and Pete Babando, both filled in for Howe on the Production Line. Couture had enjoyed a fine season that year, scoring 24 goals, and would end up tied for second place in playoff scoring with Raleigh and Gee.

A film documentary exists of the 1950 finals; intended to promote the NHL among the uninitiated in the U.S., it gushingly describes hockey as "the fastest sport in the world in which human beings participate without mechanical assistance—a matchless spectacle of speed, stamina and red-blooded courage." To judge from the film, the gush was accurate.

Raleigh's two spectacular game-winning goals, both in over-time, gave New York a 3-2 series lead going into the sixth game. Ahead 3-1 in the second period of that game, the Rangers looked unstoppable until Abel and Couture both scored. In the third period, Leswick and Lindsay swapped goals to make it 4-4. Finally

Abel, in a truly astonishing and literally breathtaking effort that deserves to be remembered for as long as anyone remembers hockey, drove in on the Ranger net, tripped over Rayner's pads and, flying upended across the goalmouth with his skates higher than his head, somehow managed to control the puck and slide it around Rayner. Detroit had stayed alive for a seventh game.

Fortunately for the Red Wings, the deciding match was scheduled for the Olympia. The Rangers had been ousted from Madison Square Garden by a circus; hence New York had elected to play its "home" games in Maple Leaf Gardens, the seat of Detroit's archrivals. The Toronto fans adopted the Rangers as their own and cheered them lustily.

The seventh game developed into another cliffhanger. Trailing 2-0, the Red Wings drew even with goals by Babando and Abel within twenty-two seconds of each other. With the score tied at three by the end of the second period, the teams proceeded to play more than fifty-two scoreless minutes before the deciding goal at 8:31 of the second overtime period.

It was fired through a melee of bodies by the Red Wings' Pete Babando, on a pass from George Gee—although some in Saskatoon say Gerry Couture tipped the puck into the net and deserved the credit—and it was the very first overtime goal to decide a Stanley Cup in the seventh game.

The fans in the Olympia went absolutely wild. At last, after years of playoff defeat and frustration, they could surrender to the delirium of victory. The Detroit players threw their gloves into the air, kissed and embraced, and hoisted little Tommy Ivan onto their shoulders. As the Cup was presented to Sid Abel at centre ice, Jack Adams waddled joyously up behind him and gave his captain a smothering bear hug from the rear. Abel set the Cup onto a small wooden table and skated around the ice with it, pushing the table ahead of him so that fans in every section of the Olympia could get a better look. Then Lindsay, with his native flair for the dramatic, seized the Cup, hoisted it high over his head and paraded it around the ice followed by those new witnesses of NHL history, the television cameras—thus coining an enduring image of Stanley Cup triumph, a victory gesture that would be repeated year after year unto the present day.

In the midst of their excitement, the fans chanted, "We want Howe. We want Howe." And they got him. Well launched on his recovery, Howe was out there on the ice, wearing a suit and a hat to cover his scarred and shaved head, still tender from the operation twelve days earlier. In jubilation, Lindsay snatched his best friend's fedora and whipped it into the crowd. Then Adams ruffled the stubble on his young favourite's scalp and held his arm aloft like a heavyweight champion's.

And yet, glad as he was for his team, Howe couldn't help feeling set apart from the celebrations. He couldn't quite allow himself to let go and believe that *he'd* won, too. Over forty years later, he'd explain that his injuries had prevented him from feeling he could take any credit for the victory. "I like to earn things," he said. "To be on the ice, and sweat and bleed with the boys."

There would be plenty of blood, sweat and ice, and three more Stanley Cup celebrations, in the seasons to come.

CHAPTER SEVEN

All in the Family

"Howe would stay on skates twenty-four hours
if you let him."

—Harry Lumley, 1994

THE YEAR OF GORDIE HOWE'S brush with death coincided with the beginning of the Detroit dynasty. In the seven post-seasons between 1950 and 1956, the Red Wings would reach the finals five times. They'd win four Stanley Cups—three in four years against the Montreal Canadiens.

It's a terrifically impressive record, one of the finest in Stanley Cup history. And yet, to hear Red Wing players from that period tell it, they should have done even better: that's how much talent and power the team possessed, and that's how badly they wanted to win. As we'll see later, some of them are still bitter that it was the Canadiens, and not the Wings, who eventually won five Cups in a row.

But all of that lay in the future for Howe and his team. First, he had to finish mending after his frightening injuries.

The vigil kept by his mother and sister at his Detroit hospital bed shows how close he remained to his family at that time. After the Wings triumphed without him in the 1950 finals, Howe returned as usual to Saskatoon, spending the spring and early summer completing his recovery at home. Physically and psychologically, it was the most conducive atmosphere for healing.

Gradually, he was able to return to his summertime pursuits— baseball, fishing, golf. In those days, it was baseball that Howe loved most. It was considerably less punishing than hockey, and it gave him the chance to test his recovery and rebuild his strength before the new NHL season began. One thing he could count on: at twenty-two, he had the resilience of youth on his side.

Both softball and baseball were big draws in Saskatchewan in the 1940s and '50s. Major-league scouts used to say the calibre of western Canada semi-pro baseball was equivalent to that of double-A in the States. Small Saskatchewan towns such as Delisle, Rosetown and North Battleford, as well as the larger centres, fielded strong teams of local ballplayers supplemented by American imports, some of them recruited from the Black leagues in the midwest. In addition to their league schedules, Saskatchewan teams competed for prize money offered by numerous tournaments throughout the province, such as the annual Dominion Day tournament held at the old Cairns Field (now gone) on Avenue A (now Idylwyld) in Saskatoon.

For several summers, Howe was a familiar figure on the base paths at Cairns Field. It was a comfortable, roofed ballpark that could normally seat up to 5,000, but the July 1 tournament drew as many as 10,000 spectators, jamming the stands and extra bleachers and ringing the outfield. Baseball and softball tournaments were major local attractions in the days before television kept people at home and before cars, motor homes and cottages took them out of town for the summer holidays.

Howe had been playing ball since his school days; he'd once pitched for the King George softball team in the city finals. In semi-pro baseball, he played first base and sometimes third and was one of the most powerful and consistent hitters, batting .370 one season for Saskatoon. He was far from being the only Saskatchewan NHLer playing ball there in the off-season. Bert Olmstead played for Moose Jaw. Emile Francis was the playing manager for North Battleford. And the powerful team from Delisle, which took the money at many provincial tournaments, starred and was run by the Bentley brothers, Max, Doug and Reg.

Ned Powers, the veteran sports columnist for the Saskatoon *StarPhoenix*, likes to relate the local Howe legend of "the longest home run ever hit at Cairns Field." The Canadian Pacific Railway tracks ran right behind the ballpark; one day Howe, playing baseball for Saskatoon, drove a towering home run over the right-field fence. The ball landed on a moving CPR flatcar and didn't stop until it reached the town of Unity, eighty miles to the west. Of course, over the years the tale has grown taller, with the train not stopping until Calgary, or even Vancouver.

In any case, anyone who watched him play agrees that Howe's exceptional reach, coordination and physical strength made him a superb ballplayer. Long before Michael Jordan's quixotic attempt to cross sports, Howe's off-season prowess led people to speculate he could have made it big in the majors. But Jack Adams would put a permanent damper on such fantasies. In summer 1952, after hearing Howe had been spiked while playing and had developed blood poisoning, Adams wired his young favourite in Saskatoon: "Quit baseball Stop Who will pay bills if you are hurt."

Howe sent a return telegram: "Dear Jack Adams are you serious."

And Adams wired back: "Dear Gordon Howe I am serious."

After that, Howe had to content himself with invitations to join batting practice with the Detroit Tigers—and, on one occasion well-remembered by former teammates, the Cleveland Indians. He's said to have driven a few out of the park then, too, after Cleveland manager Lou Boudreau offered him the chance to try his luck against major-league pitching. It may just have been coincidence, but when Howe was able to afford a new house for his mom and dad, it would be located right across from Cairns Field, the site of his old baseball triumphs.

When he returned east for training camp to start the 1950-51 season, Howe was determined to prove two things to himself and everyone else: that he was completely recovered from his injuries of five months earlier, and that he was tougher than ever, unaffected by his mishap. As always, it was vital to him to demonstrate he couldn't be intimidated on the ice. It was his perennial application of Ab's old maxim, and he'd uphold it as long as he played professional hockey. That season, in addition to being his highest-scoring yet, would also be his most penalized so far.

Reinforcing Howe's determination was a recurring—and, from this distance, inexplicable—fear of losing his spot on the team.

He dreaded being sent down to Indianapolis, suffering the painful sense of failure and the inevitable cut in pay. Ted Lindsay has attested, with a trace of wonderment, to Howe's insecurity at training camp: "Genuinely, sincerely, he felt he had to worry about his position. He would say, 'Gee, I hope I make the team.' Or, 'That guy isn't going to get my job. He'll do it over my body.'"

In a sense, this was Howe's big secret: he ran scared. Just as he'd use his elbows and stickwork for preemptive strikes, designed to discourage opponents' attacks before they happened, so he used his fear of demotion as a goad to make himself try harder, practise longer, play better than ever. He learned to use his own psychology to his profit.

This too seems a reflection of an attitude Ab Howe had taught his children: never be too sure of yourself. If your head swells too full, you'll just suffer a comeuppance. It was essentially an underdog philosophy, and if Gordie was able to turn it to advantage as a hockey player, sometimes Ab took it to strange extremes.

Howe's sister Joan recalls her father telling her and her brothers and sisters, when Gordie was becoming well-known in the NHL, not to boast to outsiders about his success. "If Dad ever caught one of us bragging about Gord, we were in for it. We weren't even supposed to say we were related. I guess he didn't want us to be smart-alecks. We were all proud of Gord, but Dad didn't want us to go around and make ourselves look stupid."

Although never in real danger of failing to make the team, Howe *was* joined on the 1950-51 team by some very talented new players, whose presence egged him on to show what he could do. The new recruits were a mixture of youth and experience, and several would be highly instrumental to the future success of the Detroit dynasty.

A major trade in the off-season between the Wings and the Black Hawks involving nine players—one of the biggest NHL trades to date, and one of many that Adams would engineer with Chicago over the years—had brought high-scoring forward Metro Prystai, veteran defenseman Bob Goldham and two others onto the team. Sacrificed to the Black Hawks were goaltender Harry Lumley, all-star defenseman Jack Stewart, whom Adams considered over the hill, Pete Babando and two others. In addition, up for their rookie seasons came two future standouts—centre Glen Skov and defenseman Marcel Pronovost. But even more important would be the player brought up from Indianapolis to take Lumley's place: Terry Sawchuk, who had played seven games in the previous season while Lumley was injured, and who in the opinion of many would develop into the greatest goaltender the game has ever seen.

Thus the Red Wings, while retaining the nucleus of Abel, Howe, Lindsay, Kelly and Pavelich, would be substantially different at all positions from the team that had just won the Cup. Sweeping shakeups like this were typical of Adams's management style. He thought he knew when a player was losing career momentum before anyone else did, and he prided himself on shrewdly dealing for new blood to rejuvenate his remaining players. Adams, too, ran scared, trying to second-guess his own players' legs, longevity and dedication to the team. According to Bud Lynch, the Red Wings' veteran broadcaster and announcer, "Adams believed even a winning combination had to be broken up, because they weren't hungry any more."

The problem with tampering so fundamentally with the dynamics of a championship team was that a season or more was required before the new dynamics worked themselves out and produced another winner. This partly explains why Adams's teams seldom won Stanley Cups in succession.

On the other hand, for players who came to the Wings of that era, the move was a happy event. The team was successful on the ice and at the box office, and with a perennial contender at the Olympia, Detroit had become an excellent hockey town. Metro Prystai, living today in retirement in his native Yorkton, Saskatchewan, recalls: "Everybody wanted to play for Detroit at that time. It was such a good outfit."

Prystai's new teammates also knew they were fortunate. With 29 goals, he'd been the NHL's fourth-highest goal-scorer the previous season, after Richard, Howe and Abel, and they gave him a warm welcome: "When Ted Lindsay heard I was coming to Detroit, he asked me if I had a place to live yet. Well, that just eased everything—I went to stay at Ma Shaw's. At training camp, they treated you like a brother."

The Red Wings' team culture was like that: governed by a family spirit, with a family's loyalty and closeness and continuity, and a family's sense of pride in playing for Detroit. Like any NHL team of the Original Six era, this was a collection of young Canadians who lived for hockey, who came mostly from working-class backgrounds and small towns scattered across Canada and had to create their own sense of community within an alien, industrial metropolis. But the Wings were even closer than most. Living together at home as well as on the road, they bonded by doing practically everything together, from playing cards and drinking beer to dating women and worshipping God. In time, they would become each other's best man at weddings, each other's partner in business ventures. They were a clan, with clannish ways.

The reason there was room at Ma Shaw's for Prystai was that Lindsay had moved out. He'd bought a house in a Detroit suburb for his parents, bringing them down from Kirkland Lake and moving in with them. And, as always, Lindsay had taken Howe with him.

The two inseparables now shared practically everything. At the beginning of the 1949-50 season, they'd agreed to share any bonuses from the NHL scoring leadership equally, no matter who won—after all, they contributed equally to each other's success. So it was natural that Howe would share living quarters with Lindsay and his folks.

"It worked out nicely for us," Lindsay recalls. "We had home cooking and a nice home to come back to." Little by little, both young men were putting down adult roots, making commitments.

The Red Wings who couldn't bring their parents to Detroit brought their surrogate mothers to the Olympia to watch them play. Sawchuk, who had gone to live at Ma Tannahill's house, brought her to the games; Ma Shaw's gang, including Kelly, Pavelich and Prystai, brought her. Back home after the games, Ma Shaw would play the piano and lead her boys in a singalong. Howe still came around to the old house on McGraw to visit, even after moving out. "He was one of her favourites," Prystai remembers.

When the '50-'51 training camp was held in Pavelich's home town of Sault Ste. Marie, Ontario, the boys went over to Marty's to fill up on some of Mrs. Pavelich's good home cooking. And during the regular season, the Wings helped each other cope with the hockey player's chronic professional hazard: too much time on their hands.

They pulled practical jokes, stunts involving pails of water and exploding cigars and the usual head- and groin-shaving rituals, the kind of thing where you had to be there to see the humour. They played poker or pinochle for a penny a point. They watched the afternoon feature at the Fox Theater on Woodward. Or they walked up Grand River Avenue to the Lucky Strike bowling lanes, divided themselves into teams from western and eastern Canada and bowled for the honour of Saskatoon, Saskatchewan, or Kincardine, Ontario. The Lucky Strike, located just three blocks from the Olympia, was a favourite hangout and would soon become the site of a fateful romantic rendezvous.

Speaking of romance, the Red Wings liked to dance—or at least, in the case of some of the unattached players, to hang out where dancers could be found. Prystai remembers a Detroit ballroom he and his teammates frequented: "You couldn't go out and drink all the goddamn time, and you couldn't twiddle your thumbs, so we'd go ballroom dancing. It was something to do, and it was a way to pick up girls. Marty loved dancing. I used to like to watch. I don't think Gordie danced, but he'd go out with us anyway."

As they became better known to the Detroit fans, the Red Wings found it harder to have a good time in public. There was the clean-cut team image to maintain; worse, there were informants whom Jack Adams, a staunch churchgoer and strict teetotaller, despatched to the downtown bars to spy on his players' vices.

"We had to be careful," Prystai recalls. "Anywhere we went with Kelly, with that bright red hair of his, people recognized him. I used to say, 'Red, put on a goddamn hat.' People'd see us in a bar and send over a beer, but we had to keep moving, we couldn't stay there all night."

Although Abel remained captain, Lindsay was emerging as the new team leader, not only on the ice but off, and especially among the unmarried players. With his take-charge approach, Scarface (as Lindsay was becoming known, well on his way to

Above: Fourteen-year-old Gordie Howe starred on defense for Saskatoon's King George Athletic Club Bantams in 1942. Howe, in the back row, third from right, stands beside Mrs. Frances Hodges, whose family had an outdoor rink where Gordie practised day and night.
KING GEORGE COMMUNITY SCHOOL

Right: Howe, seventeen, is pictured with famous namesake Syd Howe at the Red Wings' training camp in October 1945. Photo shows original *Detroit News* cropping.
MacGregor / DETROIT NEWS

Far right: Gordie spent his first professional season, 1945-46, with the Omaha Aksarben Knights, a Detroit farm team. Howe is third from right in the back row. At extreme right is coach Tommy Ivan, next to goaltender Lefty Wilson.

Overleaf: Howe as he looked as an eighteen-year-old rookie with Detroit, 1946.
DETROIT NEWS

During their 1950 training camp in Sault Ste. Marie, Ontario, five hungry Red Wings fill up on Mrs. Pavelich's spaghetti and meatballs. *From left:* Howe, Bob Goldham, Metro Prystai, Ted Lindsay, Marty Pavelich. Ray Glonka/Detroit Free Press
Right: Howe, nineteen in 1947, works out on the exercise bike to build up his muscle mass. At 187 pounds, he was almost 20 pounds below his eventual playing weight of 205. Detroit Free Press
Far right: Olympia Stadium in Detroit, as it looked during the Red Wings' great years of the 1950s. Detroit News

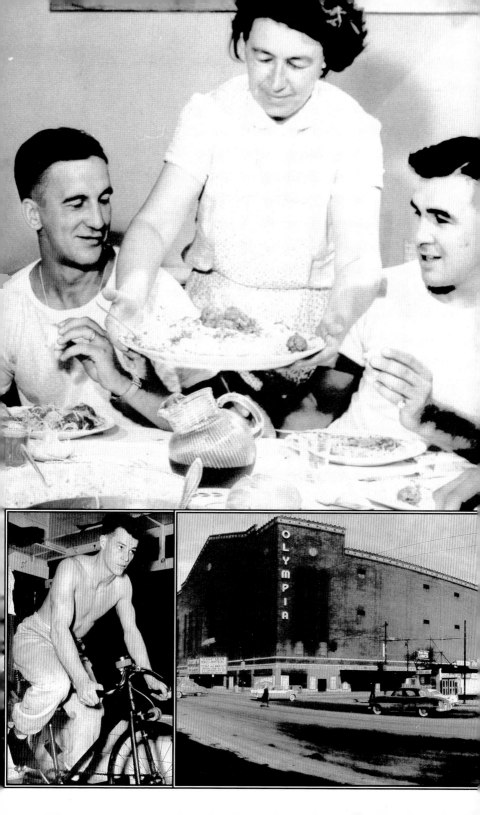

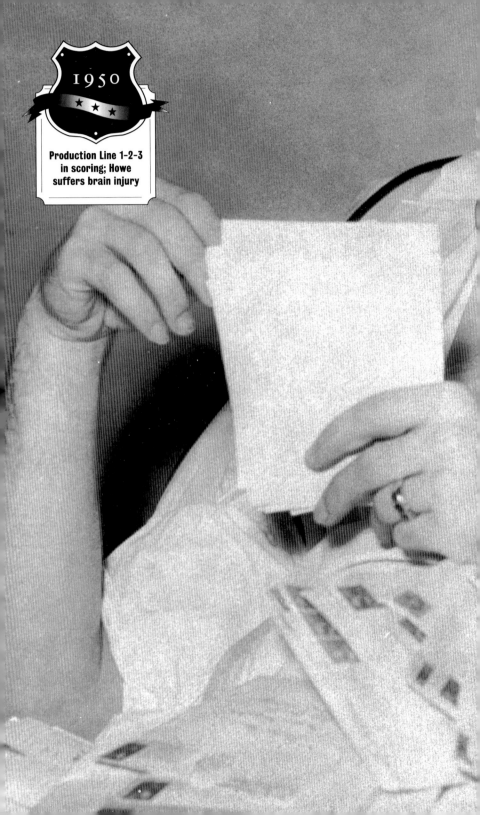

1950

Production Line 1-2-3 in scoring; Howe suffers brain injury

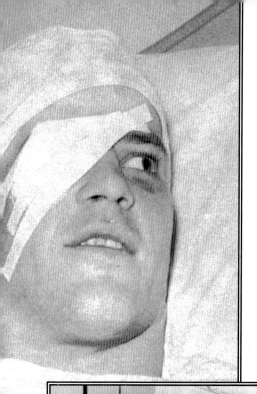

Left: Following brain surgery after his near-fatal collision with Toronto's Ted Kennedy in the 1950 semifinals, Howe is deluged with sympathy mail in Detroit's Harper Hospital. H. BURGERT / DETROIT NEWS

Lower left: Howe began playing the following season with a leather helmet, which he discarded as soon as he was permitted to. JAMES R. KILPATRICK / DETROIT NEWS

Below: In the seven-game finals in 1950, the Red Wings went on to defeat the New York Rangers for the Stanley Cup, pictured here with jubilant team captain Sid Abel. DETROIT NEWS

The official portrait of the fabulous 1951-52 Red Wings team that swept the Stanley Cup playoffs against Toronto and Montreal in eight games straight—including four shutouts, all on home ice. *Back row, from left:* Marcel Pronovost, Bob Goldham, Fred Glover, Vic Stasiuk, Alex Delvecchio, Lefty Wilson (asst. trainer); *Middle row:* Jack Adams (G.M.), Tony Leswick,

Metro Prystai, Marty Pavelich, Leo Reise, Red Kelly, Ben Woit, Tommy Ivan (coach), Carl Mattson (trainer); *Front row:* Terry Sawchuk, Ted Lindsay, Sid Abel (captain), Gordie Howe, Glen Skov, Bill Tibbs. JAMES R. KILPATRICK/DETROIT NEWS

1952

★ ★ ★

**Red Wings sweep
Stanley Cup; Howe wins
1st Hart trophy**

Left: The most famous photo ever taken of the Production Line: *from left,* Howe, Sid Abel, Ted Lindsay. JAMES R. KILPATRICK / DETROIT NEWS

Above: In 1953, Howe came within a goal of equalling Rocket Richard's record of 50 goals in a season. Gordie checks out his fan mail that year at the Olympia as goalie Terry Sawchuk peers over his shoulder. DETROIT FREE PRESS

Below: After the Red Wings were upset by Boston in the 1953 semifinals, an exhausted and dejected Howe was the last to leave the Detroit dressing room. Ten days later, he married Colleen Joffa. At rear are matron of honour Pat Lindsay and best man Vern Howe, one of Gordie's two older brothers.

UPI / BETTMAN; STYRLANDER / DETROIT NEWS

Above: Ted Lindsay and Marty Pavelich went into business together in the mid-1950s in Detroit, briefly including Howe as a partner.

1955

Red Wings win
fourth and final Cup
of Howe's career

Left: When G.M. Jack Adams alleged the players were spending too much time on business and becoming too wealthy, Colleen Howe and Pat Lindsay turned up at the Olympia in borrowed mink stoles, clutching handfuls of Monopoly money.
JAMES R. KILPATRICK / DETROIT NEWS
Below: Adams is portrayed with Howe in 1955, the last year the Red Wings won the Stanley Cup.
RANSOM / DETROIT NEWS

Left: The Red Wings vs. the Canadiens was the NHL's biggest rivalry in the early to mid-1950s. In some hot and heavy action, Ted Lindsay leaps straight up to screen Jacques Plante on the shot. *From left:* Doug Harvey, Claude Provost, Howe, Lindsay, Plante.

Below: My brother, my foe: Vic Howe, left, who played parts of three seasons with the New York Rangers, shakes hands with brother Gordie before a game in 1955. DETROIT NEWS

Overleaf: In 1957, a proud dad hoists two future teammates: Marty Howe, three years old and forty-five pounds, and Mark Howe, two years old and forty pounds.

JAMES R. KILPATRICK / DETROIT NEWS

collecting his career total of four hundred stitches) acted as a genial, broken-nosed social convenor, organizing the Monday night parties (game nights were usually Wednesdays, Thursdays, Saturdays and Sundays) and making sure everyone turned out or had a damned good excuse if they didn't. An Italian restaurant closed to the public on Mondays was regularly reserved for the Red Wings' private soirees.

"We'd go there with girlfriends and wives and let loose a little," Prystai says. "Not getting into any trouble, you know, but it was nice to have a place to ourselves, where we didn't have to worry about being seen in public. Lefty and Lil Wilson were always there. Lefty was a real partygoer, lots of fun."

At that point, Wilson had just arrived from Indianapolis as assistant trainer and standby goaltender behind Sawchuk. He relishes memories of those Monday night blowouts and snorts derisively at highly publicized drinking incidents involving latter-day Detroit players, such as Bob Probert and Petr Klima: "Hell, we *spilled* more beer than those guys drank."

Wilson recalls Lindsay enforcing team togetherness on Mondays. "You had to go, you couldn't get out of it. If you didn't go, you'd pay anyways. Lindsay'd come along and say, 'Where were *you* last night?' And you'd have to pay whatever it cost, ten bucks or something. And you'd pay up."

Then there was Sunday Mass. The Red Wings included a large nucleus of Catholics in those days, led by Adams himself. They didn't always attend church together, but Marty Pavelich says the frequency of team worship increased around playoff time: "We'd stay in retreat in Toledo during the playoffs, and a bunch of guys used to get up in the morning and go to Mass. There was Kelly, Lindsay, Sawchuk, Prystai, Pronovost, Benny Woit, Lefty Wilson and I. And Adams, of course. Protestant guys like Bob Goldham would give us a couple of dollars and say, 'Light some candles for us.' "

Howe too, being Protestant, was in the group that worshipped vicariously, or elsewhere. But Goldham, who was notoriously superstitious, liked to cover his bets; team folklore had it that a well-placed prayer or votive candle could turn the tide in crucial games.

Les Costello, who played briefly for Toronto and later became better known as Father Costello, a member of the Flying Fathers who played hockey for charity, once spotted Adams praying in the chapel at St. Michael's College. As they travelled together on the train back to Detroit for the next game, Costello grinned at Adams and said, "Jack, you won't be winning tonight. After you left, I blew out all your candles."

The Red Wings' active churchgoing continued for a number of years. When Father Costello's younger brother, Murray, arrived to play for Detroit in 1955, the team was still turning out in force for Mass. "By then it was kind of a tradition," Murray Costello remembers. "It kept them close."

Nonetheless, the glue bonding the Red Wings wasn't Christianity or ballroom dancing or boozing, but raw desire: the burning will to be the best of the best.

"The chemistry on the team was just fantastic," Pavelich says. He believes Detroit had solid coaching, certainly when Tommy Ivan was there, but that the players themselves supplied the vital element: "You always need a few guys who really want to win—who'll do whatever it takes to win—and can instil that desire in the rest of the team. We had that: guys like Lindsay, Howe, Kelly, Pronovost. We had a lot of hungry individuals. If we lost two games in a row, we'd be so mad at ourselves. The next team we played had to watch out, we'd kick hell out of them. Yet it wasn't just money we played for. It was love of the game."

That may sound like a hoary, sentimental cliché, but so many players of the era—certainly a Howe or a Kelly or a Lindsay or a Prystai—will use that same phrase, "love of the game," that same emotional language, no matter how much they've focussed in recent years on their relatively low salaries at the time, or the inequities and rip-offs involved in the pension issue. "We loved our game," Lindsay says. "We had a wonderful game that we loved to play."

But it wasn't as if they wanted to play it in the International League or the American League or the senior leagues of Ontario or Quebec or western Canada. Whether for love or money or pride, or simply to play with the best in the world, everyone desperately wanted to play—and stay—in the NHL.

It wasn't that easy. With only six teams, compared to twenty-six today, a mere 120 players could wear NHL sweaters at any given time. Consequently, they tended to be not only the most talented but the hungriest, the smartest, the most driven. Competition was ferocious, within teams and between teams. As Pavelich explains it, "You played every team fourteen times a year, so everybody had a book on you. The players you'd go against knew all your moves; they practically knew when you went to the bathroom."

And if the opposing players weren't enough to worry about, there was your own management. Since so few NHL positions were available, and so many hundreds of skilled minor-league players were eager to move into them, the law of supply and demand played heavily into management's hands.

"You played and played and played," Pavelich says, "and if you let down, somebody'd take your job. If you had some little injury, you kept right on playing over it." This gave general managers and coaches tremendous leverage over the men on the ice, almost the opposite of the situation in the NHL today. "They controlled us, we were at their mercy. If they didn't like you, they'd railroad you out of the league. If Adams didn't like the way you parted your hair, he'd get rid of you."

In that light, Howe's anxiety about losing his place on the team becomes a little more understandable. Prompted to excel by his native competitiveness and the theoretical threat of displacement, he never ceased practising his shooting and stick-handling and puck control. He became notorious for being the first guy on the ice before practice, the last guy off afterwards. Then, and for years later, Howe's coaches literally had to order him to the dressing room to get some rest and let the arena staff go home for dinner.

"He used to stay out on the ice after practice and try everything he could think of," Harry Lumley remembers. "Howe would stay on skates twenty-four hours if you let him."

But then Howe enjoyed practising in a way that is beyond the comprehension of ordinary mortals. The ice was his natural element, just as in the old days when he had spent long, solitary hours on the Hodges' backyard rink in Saskatoon. Playing and practising the game of hockey remained as much as ever his idea of heaven: a case of equal parts love, dedication, perfectionism and insecurity—a potent combination that led, sometimes, to perfection itself.

One of Howe's favourite practice rituals occurred when he was all by himself, after the other players had left the ice. He'd take two buckets full of pucks, emptying out one at the blueline against the boards and the other diagonally across the ice at the other blueline. Then he'd begin a continuous circuit of the rink, and as he passed the mound of pucks at each blueline, he'd pull a puck out and let it fly at the net—around and around, not pausing, until the pucks ran out. Former teammate Murray Costello, now director of the Canadian Amateur Hockey Association, recalls watching this solitary, single-minded, obsessive ritual.

"He'd just lope around the ice with that long stride of his and that big shot and that little curve in his stick. And he'd pull a puck out and just *snap* it with his wrists. If he didn't hear the *ping* against the goalpost, in or out, he'd be mad at himself. He'd just lope around and *ping*, *ping*, and he'd shoot that snap shot of his— he was the one who perfected it first. It was unbelievable. He felt he had to be able to shoot the puck right to a spot, and he used the goalpost as his mark. You never shot *at* a goalie, you shot to just miss him, and so he used the goalpost, and he was amazing. And they'd yell at him, 'Gordie, get the hell off the ice, you've got a game tomorrow night!'"

Somehow, all that extra practising never wore him down or tired him out for the next game. It just helped him get better and better.

CHAPTER EIGHT

When the Red Wings Ruled

"We could have played all summer and kept on winning."
—Marty Pavelich, 1993

WITH THE MOST SERIOUS INJURY of his career now behind him, Howe proceeded to play the first of his truly outstanding seasons in 1950-51. His natural talents converging with his growing NHL experience, he now began, in his fifth year in the league, his long assault on the record book.

The only dark note came early in the season. In a disturbing echo of his head injury, Howe found himself suffering in November from repeated headaches and dizzy spells. Adams required him to wear a leather helmet, and for a short while Howe became the only NHL player wearing headgear (although not the first to do so). This was ironic since, after discarding the helmet, he would continue playing well into the era of plastic helmets and would support their use by others, yet refused to wear one himself. "They're great," he always said, "for kids."

As the season progressed, the headaches wore off, and Howe found himself neck and neck in a race for the scoring title with fellow-right wing Maurice Richard. The Rocket was burning up the league. Scoring the 271st goal of his career, he surpassed the career total of Aurel Joliat; three goals later, he passed another and even greater Montreal legend, Howie Morenz. But Howe, who had finished three points ahead of the Rocket a year earlier, burned just as brightly, staying with him point for point, and in February adding fuel to their accelerating rivalry by scoring the winning goal against Montreal—the 100th of his career—before a record crowd at the Forum. To add insult to injury, it was Maurice Richard Night. It wouldn't be the last time Howe would steal the Rocket's thunder.

That season a less edifying rivalry, which had been continuing for years, erupted once again between Lindsay and fellow policeman Bill Ezinicki, then with Boston. One night in January, the two fought a vicious battle with sticks and fists that stands as some sort of landmark in hockey violence. After taking the butt-end of Ezinicki's stick in his left eye, Lindsay retaliated with a stick-blow that carved Ezinicki's forehead.

"With the gentle stuff out of the way," wrote David Cruise and Alison Griffiths in *Net Worth*, "they went at it with their fists. Lindsay was leading on points by the time the officials separated them . . . Ezinicki slipped away from the scrum and circled wide around Lindsay, whose back was turned. Lindsay saw him coming but feigned unawareness. At the perfect instant, he wheeled and landed a right that felled Ezinicki to the ice head first."

It was typical of "Terrible Ted," as the sportswriters liked to call him, to use his brains as well as his unforgiving fists; but when he leaped on Ezinicki's fallen body to prosecute the fight, Lindsay discovered his foe was already unconscious. Condemning the incident in outraged tones, league president Clarence Campbell suspended the two brawlers for three games and fined them both $300—a lot of money in those days, especially for a professional hockey player.

By the end of the regular schedule, Howe had played the full 70 games, leaving no doubt whatever that he'd sprung back from his injuries healthier than ever. It would be the first of five straight 70-game seasons for him, the beginning of a string of 382 consecutive games—early signs of a durability that no one could have predicted at the time.

Just as importantly, his performance was so consistent during the second half of the season that he pulled steadily away from Richard in scoring. Howe scored a nicely symmetrical 43 goals and 43 assists to capture the first of his six scoring titles with 86 points—a goal and 19 assists more than Richard, who came second. Even allowing for the fact that the Rocket had missed five games because of injury, he'd been decisively outscored. Howe rudely bumped him from his accustomed position on the first all-star team.

This was also the first time Howe had surpassed his two partners on the Production Line. Abel finished tied for fourth place in scoring with 61 points, and Lindsay was seventh with 59. With Red Kelly leading all NHL defensemen at 54 points, Detroit had four scorers in the top nine.

Not surprisingly, then, the Red Wings earned first place for the third straight year; they also became the NHL's first 100-point team, hitting 101. They had such a potent offense, stout defense and excellent goaltending from twenty-one-year-old Sawchuk, whose classy 1.98 average placed him second for the Vezina after Toronto's Al Rollins and earned him the Calder trophy as top rookie, that the Wings were favoured to repeat for the 1951 Stanley Cup. But something happened on their way to the finals.

In the semifinal round, they drew the Canadiens, who had finished third between Toronto and Boston, a distant 36 points off the pace. In the midst of rebuilding, Montreal coach Dick Irvin had replaced Bill Durnan in goal with Gerry McNeil, and had added several new players, notably Tom Johnson, Bert Olmstead and a junior named Bernie Geoffrion, who would score a decisive goal in the semifinals.

Montreal were the underdogs, but they stunned Detroit by winning the first two games—at the Olympia, no less. Both went into overtime, and Richard showed why he was considered the ultimate clutch player by scoring the winning goal both times. Overtime games are commonplace in playoff competition, but these two were uncommonly long: the first ran into a mind-boggling fourth overtime period, the second into a third. Not only that, the second game was scoreless for over five periods, an epic marathon duel between two rookie goaltenders. Sawchuk tirelessly held off the Canadiens, while McNeil brilliantly foiled Howe (who had scored in the first game), Lindsay and Abel again and again and again. Finally, the Rocket, on a pass from balding Billy Reay, zoomed in on Sawchuk and fired a backhander behind him to win the game 1-0 in the 103rd minute.

The Red Wings reasserted themselves by winning games three and four at the Forum: Pavelich's fanatical checking neutralized Richard both times. In the third game, Howe marked his twenty-third birthday by scoring one of Detroit's two goals in a shutout victory. In the fourth game, Detroit's winning margin was three goals, scored by three other players from Saskatchewan, Prystai, Couture and Abel.

But going against form, Montreal pulled ahead in the fifth game on Geoffrion's deciding marker, which the Boomer has called "my first big goal." Then, in the sixth game, two unthinkable things happened: not a single penalty was called; and, despite a heroic effort by the Production Line, the Canadiens eliminated the powerful league champions with a 3-2 victory.

The Red Wings were deeply disappointed in themselves. They didn't even get the satisfaction of being beaten by the Stanley Cup winners; Montreal went on to lose to Toronto in five games, every one of them ending in overtime. The Maple Leafs won their fourth Cup in five years on the famous flying goal by Bill Barilko, who died in a plane crash a few months later.

Why hadn't Detroit done better that year? Having a rookie in goal had been no liability—Sawchuk had been hot, although McNeil had been even hotter. The Rocket had been formidable too. But Detroit continued to lack the necessary balance on offense, still relying too heavily on the Production Line for scoring power and getting great checking but too little production from its other two lines. The revamped version of the Red Wings hadn't quite jelled yet, hadn't realized its full, awesome potential. That potential would arrive the next season, with the inauguration of the great Stanley Cup final wars between Detroit and Montreal.

Veteran hockey fans and mere experts will argue all night about which was the greatest team in postwar NHL history. Was it Hap Day's Leafs of the late 1940s? Toe Blake's Canadiens of the late 1950s, when the Richard brothers played with Beliveau, Geoffrion and Moore? Was it Scotty Bowman's Canadiens of the late 1970s, with Lafleur and Dryden? The Bossy-Trottier Islanders of the early 1980s? The Gretzky-Messier Oilers of the mid-1980s?

But for many, the best team ever—at least, the best in a single season—has to be the 1951-52 edition of the Detroit Red Wings.

Marty Pavelich says it well: "The team we had that year was the greatest. We could have played all summer and kept on winning." And Metro Prystai: "We had a helluva club, a *powerful* team that year—the greatest Detroit team ever."

Pavelich and Prystai shouldn't be accused of partisan hyperbole. In the 1952 Stanley Cup playoffs, theirs was a miracle team that may briefly have come closer than any, before or since, to perfection.

Like all great teams, the Wings that year had a distinctive personality. They're portrayed in full colour in a superb *Detroit News* photograph by James Kilpatrick, and their spirit is evident in the open, confident, grinning faces: a spirit of blithe optimism and youthful insouciance and joie de vivre. They combined mature professionalism and reckless abandon, disciplined self-control and explosive intensity, unselfish teamwork and inspired, individual spontaneity. With their fearless dash and madcap hustle and sheer will to win, they were a joy to watch in action.

What those Red Wings accomplished in the playoffs against strong Toronto and Montreal teams was extraordinary. But first they played another exceptional regular season. All year long, the Red Wings swept the opposition before them. They ended the schedule in first place for the fourth consecutive year, racking up an even 100 points and a wide margin of 22 over the second-place Canadiens, whom they shut out four times in fourteen meetings, and 26 over the defending-champion Maple Leafs.

Terry Sawchuk had a wonderful sophomore year. At 205 pounds, Sawchuk was on the lardy side, but he filled the net, and his quicksilver reflexes made him unbeatable many nights. Playing the incredibly gruelling (and today, unthinkable) full schedule of seventy games (although only one of *five* goalies to do so that season), Sawchuk recorded a remarkable twelve shutouts. His goals-against average of 1.90 earned him the Vezina trophy, the first of four in his career. Many believe, with Ted Lindsay, that Sawchuk was at the peak of his game in those early years, before he lost twenty-five or thirty pounds and became nervous, morose and depressive.

Sawchuk was protected by a dream defense. Quarterbacked by Red Kelly, it included Marcel Pronovost, Bob Goldham and Leo Reise, with capable backup from big Benny Woit. Kelly, equalled as a rushing defenseman only by Doug Harvey and later Bobby Orr, was so skilled offensively he was often moved up to forward; later he'd complete his remarkable career as a centre in Toronto. Pronovost and Reise were also solid, steady playmakers, and Goldham went down so often to block shots with every conceivable part of his anatomy, including his helmetless face and head, that it was like having a second goaltender on the ice. Like Bill Quackenbush and Jack Stewart before them, the Red Wing defenders relentlessly patrolled their zone, taking either the puck (as in the case of Quackenbush and Kelly) or, more often, the man. Detroit television commentator and announcer Bud Lynch says Sawchuk's defenders shared a kind of code of honour: "Their pride and burning desire was standing up at that blueline and never letting an opposing forward come across."

On offense, Adams and Ivan made the crucial addition of two players who would strengthen their attack and help achieve the balance they'd lacked in earlier years. Rookie Alex Delvecchio, who would play a major role for Detroit throughout his outstanding twenty-four-year career, eventually replacing Abel between Howe and Lindsay, centred the team's third line, which included Prystai and another talented rookie, Johnny Wilson. And in a smart trade with the Rangers, Detroit obtained Tony Leswick, a quick, mouthy, frenetic hustler who could check, score and fight, and who fit in ideally on the close-checking second line with Pavelich and Glen Skov.

With the Production Line still operating at the peak of its efficiency, in what would turn out to be Abel's final season, housemates Howe and Lindsay finished 1-2 in league scoring. Howe led comfortably by 17 points, while Abel tied for seventh despite missing eight games.

For Howe, it was unquestionably his best year to date. On top of his second straight Art Ross trophy, he'd win the Hart trophy as the NHL's most valuable player for the first time, in recognition of his increasingly central contribution to the Red Wings' success. Howe's total of 47 regular-season goals was phenomenal for the times, representing not only his career high to that point but the second-highest mark in NHL history after Richard's record of 50, set seven years earlier. (Howe would come even closer to the sacred record a year later.) Richard himself had had an abysmal season by his own standards, missing twenty-two games with a groin injury and scoring a mere 27 goals and 44 points, which placed him fifteenth in scoring, directly behind Kelly.

With a season like theirs, the Red Wings had set the stage for an even more sensational playoff series. And yet they'd had great regular seasons before—it seemed natural, almost easy, for them—without being able to follow through in the playoffs. The previous year, when they'd broken the NHL record for most points and then faltered in the semifinals, was the most painful example of their tendency to choke. As a result, the pressure on them to finally fulfill their promise was enormous, not only from the Detroit fans and media and management but most acutely from the players themselves.

The Red Wings opened the semifinals at home against their old nemesis, the Maple Leafs. Toronto had compiled a better record than any other club against Detroit during the regular season, but by the time the series moved to Maple Leaf Gardens, whatever had bedevilled Detroit in earlier playoffs between the two had been exorcised.

To the delight of the hometown crowds, Sawchuk and his defense corps were more tenacious than ever: indeed, they were invincible, racking up back-to-back shutouts at the Olympia. The Wings blanked the Leafs 3-0 when Al Rollins was in nets, then 1-0 against Turk Broda. What's more, the Wings' newfound depth and balance emerged in the fact that two of their four goals were scored by newcomer Johnny Wilson, the others coming from Abel and Kelly.

In game three, the Leafs finally scored a goal on Sawchuk, but the Red Wing attackers poured it on and scored six times against Broda—Johnny Wilson adding two more goals in Detroit's 6-2 victory. Nonetheless, Adams warned his team publicly against becoming overconfident. "I still can't forget 1942," he said, "when we beat the Leafs in three straight, then lost the series."

In the fourth game, Toronto switched back to Rollins in goal, but the Leafs lost 3-1 and were gone. Abel again displayed his uncanny flair for scoring while flying through the air as he back-handed home an unlikely airborne goal on a short pass from Howe just before landing on his kisser. The Maple Leafs' only consolation was holding Howe without a goal throughout the series. But their offense could take no consolation from Sawchuk's goals-against average in the four games: a superlative 0.75.

In the other series, the Canadiens almost failed to eliminate fourth-place Boston but finally made the finals, exhausted and bruised after seven games against the Bruins. Richard was back in form after his long layoff, scoring the series-winning goal on a spectacular end-to-end solo rush. The fierce Montreal-Detroit rivalry could now begin in earnest.

Gordie Howe had something more to prove in that series. It was the first time he'd played in the Stanley Cup finals; and, since he hadn't scored in the semifinal sweep of Toronto, he was in danger of seeming to excel in the regular season, often against the weaklings of the league, but not when the chips were down and the money on the table.

In game one at the Forum, after Tony Leswick opened the scoring in the second period, Howe stick-handled his way beautifully through all the Montreal defenders, right in on Gerry McNeil. He deftly faked the little goaltender hopelessly out of position, had him totally at his mercy—but unaccountably failed to poke the puck in. Whether it was nervousness or overanxiousness, whatever was ailing Howe would pursue him, along with the Canadiens' close checking, right into game two.

Leswick, meanwhile, who excelled as a money player and always outdid himself in the playoffs, scored another goal in the final period of game one, before defenseman Tom Johnson put Montreal on the board. When the Forum announcer declared the last minute of play, Dick Irvin pulled McNeil, and Lindsay fired a pass from Abel into the empty net at 19:44—after which it was announced that another full minute remained after all. Irvin was beside himself, claiming the timekeeper's error had made him pull his goalie too early. But the game ended 3-1 for Detroit.

In game two, the real opportunists once again were the ferociously backchecking Skov-Pavelich-Leswick line. Cutting and darting like sand fleas, working tirelessly up and down the ice, they neutralized Richard and, along with Lindsay, accounted for all Detroit's goals in those first two games at the Forum.

Pavelich scored the opening goal of game two on a goalmouth pass from Leswick. As for Lindsay, he was erupting all over the rink like a travelling volcano. Legs flailing wildly, elbows pumping furiously, hair streaming out around his head, Lindsay rushed and ran the net in his hellbent-for-leather style, with or without the puck—never a Lafleur-like model of grace, but every bit as exciting and dramatic. Defenseman Doug Harvey would check Lindsay straight into the ice, and Terrible Ted would bounce right back up and come at him again.

Lindsay scored the game-winning goal in a mad scramble around the Montreal net, retrieving the rebound from Howe's wrist shot and putting it away. Game two ended 2-1 for Detroit—but not before Montreal's big, young rushing defenseman, Dollard St. Laurent, charged at Howe and came away with a lacerated eyeball that put him out of action for the rest of the series. Howe, who had simply stood his ground against St. Laurent, was one of the players who helped him off the ice.

In the third game back at the Olympia, where the Stanley Cup shared top billing with the Hollywood Ice Revue, Howe finally and superbly came into his own. He lived up to his reputation by scoring two great goals, both on his backhand, to pace a convincing 3-0 victory and give Detroit a stranglehold on the Cup.

With his power and ambidexterity, Howe's backhand shot was as hard as other men's forehands, and often more accurate. His first goal was a masterpiece of stick-handling and timing: keeping the puck away from the desperate Canadiens, he closed in on McNeil, circled around him to the left, went to his backhand, waited until McNeil was screened, then effortlessly flipped the puck up into the exposed upper corner. On his other goal, following one by Lindsay, Howe whipped a blistering backhander past McNeil from twenty-five feet out—the kind of shot scarcely if ever seen in the NHL today.

Detroit entered game four still undefeated through both playoff rounds. "The Red Wings," declared Canadian Press, "stand on the threshold of the greatest Stanley Cup sweep in the modern-day big-league game." It was now up to Montreal to try to mar the Wings' perfect record.

To salvage at least one victory, the Canadiens knew they had to shut down Howe, Lindsay and Abel. And in that fourth game, they succeeded in keeping the Production Line off the score sheet. But the Red Wings were no longer a one- or even two-dimensional team; their league-leading goaltending and defense were now complemented by an uncontainable, multithreat attack. The Red Wings would capture the Stanley Cup, and in the process establish a brilliant Cup record, on the unheralded strength of their new third line—Metro Prystai, Alex Delvecchio and Johnny Wilson.

Playing with the two rookies, Prystai ("Meatball" to his teammates) was the line's spark plug and veteran, relatively speaking, then in his fifth NHL season. He was no fancy skater or stickhandler, but as a checker he went all-out all the time, and as an opportunist he was determined and dangerous, pouncing on the puck and rushing the net in a headlong, forward crouch. He could be tricky around the back of the net, too, an inventive playmaker. Cast from the same mould as Pavelich or Leswick, he was an endlessly game battler (although not a fighter), who could take his lumps and always come back.

Prystai remembers the dressing-room talk that Tommy Ivan gave the line just before that fourth game began. It's one of those sports anecdotes hinting at predestination of some kind or, at the very least, illustrating the uncanny workings of the athlete's psyche.

"Ivan came up to Delvecchio and Johnny Wilson and me, put his arms around us, and said, 'I'm expecting you guys to come through tonight and do things for us. I'm expecting you to *win* this game.' And by golly, we did—I don't know how he knew. But we beat Montreal 3-0 in that last game, and I scored two goals and an assist. Usually we focussed on checking, checking, checking all the time, but if you got a chance, boom, you scored, and that's exactly what happened that night."

Given Montreal's success in tying up the Production Line, it was the kind of thing that had to happen if Detroit was going to preserve their unbeaten streak. Prystai scored his first goal on a point-blank shot, after taking Delvecchio's pass from behind the net. His assist came on Glen Skov's goal in the midst of a line change with the Skov-Pavelich-Leswick line (scrappy Leswick resuming a duel with scrappy Dickie Moore begun in game two). And for his other goal, Prystai stole the puck and made an exciting, long solo rush on a breakaway, firing the puck over McNeil's stick into the upper-left-hand corner.

Prystai was named the first star of a game in which the Red Wings sealed their perfect record, becoming the first team ever to sweep the Stanley Cup playoffs in eight games straight.

But overall, the *most* remarkable part of this remarkable achievement had been the indomitable Detroit defense, and especially the magnificent goaltending of Terry Sawchuk, who earned four shutouts in eight games (tying the record of Davey Kerr from the 1930s and Frank McCool from the 1940s); registered an astonishing goals-against average of 0.63; and—miraculously—*didn't allow a single goal on home ice.* Among the many superb goaltending performances in Stanley Cup history, it's doubtful that any have matched Sawchuk's series. What's more, he achieved it against some of the best marksmen in the league, including Maurice Richard. The Rocket told the press that Sawchuk had made all the difference. "He is their club," he said sullenly, refusing to give any credit to the Detroit offense he hated so much, especially Lindsay and Howe. "Another guy in the nets and we'd beat them."

As the fans in the Olympia went nuts celebrating their second Stanley Cup in three years, a new Detroit tradition began. Since the Red Wings had strangled their opposition like an octopus, and in eight games at that, a local fish merchant decided to symbolize their ascendancy by hurling an eight-tentacled sea creature onto the ice. "Over the years, galoshes, girdles, beefsteaks and buttons, and all brands of normal fish have appeared upon the ice," reported the *Detroit News* the next day, "but never an octopus." It would not be the last; octopi have been linked with the Red Wings ever since.

Dick Irvin achieved a low point in NHL sportsmanship by refusing to shake hands with the victors. He took Richard and Elmer Lach with him straight to the Montreal dressing room, refused to congratulate Detroit verbally and barred the media from the room.

After Clarence Campbell had presented the Cup at centre ice to captain Sid Abel, who had just completed his final season as a Red Wing before becoming playing coach with Chicago, Jack Adams regaled reporters with self-congratulation in the Detroit dressing room.

Standing on a bench above the melee of sweaty players, the buttons on his bulging vest popping with pride, Adams crowed rhetorically, over and over again, "What do you think of this club, eh? What do you think?" Of Tommy Ivan's team, he proclaimed, "For balance, for depth, for anything you want to call it, this is the best Red Wing team I've had in my twenty-five years in the NHL. I'll let the figures speak for themselves. Let any other club in the league try to match them."

As galling as Adams's boasting may have been to his rivals, he had, for once, a good point.

CHAPTER NINE

Stars and Lovers

"Don't leave your game between the sheets!"
—Jack Adams, frequently

JACK ADAMS HAD THIS OBSESSIVE IDEA about hockey and sex. In Adams's lopsided view of the world, women and all they represented—bed, marriage, babies, family obligations—stole a player's energies away from hockey, and therefore interfered with Adams's other obsession in life: winning.

Like his chief rivals, Conn Smythe of Toronto and Frank Selke of Montreal, Adams's prime directive was the need to win, and every other consideration was secondary. This was fully acknowledged even by Adams's sycophantic biographer, Phil Loranger, who described him as "a man who judged everybody and everything by results. Winning meant everything to him and he never tried to make people understand otherwise."

According to Loranger's *If They Played Hockey in Heaven: The Jack Adams Story*, "His players . . . had to deliver or were stunned by just how fast he could send them down to the minor leagues . . . Once-valuable players meant nothing to Jack when it came to winning. He didn't waste any time in useless regret or indulge in sentimentality when he cast off a former star."

To show that Adams had a heart in there somewhere, Loranger noted approvingly that he'd press a crisp twenty-dollar bill into the palm of any pathetic former player down on his luck. But if the current Red Wings' performance displeased him, Adams had not a shred of charity for his boys. He'd promptly dangle the sword of a trade or demotion over their necks: "You're all a bunch of gutless wonders!" he'd scream in the dressing room. "I'm going to send some of you so far away from the NHL, they won't be able to reach you with a postage stamp!"

Worse, his players knew he meant every word of it. Despite the Stanley Cup victories and successive league championships, no Red Wing ever dared dream he was irreplaceable—except for Adams's two avowed favourites, whom at various times he declared untradeable: Howe and Kelly. And that didn't prevent Adams from chewing them out, too, even when they'd played up to their usual high standard. Once, after a 4-3 loss in which Howe scored all three Detroit goals, Adams ranted at every player in turn. Coming to Howe, he said, "And you—three goals, wasted! Why didn't you save them for some night when we could use them?"

All this was good clean fun by NHL standards of the day. But even by that measure, Adams's suspicion of female influence was excessive. Like Jack D. Ripper, the demented U.S. Air Force officer in the movie *Dr. Strangelove*, he harboured a paranoia about a player's being robbed of his "precious bodily fluids." The old athletic/military school of thought that sex saps strength, drains energy, weakens legs and lowers aggression had no greater exponent than Jack Adams. His former players agree that his bottom line on the subject was the oft-repeated admonition, "Don't leave your game between the sheets!"

Adams took his prurient interest farther than admonitions. He'd actually keep players under surveillance, serving them with a warning if he considered them to be overindulging in sex to the detriment of their game. Among the authorities Adams consulted on this pressing matter were his scouts, trainers, other players and Ma Shaw, who was sometimes in a position to know.

As in many families, there was little privacy in the Red Wing "family." Management even poked its inquiring nose into the marriage bed. The manager of the Olympia in those days, Lincoln Cavalieri, told the authors of *Net Worth*, "If they thought one guy was screwing around with his wife too much they'd call him in."

How management thought it knew about such private matters is an interesting subject for speculation. Dressing-room bragging and gossip are probable sources; there was undoubtedly a management stool pigeon or two in the room. And when the team was on the road, Adams was able to wield even greater control over his players' marital relations. Wives were not only prohibited from visiting their husbands' hotel rooms—that would have presented an irresistible temptation to a lonesome left wing or randy defenseman—but also forbidden to telephone them directly. In an emergency, a wife was supposed to route her call through team management.

As a good Catholic, Adams might have done well to adopt St. Paul's position that it is better to marry than to burn. But "Jolly Jawn," as he was unfathomably known, wanted his boys to do all their burning on the ice: he actually preached sexual abstinence for the duration of the hockey season. At the very least, he told his players, if they really must surrender to the demands of the flesh and get married, they were to wait until the day after the season ended. That way, they'd have the maximum stretch of time to get over their excitement before the new season began.

One player who contravened this rule was Detroit's tall, smooth-skating centre, Glen Skov, from the notorious sin-city of Wheatley, Ontario. Trainer Lefty Wilson's wife, Lil, remembers the consternation Skov's wedding caused Adams.

"When Glen got married in the middle of the season, well, that was tantamount to every mortal sin conceivable. Poor Glen was having a bad game one night, and Adams came into the room and started throwing oranges. He said to one guy, 'The way you're playing, you're getting money under false pretences—you ought to be ashamed of yourself!' Then he looked at Skov, the new bridegroom, and said, 'And *you*—you're spending too much god-damn time in the *crease*!' Adams's face was livid, purple—all the guys put their heads down because they couldn't help laughing. And poor Glen, he was such a saintly kid."

Oddly enough, this was one rule Ted Lindsay didn't flout. Lindsay waited until just after the Red Wings' 1952 Stanley Cup victory before wedding his first wife, Pat. This was all the more surprising since he'd been subjected to the usual meddling and harassment during his courtship. Adams took it into his head that Lindsay was growing tamer on the ice because of dalliances with his fiancée: "I think he's so much in love, he may be softening up,"

Adams coyly told *Look* magazine. He even took the step of summoning Lindsay—who was, at that point, a mature twenty-six years old—and speaking to him about it. Not unreasonably, Lindsay exploded, widening the rift between them that had been inevitable from the start and was now growing with every passing season.

If Terrible Ted *had* been "softening up," it was in fact because he was playing with a separated shoulder. But Adams wouldn't admit the injury publicly, out of fear of making his star a sitting duck for opposition checkers. Adams just found it easier to pin the blame on women and sex.

Later, Adams would widen his accusations and place general blame for any Red Wing letdown on all the trappings and responsibilities of marriage. To explain away a prolonged Detroit slump, he once told the press, "The Red Wings are pushing supermarket wagons instead of the puck. They're thinking about how they're going to fix up their rec rooms instead of how to rack up the Rocket. They're singing babies to sleep instead of knocking their enemies unconscious."

In truth, Adams didn't like to see his boys growing up. A controlling patriarch, he was saying, in effect: "Thou shalt have no other family before me." And by scapegoating his players' wives, he also diverted scrutiny from any possible shortcomings of his own in managing the Red Wings.

When Lindsay married at the end of April 1952, Gordie Howe lost his housemate—but only temporarily, while the newlyweds went off on their Florida honeymoon and Howe summered in Saskatoon. At first, Pat Lindsay joked that the two friends had been so inseparable as bachelors, Gordie might just show up for meals every day with her and Ted, or even (giggle) move in with them! And after the summer, that's exactly what he did, for the better part of a year. Howe still had as big an appetite as ever for home cooking, but not for independence.

Something else had changed in Howe's life, however. By the time he moved in with Ted and Pat Lindsay, he had been enjoying regular female companionship for some months. She was six years younger than he, and hardly his first girlfriend, but she was already considerably more worldly.

Colleen Joffa liked to bowl in a women's league in downtown Detroit. Seventeen years old in 1951, athletic and competitive, she found bowling at the Lucky Strike lanes on Grand River Avenue relaxing after her working day as a secretary with Bethlehem Steel.

Colleen had grown up in the small Michigan town of Sandusky and in Detroit. She was an only child who had been raised by her divorced mother, with the help of an aunt and uncle, until her mother remarried. Colleen liked her stepdad, Budd Joffa, who owned a bar and who also frequented the Lucky Strike. The two of them would often bowl together after their league games; the loser bought the Cokes.

The Lucky Strike was one of the Red Wings' favourite hangouts. Twenty-three-year-old Howe had been watching the blonde teen-ager for weeks, slowly trying to work up the courage to say hello. But somehow he couldn't seem to do it. So he asked the Lucky Strike's manager, Joe Evans, to introduce them, and then arranged to bowl a game with his new teammate, Vic Stasiuk, in the lane next to Colleen and her father.

After the introduction, Colleen still had no idea who this tall, good-looking fellow was; she was no hockey fan, and the Stanley Cup might as well have been a badminton trophy. But she was definitely interested. She found him "cute," she wrote in her lively and personable 1975 memoir, *My Three Hockey Players*, and she admired his expensive suede sportcoat. But she already had a steady, a baseball player she had dated during her school years.

Howe asked if she'd like a ride home, but she had to decline since she had a car. After this setback, he hesitated to come right out and ask for her telephone number. However, he obtained it through Joe Evans and then called her. He phoned her several times that week, sometimes talking for up to three hours at a stretch—not about playing in the NHL, significantly, but about his family and childhood back in Saskatoon. Clearly, there was a lot of himself he wanted to share with her. Yet after each marathon conversation, he'd say good-bye without asking for a date.

Her stepfather, an avid Red Wings fan, was impressed by the identity of her new beau, and Colleen discovered who Gordie Howe was in the eyes of the world. At last he invited her to a movie. Nibbling shrimp cocktail afterwards at Carl's Chop House, another Red Wing habitat near the Olympia, Howe startled her by asking, "How old do you think a man should be before he gets married?" Colleen didn't know what to say.

But Howe was in no rush to storm the altar. His courting style was distinctly slow-moving, drawn-out and low-key, marked by such romantic highlights as card nights at Ma Shaw's and complimentary seats at Red Wing home games. As an unavoidable condition of getting to know him, Colleen began her hockey education, sitting in the place of honour at the Olympia, right next to Ma herself. She also met his closest friend, Lindsay, whose self-assured, forceful personality was much like her own—and whose shaping influence on Gordie she would gradually displace.

Colleen was so sure she was in love, she broke off with her baseball player. During the summer, while Gordie was home in Saskatoon and they were both dating other people, they wrote each other almost daily—"long, loving, silly letters," she called them in her book. She has also told the story of how they almost drifted apart once their relationship resumed in the fall.

On the afternoon of a big date, Howe called and said he was sorry, but he'd just been assigned to represent the Red Wings at a banquet that night. (Banquet appearances by his star players were one of Adams's favourite ways of marketing his team.) Feeling jilted, Colleen accepted the offer of a date with an old boyfriend for that same evening; they went to a club to hear the popular vocal group the Four Freshmen.

Later, Howe walked into the club with some people from the banquet and saw her sitting there with her date.

The next day, Howe failed to make his usual call to tell her there would be a game ticket waiting for her at the Olympia that night. Upset but undaunted, Colleen bought her own ticket, then telephoned him ("a very brazen thing" in those days) to suggest getting together after the game.

"I have a date," he told her.

Colleen went to the game anyway. She marched down the aisle to where Howe's date was sitting, in her seat beside Ma Shaw, and very audibly asked the landlady to give Gordie a message for her: she was sorry she had to break their date that night, but she'd speak with him the next day.

Howe didn't understand why his post-game date went so badly until Colleen told him the story much later—years after they were safely married.

Getting to that point took two full hockey seasons. Howe was on the road a great deal; and when he was back in Detroit, he often had game days, especially on weekends. Colleen had to work during the week, so their opportunities to see each other were limited. But Colleen knew what she wanted, and she knew the best way to stay close to Howe was to attend his home games faithfully. She was there in the Olympia throughout the 1952-53 season to watch him make his best run ever at Rocket Richard's famous 50-goal record.

The 1952-53 season was a year of milestones, breakthroughs and one enormous upset.

On the Canadian Broadcasting Corporation's new television network, *Hockey Night in Canada* began appearing regularly for the first time. Rocket Richard scored his 325th goal, thus breaking the all-time NHL record held by Nels Stewart; Old Poison immediately sent a telegram of congratulations to the Montreal dressing room. Three great goaltenders of the future, Glenn Hall, Jacques Plante and Lorne (Gump) Worsley, made their NHL debuts. Jean Beliveau was brilliant in a three-game trial with the Canadiens, but Montreal couldn't pry him loose from his senior team, the Quebec Aces, who were paying him the equivalent of a top NHL salary. And the Red Wings' imperious owner, James Norris Sr., who had played hockey for the Montreal A.A.A. Winged Wheelers over half a century earlier, away back in 1898, died of a heart attack. Now Jack Adams would be dealing directly with Norris's offspring, Marguerite and Bruce; in the meantime, he was appointed to the powerful post of Detroit's representative on the NHL Board of Governors.

Coming off its amazing eight-game sweep in the 1952 playoffs, the Detroit juggernaut hadn't lost any momentum. Sid Abel had gone to Chicago as playing coach, but his role as playmaker between Howe and Lindsay—and consequently as one of the league's top scorers—was quickly filled by twenty-one-year-old Alex Delvecchio. The Red Wings powered to another first-place finish, their fifth league championship in a row. They dominated the scoring leaders by placing five players in the top eight: Howe, followed by Lindsay, Delvecchio, Prystai and Kelly. Howe's scoring championship was his third in a row, making him the first player ever to win three consecutive Art Ross trophies.

The Wings also dominated the other trophies: the Hart (Howe's second), the Vezina (Sawchuk's second) and the Lady Byng (Kelly's second). And for the third year running, Howe, Lindsay, Kelly and Sawchuk captured two-thirds of the positions on the NHL's first all-star team; Delvecchio made the second team at centre.

But the biggest story of the regular season was Howe's prodigious goal production. First of all, he scored his 200th career goal in a game against Chicago in February. Then, in the sixty-eighth game, he scored twice against Boston, giving him 49 goals and putting him one away from tying Richard's single-season record. Late in that game, he came painfully close to scoring number fifty when Lindsay, who had a chance to equal his own career-high 33 goals, passed to him instead. "The net was open," Howe recalled, "but before Ted's pass got to me it nicked Hal Laycoe's skate and skidded away."

With two games left to play—against Chicago and Montreal—Howe looked like a good bet to set a record of his own. But the Black Hawks had an improved team that year, strong enough to beat out Toronto for the last playoff spot, and they held Howe scoreless, even though his teammates kept trying feed him and he stayed out on the ice for extra shifts. That set the stage for some Howe heroics at the Olympia on the final night of the schedule against, fittingly enough, Richard himself.

As Dick Irvin Jr. has noted of the Rocket in his oral history, *The Habs*, "He was passionately proud of his record. The press had a field day, especially in Detroit, where they were blatantly hoping Howe would first tie, then break the record, on a night when Richard would be forced to watch him do it."

Again, Howe skated extra shifts all night long. But this ultimate humiliation for the Rocket, this ultimate triumph for his archrival, would be thwarted by two Montreal defenders: little goaltender Gerry McNeil and big left wing Bert Olmstead, from Scepter, Saskatchewan.

As McNeil has said, "It was quite a thrill for me, one of my biggest. [Howe] had a couple of good chances and one of them was kind of a breakaway . . . But I was able to stop him."

Howe had only five shots on goal. McNeil gave credit for that miracle (considering that Howe's teammates were constantly trying to set him up) to the glue-tight checking of Olmstead, who took his coach's orders—"Go where Howe goes"—quite literally.

"I think Howe was a little bit disappointed when he saw what I was doing," Olmstead has recalled. "He'd go back to talk to Sawchuk, so I'd go back with him and there'd be the three of us standing there. They would yell at me, 'What are you doing back here?' I wouldn't talk to them. I knew I was getting their goat. Gerry was good that night and made a couple of big saves off him . . . After the game Gerry said [to Richard], 'Well, Rock, he's got to start at one again.'"

Montreal coach Dick Irvin Sr. twisted the knife by gloating publicly over Howe's disappointment. Irvin taunted the Red Wings and their fans by sliding across the Olympia ice after the game and holding Richard's arm high in the air. "The winner and still champion," Irvin trumpeted to the press. "The way Howe went tonight, I think he's all burnt out. He's been playing too much, too hard. He won't be worth much over the next couple of weeks."

Like so much coaches' talk at playoff time back then, this had a silly ring of bluster and bravado about it. But in hindsight, Irvin may have been right. Metro Prystai, who remembers the moment vividly, tends to agree.

"We had first place all locked up, and yet in those last few games Gordie must have played close to forty minutes [in fact, he played thirty-three in the final game against Montreal]. I kind of blame that for our poor showing in the playoffs later, because he was so damn tired he could hardly shoot the puck—he'd been out on the ice while we tried to get him that 50th goal. Everybody was looking for him, trying to get the puck to him, and he was hitting the goalpost, putting it over the net and stuff like that, trying too hard.

"Maybe he should have been rested for a game. If he hadn't played so much, he'd have had a little more left for the playoffs, and we'd probably have beaten Boston."

But that's what didn't happen: it was the upset of the year. During the regular season, Detroit had defeated the Bruins ten times in fourteen meetings, sometimes by very one-sided scores. In the first game of the semifinals, the Red Wings stayed true to form, winning 7-0, with Pavelich and Lindsay scoring 2 goals each. Howe was held scoreless, but it didn't seem to matter at the time. However, during the next three meetings, the Bruins stunned everybody, including themselves, by winning every time; Howe managed to score only once. Detroit stayed alive by winning the fifth game 6-2, Howe scoring one more time. But in the next game, the third-place Bruins shocked the mighty league champions by eliminating them 6-4.

Could one star's fatigue have made that much difference to Detroit? Perhaps, although the Red Wings had already shown they had the depth to compensate for a lacklustre performance by a single player. But there had also been a team-psychology factor at work: a collective sense of letdown by all the players, after trying so hard, but failing, to boost their teammate into the record book alongside or even above the Rocket.

"It was the whole team that wanted him to get 50," Prystai explains, "not just Adams or Ivan. But Gordie never got it, and we felt bad about it."

So much attention was paid to the anticlimax of Howe's "failure" that people almost forgot he'd achieved a stunning single-season record for total points that year: 49 goals and 46 assists, for 95 points. It had not only been the best-ever individual performance in NHL history but it had put Howe an impressive 24 points ahead of second-place Lindsay, and an even more impressive 34 ahead of third-place Richard. By that measure, there could no longer be any doubt about who was the best offensive player in the league. Nonetheless, the quest for the Holy Grail of 50 goals had mesmerized everyone, including Galahad himself. By season's end, he was vastly relieved to forget it, like a bad dream, and go fishing instead.

Inevitably, the Dr. Strangelove school of hockey commentators couldn't resist suggesting, however tongue-in-cheek, that Howe had been distracted in the playoffs not only by Richard's record but his own imminent marriage to Colleen.

At least Howe obeyed Adams's condition of waiting until the season was over. On April 15, 1953, ten days after Boston eliminated the Red Wings, Gordie and Colleen became Mr. and Mrs. Howe in Detroit's Calvary Presbyterian Church. (The church overlooked Grand River Avenue, thus allowing Gordie to maintain his habit of not straying far from the Olympia, no matter what.) Lindsay and Pavelich were both in attendance at the wedding. And although the Church forbade Lindsay's being best man because he was Catholic, Pat Lindsay was Colleen's matron of honour. Howe's brother Vern filled in as best man.

Howe was also obeying a condition of Colleen's. After such a long courtship, she felt she'd waited long enough for marriage, and hadn't been interested in a formal engagement. With Howe planning to return to Saskatoon for the long summer as always, she'd been unwilling to wait for his return and had refused to accompany him to meet his family unless she was his wife.

Howe complied. When Colleen visited Saskatoon for the first time and was introduced to Ab and Katherine, and to Gordie's brothers and sisters and friends and relatives, she was already Mrs. Howe.

As a young adolescent leafing through the Eaton's catalogue, Howe had promised his mother he was going to make *real* money someday so he could buy her things the family lacked, luxuries like an indoor toilet. Shortly after turning pro in 1945, he'd devoted some of his first earnings to that very purpose. A grander promise had been a brand-new home for his parents, and now he managed to make good on that one, too. The house went up at the corner of Avenue A (Idylwyld today) and Twenty-fifth Street, and in addition to paying for it, Howe pitched in and personally helped dig the foundations and install the kitchen fixtures. His parents would live there until they died.

In the early days of their marriage, after Colleen had made the acquaintance of the Howe family and their community, she began sharing her new husband's main recreations of fishing and golf. (Baseball had been off limits to Gordie since Adams's telegram of the previous summer.) The young couple journeyed up into northern Saskatchewan to the relative wilderness of Prince Albert

National Park. They socialized with Johnny Bower and his wife, Nancy, who were also newlyweds and who ran a coffee shop at Waskesiu Lake in the park during the tourist season (later they'd operate the Lakeview Hotel in the same area).

A Prince Albert native, Bower was playing in the American Hockey League at the time—he wouldn't make the NHL permanently with Toronto until 1959. He remembers Howe bringing his own boat and combing the lake for the best holes.

"Gordie didn't say too much: he was all business in the boat. He just concentrated on getting that fish. And he caught them all over the place—he'd come up with an eighteen- or nineteen-pound pike, and I'd tell him he was a lucky fisherman, just like he was a lucky goal scorer."

Howe and Bower went out on the lake together with an elderly fishing guide known as "Grandpa," who was in fact the grandfather of Ed Van Impe, later a player for the Chicago Black Hawks. Bower recalls Howe's vast appetite after a day on the water. "Gordie just loved to eat fish. He and I would fillet them—he was a great filleter too, there was nothing he couldn't do—and Nancy and Colleen would fry them up with margarine and green peas. It was nothing for him and me to go through five or six fillets each."

The following year, Howe would take a summer job at the park's Lobstick golf course. Built on muskeg in an unspoiled natural setting, the course wound through hills and was regularly visited by deer, moose, foxes and wolves. The Howes rented a cottage nearby, and Gordie cut and maintained the greens and fairways and golfed to his heart's content. As far as he was concerned, it was the perfect off-season employment. He won prizes in the club tournament and gave Colleen lessons; eventually, both of them would be prize-winning golfers. Competing in numerous pro-am tournaments over the years, Howe routinely shot in the seventies and even sometimes the high sixties, and was celebrated for his prowess in keeping up with professionals from the tour.

"Gordie loved working at Lobstick," Bower says. "He just had to be out in the open. He redesigned the course, cutting new holes and moving the pins. You couldn't even see the pins because he put the holes in such difficult spots—said it was more of a challenge that way."

The great Maple Leaf goalie also notes that, just about nine months after that first summer devouring lake fish in Prince Albert National Park, both the Bowers and the Howes had their first children. Gordie and Colleen were living in their ranch-style bungalow in northwest Detroit when Marty, the future defenseman (named after Pavelich), was born on February 18, 1954.

In the 1953-54 season, the Red Wings-Canadiens rivalry reached its peak of intensity and would stay red-hot for several years to come.

Such rivalries just aren't possible in today's NHL. With its divisions being perpetually realigned, its twenty-six teams playing each other so infrequently, and so many new teams representing cities with no hockey tradition whatsoever, the league will take years to recreate such fierce competition, if indeed it does. But in the hockey wars of the mid-1950s, the players battled each other so often during the season that they took it all very personally.

"When we used to face the Canadiens," Howe has said, "the first name that always came to mind was Richard. I respected him but I didn't like him . . . He was the man who led the way for the rest of us. Without a pacemaker there's nothing to shoot for. He was my pacemaker, first for career points, then for career goals."

Richard has stated, "Detroit was our big rival, there's no doubt about that. I remember I used to meet their players in the aisle way of the train. We'd pass by each other and I wouldn't say hello to anybody. I didn't hate too many players, except the guy who played with Gordie Howe. Number 7. Ted Lindsay."

Lindsay was even more competitive. "I hated 'em all," he says.

Train travel was a big feature of the feud. The NHL often scheduled back-to-back games on weekends, necessitating back-to-back train trips between the two cities. The teams would play at the Montreal Forum on a Saturday night, then proceed to Westmount Station directly after the game to board the overnight train to Detroit for the Sunday rematch. One car would be designated "RW1" for the Detroit players. Like Richard, Lindsay remembers the tension between the two teams spilling over into the train journey and lasting until arrival in Detroit at two-thirty in the afternoon: "No fights, but there were times it wasn't too far away from that."

Detroit broadcaster Bud Lynch relates how certain Red Wings would be designated to get up early on Sunday morning and line up at the breakfast car, in order to occupy all the tables when the car opened at nine. "They'd sit one to a table, so no Canadiens could get in for breakfast until eleven, after all the Red Wings had eaten."

After being upset by Boston the previous season, Detroit had something to prove. And they had to prove it to the Canadiens, who had gone on to defeat the Bruins and win the 1953 Stanley Cup, their first in seven years. The Red Wings came back to lead the league throughout most of the 1953-54 season, finishing strongly in first place yet again, ahead of Montreal. Earl (Dutch) Reibel, one of two talented rookies with Detroit (the other was Bill Dineen), was now at centre between Howe and Lindsay, and the three linemates took up where the Production Line had left off.

At 33 goals, Howe fell well below his output of the previous year, but with 48 assists and 81 points, he still won the scoring championship, his fourth in as many years—another record. Richard and Lindsay switched places in the scoring race: the Rocket came second, 14 points behind Howe, and Lindsay third.

In fact, all of the league's seven top scorers that season played for either Detroit or Montreal; the other four were Geoffrion, Olmstead, Kelly and Reibel. The record shows that whoever centred the Odd Couple would improve his points total considerably. Delvecchio, now back playing on a line with Prystai and Johnny Wilson, was well down the list with just 29 points.

The Rocket had stirred up a hornet's nest at NHL head office that January. His ghostwritten hockey column in Montreal's *Samedi Dimanche* had called Clarence Campbell "a dictator." Plain speaking on the part of the players, no matter how celebrated they are or which official language they use, has never gone down well with NHL brass hats, and all the other league dictators, including Adams and Conn Smythe, frothed and fulminated in indignation.

"I have always felt that Richard is getting too big for hockey," postured Adams. "Regardless of his ability he is the poorest sportsman in the game." This was a classic case of the pot calling the kettle black. Smythe, whose ego was gargantuan, was equally hypocritical: "Hockey is a big game and no single individual is bigger than the sport."

Flexing their muscles, the league executives collectively humiliated Richard, and in the process stomped all over freedom of speech. They banned him from writing for any publication while active as a player; forced him to issue a retraction and an apology to president Campbell and the NHL governors; and required him to post a $1,000 bond as evidence of his "good faith." An angry demonstration by Richard's legions of fans was expected at the Forum but didn't materialize. This episode, seldom recalled by hockey historians, lit the fuse that would explode into the Richard Riot the next season.

Meanwhile, the two supreme superstars headed towards a showdown in the Stanley Cup finals. The Canadiens swept the Bruins in four; the Red Wings eliminated Toronto in five. In the final game of the latter series, Howe scored the earliest playoff goal in history to that point, nine seconds after the opening face-off (the record is now six).

The 1954 Cup final in the two bustling river-port cities was an epic, one of the most hard-fought and excitingly dramatic in NHL history. Like the Detroit-Montreal battle of the following year, it would not be decided until the seventh game; but unlike the '55 series, it was fought on even terms, without the interference of suspensions decreed by league headquarters, and would require a sudden-death goal to settle the winner.

As first-place finishers, the Red Wings drew home-ice advantage. They won the opening game 3-1, shutting down Richard. The Rocket hadn't scored a point in the semifinals either, and all he collected in this game was a ten-minute misconduct penalty, although he had Lindsay for company.

But Richard recovered his touch with 2 goals in the second game to even the series. While Howe served time, and Detroit played two men short for an agonizing minute and forty-one seconds (in those days a penalized player didn't return to the ice after a goal was scored), the Canadiens' power play scored twice. Dickie Moore got the first one on a brilliant rush with Geoffrion and Beliveau, using Geoffrion as a screen. Then Richard blazed a shot past Sawchuk on a pass from Moore. As the game wore on, the warm April weather turned the Olympia ice slushy and sent the players' temperatures rising; near the end, with Detroit going down to defeat 3-1, a big, young and now-forgotten Montreal forward, Lorne Davis, came away streaming with blood from a close encounter with Howe's elbow.

The Red Wings seemed to take command of the series, winning both of the next two games at the Forum. Tommy Ivan had put Delvecchio back between Howe and Lindsay for the series, and each of the three linemates scored a superb goal.

Delvecchio, retrieving the puck from a goalmouth scramble in front of Sawchuk, put a perfect pass onto Howe's tape at centre ice; Howe skated across the Montreal blueline, drifted over to the right boards, apparently too far away to do any damage, then delicately feathered a pass through the defensemen's skates back to Delvecchio, cruising in on goal, who neatly backhanded it past Plante. The second goal was less elegant but just as impressive: Lindsay took a long lead pass up-ice from Kelly, burst between the Montreal defensemen, and slapped it up high while being checked headfirst into the ice from behind.

On Howe's goal, he took a nifty drop pass from Delvecchio and nonchalantly powered a tremendous wrist shot past Plante's glove side. Johnny Wilson also scored, then linemate Prystai, on a Gretzky-style wraparound: resolutely shaking off Dickie Moore, Prystai swooped behind the Montreal net, emerged on the left side and tucked the puck into the corner, jumping for joy as the red light flashed. The game ended 5-2.

By contrast, game four was a defensive duel highlighted by Sawchuk's brilliant goaltending. The one real goal of the game, scored by Wilson while Richard was in the penalty box, came off a long, soft backhand shot that somehow eluded Plante. During a five-minute major that Howe received for slashing Doug Harvey, the Red Wings' penalty killers were everywhere, and Kelly's empty-net goal with seven seconds to play made the final score 2-0.

With Detroit leading the series 3-1 and his back to the wall, Dick Irvin radically changed his line-up in the hope of sparking a victory. Five players were benched; Plante was replaced by Gerry McNeil, who hadn't seen action for two months. Despite the long layoff, McNeil was extraordinarily sharp for the rest of the series.

In game five at the Olympia, the teams battled for three scoreless periods. One of the highlights, apart from the two goaltenders' stalwart play, was the fighting effort of little Tony Leswick. At one point, Leswick was dumped in the corner by the Canadiens' rugged defenseman Butch Bouchard; as he was scrambling to his feet, Leswick had his legs pulled out from under him by Jean Beliveau; falling flat on his face, Leswick leaped to his feet yet again, literally hopping mad, and swung his stick at Beliveau, who swung his own right back, then punched Leswick hard in the face. Undeterred, Leswick took possession and roared back with a furious rush on goal; he was foiled only at the last moment by McNeil's great save, which sent Leswick crashing into the boards.

Finally, in the sixth minute of overtime, Montreal centre Ken Mosdell, not much remembered today but a first-team all-star that year, carried the puck on a rink-length rush into the Detroit zone. Bob Goldham was the last man back; he threw a solid check, but Mosdell spun around him, held onto the puck and fired a hard backhander past Sawchuk to win the game 1-0.

Back in Montreal for game six, the Canadiens thrilled their fans by tying the series at three. Boom Boom Geoffrion unleashed what was then a relatively new weapon: the slapshot. On what broadcaster Danny Gallivan would have called "a blistering blast" or "a cannonading drive," Geoffrion blinded Sawchuk, who did the splits but didn't get even a piece of the puck as it whizzed by him into the net. Floyd (Busher) Curry scored the next 2 goals for Montreal, before Prystai finally put Detroit on the board in a spectacular two-man rush with his old buddy from Ma Shaw's, Red Kelly.

Rescuing the puck from his own goalmouth, Kelly rushed up the right side with Prystai keeping pace on his immediate right along the boards; they moved up-ice so swiftly no Montreal player even touched them. Kelly crossed the Canadiens' blueline and passed just ahead to Prystai, who cut in sharply to the net and punched it through the defenseman's legs into the right corner of the net. By the time Richard scored in the third period to close the scoring at 4-1, Tommy Ivan had Kelly filling in on left wing for Lindsay, whose efforts had utterly exhausted him.

Thus it all came down to the final game, played at the Olympia before 15,791 roaring fans—well beyond the Olympia's official capacity, and the largest crowd ever to see a hockey game in Detroit.

The Red Wings came close to opening the scoring on another give-and-go between Delvecchio and Howe. Taking a pass from his centreman, Number Nine sent it right back to Delvecchio, putting him in close, but McNeil kicked out a leg and robbed them. Detroit had another great chance when defenseman Marcel Pronovost made an end-to-end rush, slipping the puck between the skates of a Montreal defender, then retrieving it and making the Canadiens' two defensemen collide in the process—but when Pronovost drove in alone on McNeil, the goalie made another big save. Finally, Montreal drew first blood on a soft shot by Curry while Sawchuk was screened.

In the second period, Detroit went on the power play after Prystai was hooked from behind by Paul Masnick. Kelly led the rush, eventually getting the puck back from Lindsay and scoring on McNeil from close range to tie the game at 1-1.

The bitterly contested third period was scoreless, and as always in such do-or-die situations, both teams' superstars were clutched, grabbed, roughed and mauled without mercy. Howe took two ferocious hits from Harvey. When Howe had the puck in the slot, the Montreal defenseman collided with him so hard that he rode him, still with the puck, like a bucking bull—no mean feat, given Howe's superior height, twenty-five-pound advantage and enormous strength—practically through the boards. Later, Howe was bringing the puck around behind the Canadiens' net when Harvey slammed an elbow into the side of his face, knocking him dazed to the ice.

Richard was frustrated time and again by the Red Wing defenders, especially the pesky Pavelich-Skov-Leswick line. Leswick, who referee Bill Chadwick once said "could bring out the worst in a saint," played left wing on Richard's side and infuriated the Rocket by taunting and heckling him in pidgin-French while pronouncing his surname in English. By the game's late stages, driven to desperation and breaking his stick on a failed attempt to score, Richard was so upset he swept the puck into the net with his glove.

The game, the series and the season went into sudden-death overtime, which would be decided by one of the most famous goals in Stanley Cup history. Picture the scene: With over four overtime minutes gone, Prystai lugs the puck up the ice. He passes to Skov, but it's time for a line change, and the puck ends up loose down in the Montreal end. Harvey collects it in the corner and fires it behind his own net and around the boards. The puck reaches Leswick just as he's coming over the boards on the line change; he's on his wrong wing, just inside the Montreal blueline. Leswick glimpses the disquieting spectacle of the Rocket, whom he has wronged all night long, charging straight at him, so he quickly unloads the puck towards the net—a wrist shot, by a player whose shot (his teammates often remarked) couldn't break the proverbial pane of glass. Among the players standing between Leswick and the net is Harvey, who plays double-A baseball and has a sure glove hand and who is to say later that the shot was so soft he could read the label on the puck as it floated towards him. McNeil, too, has the shot all lined up: no problem. What Harvey decides to do is field the puck like a baseball, palming it, then letting it drop immediately to his stick so he can play it. But somehow, Harvey misjudges the puck's trajectory, or it drops unexpectedly, like a sinker, or his reflexes are misfiring at the end of a long, exhausting seventh game, at the end of a long, exhausting season. When Harvey goes to play Leswick's shot, the puck bounces off the side of his glove instead of nestling sweetly in his palm. The puck deflects at an angle McNeil isn't expecting and, to the goalie's horror, flips straight into the corner of the net.

And suddenly the season is over. The Stanley Cup is Detroit's. The previously unsung Leswick is the unlikely hero of the hour and the series and the season and the city, and is immediately elevated onto his delirious teammates' shoulders as the crowd gives him a thunderous standing ovation and the flashbulbs pop incessantly. And Gerry McNeil is skating slowly, slowly down the endless, infernal length of the deafening Olympia ice to his dressing room at the distant end of the rink.

"There's no way you can express how you feel at a time like that when you're a goalie," McNeil will say. "It's like the end of the world." On that note, he retires from hockey, while the Red Wing stars and lovers party long into the night.

CHAPTER TEN

The Wings' Unravelling

"There's always some reason to trade a player—
maybe he's a clubhouse lawyer."
—Jack Adams, 1962

THE 1954 STANLEY CUP WINNERS were Tommy Ivan's last Red
Wing team. Before the next season began, Jack Adams despatched
Ivan to the sinking Chicago Black Hawks—who had regained
their losing ways—as part of a concerted league attempt to rebuild
the Norris family's other NHL franchise. The three strongest teams,
Detroit, Montreal and Toronto, all contributed quality players to
the effort. In the Red Wings' case, Metro Prystai reluctantly
accompanied his coach back to his former team (although he'd
return to Detroit the next season).

Adams was now in an interesting position: with Ivan and James
Norris Sr. both gone, he had an increasingly freer hand in running
the Red Wings—a situation that, before long, would have ruinous
consequences for the club.

Norris, the crusty old owner who had wielded a restraining
authority and held the purse strings for twenty years, had been
replaced after his death by his quarrelling daughter and son, Marguerite and Bruce. Although Marguerite Norris had learned from
her father how to handle Adams and his excesses, Bruce Norris
had not; after Bruce assumed the presidency from his sister in
1955, Adams's leash unfortunately grew longer. And almost simultaneously, the buffer between Adams and the Detroit players had
also been removed. Adams's compulsion to meddle with the inner
workings of the team, and his deep and irrational suspicions of

certain players, which grew deeper and more irrational as he got older, would devastate the Red Wings' dynasty.

All the men who played under Adams have their stories about his erratic, capricious, domineering, sometimes incomprehensible behaviour. Individually, those incidents might have seemed minor at the time; together, they added up to a pattern that kept his players perpetually off balance and irredeemably damaged their morale. Part of Adams's troubling inconsistency was that, on occasion, he could also be appreciative of and even affectionate towards his men. But one thing they could count on: the moment never lasted long.

Marty Pavelich recalls a night in Montreal when the Red Wings had defeated the Canadiens. Adams had seemed exceptionally pleased. While Pavelich was standing on the platform at Westmount Station, waiting to board the train back to Detroit, Adams came up and put his arm around him. "Geez, Blackie," Adams told him, "you played great tonight. Your line was really flying out there!" Figuring he was in the Old Man's good books, Pavelich was completely baffled when Adams scarcely played him the next night in Detroit. Had Adams changed his mind about him? Had he wanted to bring Pavelich down a peg or two, so the praise wouldn't go to his head? "Why?" Pavelich still asks himself today. "Who knows?"

Adams's compulsion to put his players in their place had a damaging effect on a rising young Red Wing who joined the team in 1953. Bill Dineen, who later became a respected coach (twenty years later he'd be Howe's first WHA coach in Houston), was having an excellent rookie season; he'd scored 17 goals with three games still to play when he suddenly found himself benched until the playoffs. The reason? Adams didn't want him to reach 20 goals: that was the benchmark of NHL stardom in those days, and reaching it would have put Dineen in a position to demand more money.

According to CAHA Director Murray Costello, who roomed with Dineen, Kelly and Prystai at Ma Shaw's, being sidelined knocked the stuffing out of the young right winger. "Bill was really contributing, and he had all the enthusiasm of a rookie. He'd been replacing Howe at right wing on the power play, when

Gordie dropped back to the point. But Bill was so disappointed at his treatment, I'm not sure he ever recovered from the experience." In fact, Dineen would never do as well again; after five years, his NHL playing career would be over.

Such methods obviously hurt Adams's players, and in some cases their careers; but they also hurt the team. In that respect, Adams was his own worst enemy. There are real and legitimate questions about his acumen and judgement as a manager of hockey players. Costello tells the sad tale of Guyle Fielder, a top scorer and perennial all-star for Seattle in the minors, who received tryouts with the Red Wings, but never caught on because Adams didn't know how to utilize his talents.

"Fielder was just a magician with the puck. He was so good, he set records out west. So Adams brought him up for a tryout. He put him between Howe and Lindsay, and he played a handful of games, but he was shipped back down to the minors and never got another chance with Detroit.

"The reason was, when you were on the ice with Howe, he carried the puck. Well, if Guyle Fielder didn't carry the puck, he was nothing. He had no defensive skills and couldn't check his hat. All his skill lay in controlling the puck. But when you played with Gordie, you couldn't do that, so Fielder showed nothing. Adams said, 'Who the hell is this guy? He can't play at our level,' and sent him back. What he should have done is put two speedsters with Fielder, and he'd have sprung them loose. So I've always looked at that as a tragic case of mismanagement of talent. But that was Adams. He ruled the roost, and everyone ran in fear of him."

Tommy Ivan, too, had necessarily been subservient to Adams. But Ivan had exercised a moderating influence on his boss; he'd possessed sound judgement, people skills and ideas of his own, and he had been ready to use them in his quiet way—behind Adams's back, when necessary. As long as Ivan was coach, the players had someone who understood and defended them.

Metro Prystai says, "Tommy was a terrific little coach—soft-spoken, just an ordinary guy. We'd have a bad period, and Adams'd come into the dressing room and raise hell with us. Then after he'd left, Ivan'd say, 'Don't listen to that fat bugger, he doesn't know what he's talking about.' I don't know if they planned it that way, but he'd calm us down, and holy mackerel, we'd go out there and do anything for Tommy. He was that kind of guy."

Adams replaced Ivan with Jimmy Skinner, the former minor-leaguer who had been coaching the Detroit farm team in Windsor, the Spitfires. It wasn't a choice likely to inject new ideas, energy or momentum into the Red Wings. In Ted Lindsay's view, "Adams was looking for a yes-man, and Skinner was a good yes-man. He wouldn't have known a hockey player if he'd had a uniform on. He was a door opener."

If that seems harsh, the considered opinion of Murray Costello, who joined the Red Wings in Skinner's second year as coach, isn't much more flattering. Skinner's players had trouble hearing him during games because the crowds were so noisy; the team installed a little microphone and speakers behind the Detroit bench so the players at the far end could hear his orders. "But all you heard," says Costello, "was 'Gordie, Red, Ted, Alex! Gordie, Red, Ted, Alex!' Beyond that, I'm not sure Jimmy knew any other names on the team. They were the bread-and-butter guys, but if one of them was tired or in the box, Skinner would look around and have a hard time figuring out who else to put on."

The whole problem, in Lindsay's eyes, was that Adams had an inflated opinion of his own knowledge of the game. He didn't believe he needed a truly capable coach, as long as he was giving the orders; and he didn't believe anyone else could tell him anything about hockey.

"Jack was always the magician," Lindsay says sarcastically. "But he didn't know hockey players. Jack was a good salesman, but not a good hockey man."

Lindsay believes more of the credit for building the foundations of the Detroit dynasty should go to former player and chief scout Carson Cooper, who recruited Lindsay, Kelly and numerous others: "*He* was the man responsible for the good teams we had. Cooper loved the Detroit Red Wings—Red Wing blood flowed in his veins. When Adams fired him, it almost killed him. Adams was too stupid to realize who was really responsible for our success."

Despite all this, the team Tommy Ivan had nurtured was still mostly intact going into the 1954-55 season, still capable of winning under Adams and Skinner. They were a mature gang who had played together so long, they required less coaching than most. "We knew our lines, we just changed ourselves," says Lindsay.

Nonetheless, they seemed half a stride slower without Ivan. At the season's midpoint, they trailed the Canadiens in second place instead of establishing their usual dominance atop the standings. Even the normally reliable Howe was having a spotty season. In November, he'd been slowed by a shoulder injury and had missed six games—his first layoff after playing 382 consecutive games since his knee operation five years earlier. Then, after Christmas, he entered his worst scoring slump in years, scoring only 4 goals in seventeen games by late February.

Both of Detroit's big scorers were feeling frustration. In a losing effort against Toronto at Maple Leaf Gardens one night, Howe got into a scuffle with a foolhardy fan who grabbed his stick as he was skating past. After Howe extricated himself and began skating away, the fan lunged over the boards and took a wild swing at him—provoking Lindsay, who was so accustomed to defending his buddy on the ice, to whack the spectator with his stick. Retaliating against a paying customer, however, was simply not done: Clarence Campbell suspended Lindsay for ten days, which meant he'd miss four games, and the league governors upheld the penalty after Adams appealed it. A few weeks later, that incident was to play a key role in Richard's suspension and the ensuing riot.

Howe got into another, more equal battle in Toronto that winter—with the Leafs' big hot prospect Eric Nesterenko, who was having a hard time living up to the expectation that he'd become for the Leafs what another big youngster, Jean Beliveau, was for the Canadiens. After Nesterenko grabbed his stick, Howe lit into him and practically demolished him; it was as if Howe had determined to cut him down to size, demonstrating his own superiority as the biggest of the big guys. It was another emergence of Howe's mean, vindictive side—the side that would make its ultimate appearance four years later, in a more famous fight in New York.

In what was a banner year for violence, even by NHL standards, the Maurice Richard-Hal Laycoe high-sticking incident, followed by Richard's punching of the official, erupted in Boston on March 13. When the NHL held an owners' meeting just before its hearing into the incident, Adams and Bruce Norris were still smarting from Lindsay's suspension earlier in the season. They demanded Richard be given equal treatment. And not only that, they raged, but earlier in the season Richard had struck linesman George Hayes with an empty glove, and had gotten away with mere penalties from referee Red Storey and a $250 fine from Campbell. According to NHL insiders, it was the Detroit management's fury over this inequity that sealed the Rocket's fate, resulting in his suspension not only for the final three games of the season but for the entire 1955 playoffs.

For that reason, the final standings and playoffs were not as true a test of the relative strengths of the Red Wings and the Canadiens as they might have been. In the key St. Patrick's Day game to decide which of them would finish in first place, tear gas exploded in the Forum between the first and second periods. With the well-dressed crowd hacking and sputtering, the building was ordered cleared for the public's safety, and Campbell awarded the game to the Red Wings, who were leading 4-1 at the time, after both Red Kelly and Dutch Reibel had scored twice. A handwritten note on a scrap of paper was delivered to Adams in the Detroit dressing room, where Lefty Wilson had stuffed wet towels under the door to keep the smoke and fumes out. Signed by both Campbell and Montreal general manager Frank Selke, the note read, "Jack Adams: The game has been forfeited to Detroit. You are entitled to take your team on your way anytime now.

"Mr. Selke agrees to this decision as the Quebec department has ordered the building cleared."

The Red Wings dressed as fast as they could, exited through a rear door and boarded the team bus, which drove past rioters smashing windows on Ste. Catherine Street on its way to Westmount Station.

The final game of the schedule was played at the Olympia, once more against Montreal. Fearing an invasion by Canadiens' fans from Windsor, the Detroit police riot squad was present, but the fears were groundless, and the Red Wings won 6-0 to finish first for a record seventh straight season—by just two points.

As in the previous year, the semifinals were mere formalities. Detroit swept Toronto in four. Montreal recovered its confidence while playing minus Richard by eliminating Boston in five. Once again, the two superteams would extend each other to seven games in the finals. Only this time, without his rival's presence, Howe would emerge more clearly as the ascendant power of the playoffs.

Each of the seven games was determined by home-ice advantage. It therefore proved critical for the Red Wings that they'd finished first after all; four of the seven were played at the Olympia. Game one was close, until Pavelich scored the winner on a short-handed goal, intercepting Harvey's pass to go in alone on Plante. Game two was a 7-1 blowout in which the Howe-Reibel-Lindsay line was sensational, combining for 12 points—4 of them on goals by Lindsay, while Howe scored once.

Montreal rebounded strongly to win at home 4-2, and Geoffrion, who had squeaked past Richard to win the scoring title after the suspension, much to the disgust of the Rocket's fans, scored a hat trick. Two of Geoffrion's goals came only twelve seconds apart, both while Howe was serving a holding penalty.

After Montreal won again, 5-3, the teams returned to Detroit, where Howe had another big night: 3 goals, one of them short-handed, in a 5-1 victory. This gave Gordie a total of 19 points for the series thus far and set a playoff record, breaking an eleven-year-old mark belonging to the Canadiens' retired star and future coach, Toe Blake.

The Wings hoped to win the Cup in the sixth game, before the Canadiens' own fans; but Montreal was not to be denied and won 6-3. When Lindsay set up Delvecchio for a goal, it was his 12th assist, tying the 1946 record of the Punch Line's old centreman, Elmer Lach.

The deciding game was played at the Olympia, where Detroit hadn't lost a game since the previous December. The Red Wings didn't disappoint their faithful, and neither did Howe. He scored what proved to be the winning goal, which boosted his newly minted playoff record to 20 points. He also shared in another scoring feat and another playoff record with his linemates: in eleven games, he, Lindsay and Reibel had collected 51 points.

After a season like the one they'd had, climaxing in a second straight Stanley Cup, the Red Wings could reasonably have expected the team to remain intact. True, Howe's and Lindsay's point production had fallen off during the regular schedule— Howe's to 29 goals and 33 assists, dropping him to fifth place in the scoring race, Lindsay's to 19 and 19 (although he'd played only forty-nine games); and true, for the first time in recent memory, neither had made the all-star team. But that scarcely seemed to matter. Both had come up big in the playoffs, when it really counted; they and their teammates were wearing Stanley Cup rings for the fourth time in six years.

Nonetheless, Adams was again itching to play magician between seasons. Although he left Howe and Lindsay alone, as well as Kelly, Pronovost, Goldham, Pavelich, Delvecchio and Reibel, he proceeded to make two trades that can only be described as self-destructive in their combined impact on the Red Wings. In all, he traded virtually half his personnel from that Stanley Cup team—including the year's Vezina trophy winner, who had led the league with 12 shutouts, and kept his goals-against average below 2:00 in all five of his seasons with the team: Terry Sawchuk.

In retrospect, there is something preposterously dumb about the deals Adam cut in the summer of 1955. A comparison of the seasoned players he surrendered with the quality of players he received puts his reputation as a shrewd trader into permanent doubt.

To the Boston Bruins, Adams awarded not only Sawchuk but Vic Stasiuk and Marcel Bonin, in return for defenseman Warren Godfrey, forwards Ed Sandford and Real Chevrefils, and the rights to a couple of rookies. Quite apart from his championship goal-tender, whom Adams would be desperate to retrieve two seasons later, both Stasiuk and Bonin would go on to successful careers— Stasiuk as one-third of Boston's powerful "Uke" Line alongside Johnny Bucyk and Bronco Horvath, and Bonin with both the Bruins and the Canadiens.

In the other deal, Adams traded Tony Leswick, Glen Skov, Johnny Wilson and Benny Woit to Tommy Ivan in Chicago. In return, the Black Hawks gave him Bucky Hollingworth, Dave

Creighton and Jerry Toppazzini, none of whom would make any significant impact in Detroit.

Adams had his reasons, of course. As usual, he didn't want his team to become complacent after winning the Cup so often; he did a good job of fixing *that* problem. But his seemingly more credible motive was to create room on the Red Wings for four promising young prospects from the Edmonton farm club in the Western Hockey League, who, he said, represented the future. So Sawchuk was traded to make room for Glenn Hall, who had been brilliant in eight games as substitute goalie during the past two seasons; and three exciting young forwards were coming up fast in Bucyk, Horvath and Norm Ullman. And yet, in no time, Adams would even deal away three of these four rising stars, keeping only Ullman. Ultimately, the wholesale 1955 trades must be seen as the unravelling of the Red Wings.

Ted Lindsay and Marty Pavelich certainly see it that way. "It was just foolishness to break that team up," Pavelich says now. "We'd won four Stanley Cups and could have won three more if Adams had kept us together. We could have had a track record that would never be touched."

Lindsay is even more bitter. He cites Adams's chronic lack of faith in the men who had served him well as one reason Detroit didn't win the Cup more often. "We won seven championships in a row. We should have won seven Stanley Cups." At playoff time, Adams had a habit of sidelining tried and true players and parachuting minor-leaguers into the line-up as soon as they had finished their own playoffs. "Even though they hadn't been good enough to play with us all year long, suddenly these guys were going to help us win the Stanley Cup."

And then there were the bad trades. Lindsay isn't insisting a general manager should be loyal to his players at all costs, or disputing the principle of strengthening a team through trades. He just feels Adams traded unwisely.

"We had Hall coming up, so Sawchuk *was* expendable. But the only place we had a weakness was on defense. If Adams had traded Sawchuk to Montreal, we could have got Doug Harvey or Tom Johnson. With Harvey on defense, *we'd* have won five Cups in a row instead of Montreal. But Adams traded Sawchuk to Boston instead."

Lindsay adds, "One of the best players we had in the playoffs was Stasiuk, and he was traded. Two years later, Adams traded Bucyk. He wasn't good enough for Detroit, but he played twenty-one years for Boston and was one of the best players in the league.

"We should have won more Stanley Cups," Lindsay repeats grimly, nearly four decades later. "It bothers me all the time."

Something else was bothering Jack Adams in 1955. With their confounded insistence on growing up and becoming real adults, some of his players had actually gone into business for themselves. The worst offenders were Lindsay (naturally) and Pavelich. They had joined forces to form a company selling automobile parts— interior trim, accelerator pedals, heating ducts, bumper parts, and so on—representing various manufacturers on 5 per cent commission. Eventually, they would also get into manufacturing their own automotive products and would build a very substantial operation, with eighty employees. It would be an extremely smart move financially, with the North American economy in high gear and the Detroit auto industry setting new records every year. But Adams didn't see it that way. As far as he was concerned, the only records his boys should care about were in the NHL.

It upset him even more that, at first, Lindsay and Pavelich had included Howe in their business dealings. For a year or so, the three players were in partnership with a local businessman and hockey fan named Frank Carlin. After Lindsay and Pavelich broke away to start their own firm in 1955, Carlin brought Detroit Tigers' baseball star Al Kaline, whom he'd met through Howe, into the business. At that point, Adams decided this was all getting too far out of hand. He decided to use his clout with local sportswriters to embarrass his players and intimidate them into giving up their silly notions about having a life away from the ice.

Articles planted by Adams appeared in the Detroit press, suggesting Howe and his teammates were spending so much time on business, and making so much money, that they'd lost their dedication to hockey. One of the people most incensed by these insinuations was Colleen Howe, now a mother of two (Mark had been born in May of that year). Colleen didn't feel particularly wealthy on the salary her husband was making, estimated in the range of

$16,000 to $17,000 at the time. In fact, as she commented in her book, Adams's allegations about money were ridiculous, since the company wasn't putting anything into the partners' pockets. And to imply that the players no longer cared about their game was a cheap shot. Colleen put it accurately when she wrote that accusing Gordie Howe of neglecting hockey was like accusing Heifetz of neglecting the violin.

As a send-up, Colleen persuaded Pat Lindsay to turn up at the Olympia with her, both of them wearing borrowed mink stoles and clutching handfuls of play money from their Monopoly sets, which they used to light each other's cigarettes in front of newspaper photographers. "If we are that wealthy, we should look the part," they remarked. In the next day's paper, the cutline under the photo read, "Wives pan Adams' comments."

Jolly Jawn was not amused. Now he had more rebels on his hands. But "the Big Guy," as he always called Howe, would not be one of them. Even more afraid of his boss's displeasure than his wife's, the Big Guy soon decided discretion was the better part of valour; steering clear of Adams's paternalistic wrath, he sold his interest in the business back to Carlin.

Lindsay and Pavelich are both well-off today, having built their business into a large and successful venture over a period of twenty-five years before cashing out. In the early 1980s, they sold to one of several companies that wanted to buy them. They have plenty of reason to feel vindicated. As Pavelich says now, "We knew we needed to look to life after hockey. Adams didn't like that—he wanted 100 per cent of you. But I thought, 'No, you've gotta think ahead.'"

Howe, on the other hand, felt safer and more comfortable sticking to hockey. It would be a choice he'd make again and again. But it would be years before his choice would pay off in a big way financially.

The remarkable thing about the Detroit Red Wings of 1955-56 is that they performed as well as they did. On the one hand, Adams had gutted them of so many key players from their championship years—not only Sawchuk but Prystai, Leswick, Skov, Stasiuk and Wilson—and on the other, he kept harassing and bullying the stars who remained. Adams also let Horvath get away that year (to the Rangers, before he starred with Boston). So the Red Wings opened the new season with a startlingly strange look; they retained only nine players from their previous year's Stanley Cup triumph. Not surprisingly, they began to fade from contention, a long, slow fade that would take them, a season later, all the way into the wilderness of the also-rans.

At the season's halfway point, the Wings were third, well behind the Canadiens and (of all people) the Rangers. Desperate to shake the team out of its doldrums, Skinner and Adams juggled their lines, moving Kelly up to left wing in Lindsay's place with Howe and Reibel, and switching Lindsay to a line with Delvecchio and Dineen.

The team revived in the latter half of the season. On the night of February 7, 1956, Lindsay and Howe were reunited after two months apart, and Lindsay set up Howe's 300th goal, against Al Rollins and the Chicago Black Hawks. Howe became only the third player in NHL history to reach that then-lofty plateau.

By season's end, the Red Wings had recovered somewhat to finish second by a whisker, still a distant 24 points behind Montreal. Hall had proved a worthy successor to Sawchuk by earning 12 shutouts, compiling a goals-against average of 2.11 (second-best in the league) and winning the Calder trophy. But it had been Jean Beliveau's year to win the scoring title. He came within 3 goals of the Holy Grail, setting a record for centremen with 47 goals. Howe improved his output over the previous year to 38 goals and 41 assists, finishing second, 9 points behind Beliveau, 8 ahead of third-place Richard. Once again, the Red Wings-Canadiens rivalry was renewed in the Stanley Cup finals. It would be the last time for a whole decade.

In the uneventful semifinals, Detroit and Montreal had little trouble disposing of Toronto and New York respectively. The biggest excitement came when a fan phoned the *Toronto Star* three times, threatening to bring a gun to Maple Leaf Gardens to shoot Howe and Lindsay. The crank blamed the two for injuring the Leafs' Tod Sloan in the series' second game in Detroit.

The night of the third game, the Red Wings were even jumpier than usual as they dressed for the game. To break the tension, Bob

1957

★ ★ ★

**Lindsay, Pavelich,
Prystai gone;
Red Wings unravel**

Overleaf: Howe in mid-game conference
with Terry Sawchuk, who wears
fibreglass mask fashioned for him by
trainer Lefty Wilson.
HAROLD BARKLEY / MICHAEL LEONETTI
SPORTS PRODUCTS INC.
Below: Following a threat on his life, Ted
Lindsay does some shooting of his own at
Maple Leaf Gardens after scoring
overtime goal against Toronto in 1956
semifinals.
JAMES R. KILPATRICK / DETROIT NEWS

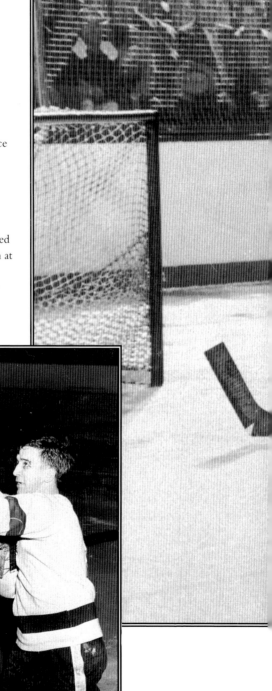

Above: Howe scores another one on New York goalie Gump Worsley, March 1958.
DETROIT NEWS

Above: Not always the perfect gentleman after all, Lady Byng trophy winner and future Member of Parliament Red Kelly decks Boston's Leo Labine in 1959. Detroit News
Right: Kelly grabs some precious time with his busy fiancée, figure skater Andra McLaughlin, between periods in 1955. Martin / Detroit News
Far right: Howe is comforted by mother Katherine Howe after breaking down in tears on Gordie Howe Night, March 1959.
Holcomb / Detroit News

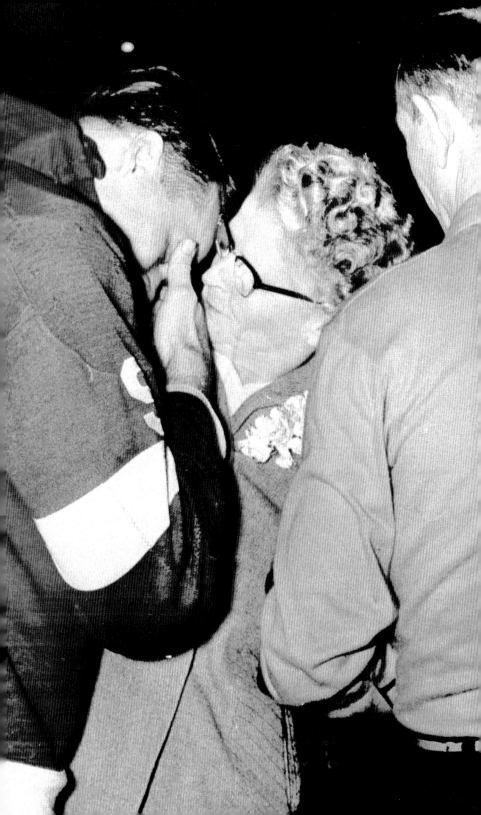

Right: It took a lot to bring Howe down. Maple Leaf defense pair Allan Stanley (*left*) and Tim Horton crisscross their sticks to box in Number Nine, December 1960.
JAMES R. KILPATRICK / DETROIT NEWS

Below: Colleen Howe seated between her parents-in-law, Ab and Katherine Howe, at a Red Wings game on Christmas Day, 1962.
DETROIT FREE PRESS

Lower right: Howe in dressing room playing Marlon Brando, March 1961.
STYRLANDER / DETROIT NEWS

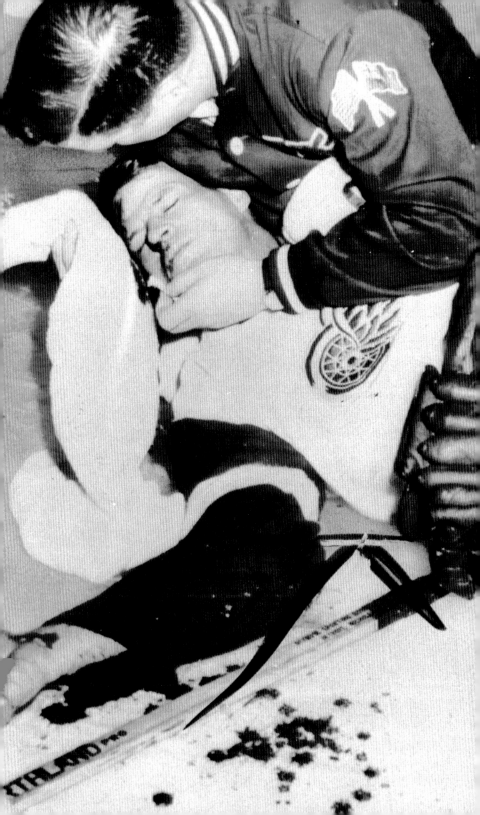

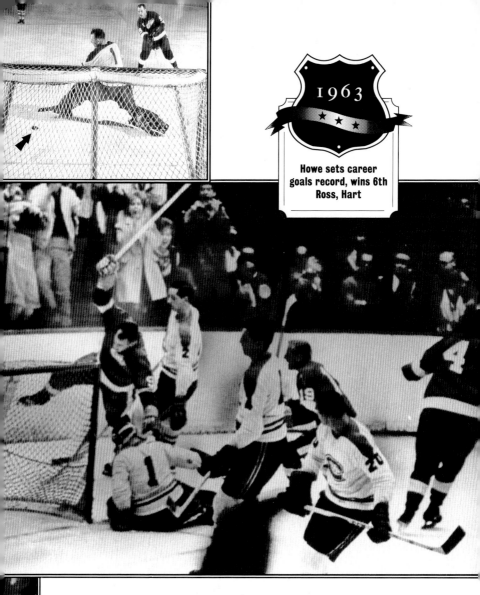

1963

★ ★ ★

Howe sets career goals record, wins 6th Ross, Hart

Left: Howe suffered a concussion and a twelve-stitch gash on the forehead after being felled by Eddie Shack's high stick in Toronto in January 1961. Here trainer Lefty Wilson ministers to Howe. He was back in action after three games. DETROIT NEWS

Top: Taken over the goal judge's shoulder, this photo captures Howe scoring against his old fishing buddy Johnny Bower on a penalty shot, New Year's Eve, 1961. JAMES R. KILPATRICK / DETROIT NEWS

Above: Record breaker! The Detroit fans go wild as Howe scores number 545, shattering Rocket Richard's career goals record, on November 10, 1963. Howe celebrates with stick upraised, while Montreal goaltender Charlie Hodge turns to look at the puck. The other downcast Canadiens are Jacques Laperriere, Jean Beliveau and Dave Balon. Detroit's Billy McNeill (19) assisted. TORONTO STAR

Right: The Happy Warrior: Forty-one-year-old Howe in September 1969, with fellow veteran and longtime linemate Alex Delvecchio.
James R. Kilpatrick / Detroit News
Far right: In his final season with Detroit, 1970-71, the old man can still dish it out: in this case, a gentle crosscheck on the Chicago Black Hawks' Keith Magnuson, nineteen years Howe's junior. Goaltender Gerry Desjardins has just taken the shot on his neck.
James R. Kilpatrick / Detroit News
Below: Tears flow during the ceremony to retire Howe's number nine jersey at the Olympia, March 12, 1972. *From left*: Mark Howe, then sixteen, Ab Howe (with handkerchief), U.S. Vice-President Spiro Agnew, Colleen Howe, Ted Lindsay, Gordie Howe. Steve Thompson / Detroit Free Press

1971

Howe's final season
with Detroit; first
retirement

Top right: Howe hams it up with the eleven-year-old who would eventually break his major NHL scoring records, Wayne Gretzky, at a minor-hockey banquet in Brantford, Ontario, 1972. JACK BOWMAN/BRANTFORD EXPOSITOR

Right: Howe often lent his support to the Michigan March of Dimes campaign. Here he shares a laugh with 1972 poster child Carmen Donessa in Detroit. JOHN COLLIER/DETROIT FREE PRESS

Above: Coming out of retirement in 1973 at age forty-five to join his sons Mark (*centre*) and Marty on the Houston Aeros of the World Hockey Association, Howe poses in the unfamiliar blue and white of the Aeros. DICK DARRELL/TORONTO STAR

Left: By 1979-80, the last of Howe's 32 seasons in big-league professional hockey, the Hartford Whalers had entered the NHL. Here fifty-one-year-old Howe zeroes in on the Leafs' Ian Turnbull as Borje Salming looks alarmed. Toronto Star

Above: Howe congratulates Wayne Gretzky on breaking his record of 1,850 career points in Edmonton on October 15, 1989, while Wayne's father Walter Gretzky and wife Janet Jones look on. UPI/Bettman

Overleaf: Howe and his long-time rival Rocket Richard let bygones be bygones at an old-timers' charity game in Saskatoon, 1987. Jeff Vinnick/Saskatoon StarPhoenix

Goldham proposed they test the supposed gunman: an obscure Detroit rookie named Cummy Burton could go onto the ice, Goldham suggested, wearing a sweater with number nine sewn on the back and Lindsay's number seven on the front. Burton vetoed the idea. In the end nothing happened, apart from Howe scoring once and Lindsay twice, including the game-winner in overtime. After the victory, Lindsay, whom the Toronto fans had booed all night, skated around the ice aiming his stick at the crowd like a rifle.

The '56 finals lacked the suspense of the previous two years' showdowns. Detroit won only once, in game three, the first game at the Olympia, and Montreal easily took the series four games to one. Just as he'd dominated the regular season, Beliveau led the playoff scoring with 19 points—just one shy of the record Howe had set a year earlier—while Howe himself was fifth, behind Geoffrion, Richard and Olmstead. It was Toe Blake's first season as Montreal's coach, and the first of his five consecutive Stanley Cups. Detroit, by contrast, wouldn't be seen in the Stanley Cup finals for another five years.

Magnetized by a potent mixture of gifted veterans, brilliant young talent and shrewd, tough-minded coaching, the Montreal dynasty had arrived. Undermined by a suspicious and senile management, the Red Wings had collapsed. It was clear that the will to win, by itself, was not enough in the modern NHL: it had to be accompanied by intelligence, insight, imagination and plain, basic common sense.

There is a sad but perhaps inevitable dénouement to this chapter in Howe's and the Red Wings' history. It was sad not only for the Detroit players at the time but for all NHL players, then and later. But it was undoubtedly saddest of all for Ted Lindsay.

By virtue of talent, dedication, courage and ferocity, Lindsay had established himself for years as the Red Wings' natural leader. His teammates looked up to him with a respect bordering on awe, tinged with both gratitude and fear. He'd taught all of them, from Howe on down, to look after themselves on the ice. "Just make sure," he'd say, "that if a guy's going to get you, he'll have to go through an inch of lumber first." They said he could carve a turkey with that stick of his.

"Teddy was the captain, and he was the mouth," Metro Prystai comments appreciatively. "If you were in a fight and you were getting the better of it, he'd be holding the other team back. If you were getting the worst of it, he'd be in there helping you."

And yet, at the start of the 1956-57 season, Adams suddenly and unexpectedly stripped Lindsay of the captaincy after four years. Adams had been angry at him, as usual, this time for criticizing the previous year's trades. Determined to assert his supremacy once and for all, the general manager provoked a final showdown with Lindsay, a man of profound loves and hates who never lacked guts on or off the ice, and who now staked his hockey career on his ultimate challenge to authority—the authority not only of Jack Adams but of the team owners and the NHL itself.

During the pre-game skate at the October 1956 all-star game, a fateful discussion took place between Lindsay and Doug Harvey. Although the two were old and bitter enemies, they had recently found themselves allied as the players' only representatives on the five-member board of the NHL Pension Society. At society meetings during the previous year, both had felt frustrated and insulted by the difficulty they'd had in obtaining the most elementary financial information about the state of the pension fund, which was administered by Clarence Campbell himself.

The fund had been started ten years earlier. Players typically contributed $900 a year, an approximately 20 per cent chunk of their salaries, which then averaged only $5,000. The owners contributed $600 per player; this money came not out of their operating profits but from the proceeds of the annual all-star game and a special surcharge on playoff tickets. Since the players took part in the all-star game for free, they were in reality subsidizing the owners' contributions.

As representatives of all the players, Lindsay and Harvey took their obligations seriously. On behalf of their colleagues, whose money it was, they wanted answers to a few simple questions: How much principal had accumulated in the pension fund? How well was it invested? How much money were those investments earning? But they felt stymied by Campbell's lack of cooperation and stonewalled by the refusal of the owners' three-man majority to agree to an independent appraisal of the fund's management.

By now, however, Lindsay had learned a thing or two about business. Harvey was no babe in the woods either, scarcely more willing than Lindsay to be condescended to by his "betters." The pair decided the time had come for collective action.

They had done a little figuring of their own. They suspected that the NHL owners, contrary to their perpetual poor-mouthing, were making healthy profits after all—which was, in fact, true. And just that summer, Lindsay had learned from Cleveland Indians' pitcher Bob Feller about the major gains negotiated by the new baseball players' association. Seeing parallels with the NHL, Lindsay had flown to New York three times at his own expense to meet with the baseball association's lawyers, from whom he'd received an eye-opening perspective on how crudely exploited and blatantly under-paid professional hockey players were. The lawyers had been especially enlightening about the players' right to benefit from the increasingly lucrative revenues from televising NHL games, of which the players received not a cent.

At the all-star game, Lindsay told Harvey they couldn't just sit tight on what they'd learned, like good little boys. They had to mobilize the players' strength in numbers, forming an association to press for better treatment. Harvey readily agreed. After the all-star game, they arranged to meet with senior representatives of the other four teams: Jimmy Thomson of Toronto, Fern Flaman of Boston, Bill Gadsby of New York and Lindsay's old friend from his Kirkland Lake days, Gus Mortson of Chicago. Against all the NHL rules, written and unwritten, forbidding "fraternization" among players of different teams, the six proceeded with stubborn deter-mination to line up support from their teammates, who were asked to chip in a $100 membership fee to cover expenses.

The NHL Players' Association—the organizers were loath to call it a union—was clearly an idea whose time had come. By Febru-ary 1957, four months later, they'd signed up every active player except one (the Leafs' Ted Kennedy, who was about to retire). In New York, Lindsay announced the birth of the new association, making it very clear the intention was not to be a militant labour organization, but to work cooperatively with the owners for the good of hockey. And from that moment, despite these carefully sent signals of good will, the NHL declared war on its own players.

Led by Jack Adams and Conn Smythe, management did everything it could to oppose and ultimately break, or at least neuter,
the association: everything from openly intimidating the organizers personally, with threats of benching, trades or demotion—
threats that were often carried out—to refusing to meet with the
association, even refusing to reply substantively to its lawyers'
letters. Through his trained seals in the Detroit media, Adams put
out inflated salary figures, making the players, and especially
Lindsay, appear greedy.

On the day after Lindsay's announcement, Adams berated his
men with more than the usual ferocity in the Red Wings' dressing
room. With all the considerable self-righteousness at his command, he lectured them about team loyalty, claiming it was
incompatible with membership in the association. Then he
demanded to know from each player, in front of the entire team,
whether he supported the association personally.

"Adams was browbeating them," Lindsay recalls. "There was no
silent vote. It was, 'Do *you* want this? Do *you*?' and it had to be yes
or no, right to Adams's face. What were they going to say? Those
kids were afraid they'd never see another hockey rink, never see
another paycheque."

Similar bullying tactics on other teams, combined with NHL
headquarters' implacable hostility to the association organizers and
their lawyers (who were characterized by Conn Smythe as "New
York Jewish socialists" out to destroy hockey), gradually wore
down the players' resolve. Some ringleaders were made examples
of. After the '56-'57 season ended, Smythe traded Jimmy Thomson to Chicago, the no-hope team where other association activ-
ists, such as the Maple Leafs' Tod Sloan, also found themselves.

In July, Adams triumphantly announced he'd traded Lindsay,
too. The eight-time first-team all-star was banished to Chicago,
along with another rebel who refused to lick Adams's boots, Glenn
Hall—himself expendable now that Adams had recovered
Sawchuk from Boston. Hall recounts that he talked with Lindsay
about the association after Adams told him not to. "He didn't like
me doing that, and I told him to fuck off."

For Adams, getting rid of Lindsay and his allies had become the
prime, the *only*, consideration. It didn't matter that Hall had just

been named to the first all-star team. It didn't matter that Lindsay had just achieved his best record in thirteen seasons with Detroit, compiling 85 points, good enough for second place in the 1956-57 scoring race, and topped only by Howe's 89. With a league-leading 55 assists, Lindsay had also boosted his linemate's goal production that year to 44, Howe's highest in four seasons, and to a record-tying third Hart trophy. But, as trainer Lefty Wilson points out, "Trades on our team were never made on the basis of ability. It was always personal. Adams'd get so bloody mad, he'd trade somebody just to get rid of him."

In Lindsay's case, it probably would have happened sooner if he hadn't been such a priceless asset to the club. But even that was forgotten in the face of the threat of the players' association. Adams fatuously justified his action as "good publicity" and proclaimed, "Teddy, he's a high-class kid and a good family man. But he got into business, then he got into the players' association, so the thing that brought him to Detroit from the mining country of Canada, he'd forgotten. It was third in his mind. So there's a time when you have to make these moves for their own good . . . There's always some reason to trade a player—maybe he's a club-house lawyer."

After his trade, Lindsay kept fighting the good fight from Chicago. But he was becoming increasingly isolated, as the owners' acts of revenge made the players increasingly nervous and fearful about their own futures in hockey. The owners still held the whip hand: who would be the next to go? More and more, the players listened to management's accusations that Lindsay was in it only for himself, that he didn't have their true interests at heart.

In October 1957, the association's lawyers filed an anti-trust suit against the NHL owners in U.S. federal court, charging they had established an illegal monopoly over the sport. But such aggressive action was too much for some players; they'd lost the stomach for playing it rough off the ice.

In the end, the players who broke the association's solidarity were none other than Lindsay's former teammates. Shortly after the beginning of the 1957-58 season, the Detroit Red Wings withdrew from the association as a team, citing the reason that the anti-trust suit had been filed without their consent. Leading the

GORDIE: A HOCKEY LEGEND

defection were two men who'd come to the conclusion, at that point, that it was smarter and more comfortable siding with management than against it: Adams's avowed "untradeables," Gordie Howe and Red Kelly.

Players still loyal to the association were furious at Howe and Kelly. They called the Red Wings "scabs" and worse. But a few months afterwards, the association's momentum petered out into meek capitulation. The lawsuit was dropped. The will to recreate the solidarity that Lindsay, Harvey and the others had forged would not return for a decade, when lawyer and player-agent Alan Eagleson revived the association in 1967.

"Two key guys folded," Lindsay says today. "They were Howe and Kelly, who still thought Adams was the second coming of Christ. That hurt." Asked why he believes they backed down, Lindsay comments curtly: "Some people can stand pressure. Some can't."

Even so, what else could have led Howe to break ranks with his close friend of ten years, whose lead he'd once followed in so many things?

For years, Adams had been publicly declaring Howe his favourite. Privately, he'd been reassuring the Big Guy that, as the NHL's best player, he was receiving the NHL's best salary, estimated at slightly over $20,000 by 1957-58 (in reality, however, Richard and Beliveau were probably receiving several thousand more). So Howe, being a trusting soul, had reason to believe he, at least, was well treated.

Before each season, when the time for contract talks rolled around, Adams would call each player into his office in turn, starting with the veterans, and talk salary and bonuses. In addition to salary, Howe received bonuses for winning individual trophies, for goal production above a certain level and for all-star selections, as well as his share of playoff winnings: in all, his bonuses in a good year might come to $8,000 or $9,000, or nearly half again his current salary.

Howe liked those incentives. To his straightforward, home-grown sense of fair play, of value given for value received, the bonuses represented a tangible reward for his achievements on the ice: the greater the achievement, the greater the reward. And as far

146

as salary was concerned, Adams seemed generous and open-handed. He'd pass the blank contract across the table and (although players didn't even get to keep a copy of their contracts in those days) invite Howe to fill in the salary figure himself: "Go ahead, Gord, just say what you're worth." Predictably, each year Howe would write in a salary figure $1,000 higher than the year before. And that was that. Who, Howe felt, could ask for anything more?

Lindsay could. At first, Howe listened to him, as he always had. There is a common assumption that Howe had to be dragged into the association kicking and screaming, but Lindsay contradicts that view: "Gordie was ready to join and be a part of it."

But by the time Howe, Kelly, Marcel Pronovost and the other Red Wings cracked, Lindsay had been traded to Chicago, and Marty Pavelich had paid the price for being Lindsay's friend and business partner by being ordered to the minor leagues. (Pavelich refused to play in another city. He knew he'd only lose the business contacts he'd built up in Detroit, and so he simply quit hockey, an enforced retirement at the age of twenty-nine. "It was the smartest thing I ever did," he says now.)

Without Lindsay's active presence and encouragement, and with a young and growing family to support—Colleen was now expecting their third child, Cathy—Howe had little will to resist the persistent pressure of the man he called "my second father." By temperament, Howe was no rebel: never had been and never would be. And Colleen was still too young, inexperienced and preoccupied with motherhood to assume the function of his backbone in business dealings, as she would later.

With Lindsay and Pavelich gone, Howe now found himself in the position of leading a team that was truly a shadow of its former self. Adams had exacted his revenge, and in the process had destroyed his own kingdom.

As the rebel angel expelled from the kingdom, Lindsay can look back today, survey the ashes and make a calmly realistic assessment. He remains adamant that he and the other leaders of the players' association didn't want to "ruin the game," as alleged by NHL management.

"We loved our game. We had a wonderful game that we loved to play. Our real reason for starting the association was that we wanted a vehicle for discussing the issues. But the owners thought we were morons—all they knew was that we wanted to play hockey. We'd never gotten together collectively before, so suddenly they thought they'd lose control of us.

"It was the same when Marty and I started the business. After all, we needed money in the off-season, and there was wonderful peace of mind in knowing you'd earn enough to support your family. It made you a more complete person, more in control of your life. We wouldn't have deserted the game. But we were human beings—we were mature, we had kids, we knew hockey wasn't going to be there for us forever."

The bitter irony of it all, as Lindsay is acutely aware, lies in what happened years later to the players' association, and to their hard-earned pension fund.

"The bad thing about the death of the association was that it gave a guy like Eagleson a chance to come in and use our game for his own purposes. If we could have kept our own association going, there wouldn't have been an Eagleson."

As for Jack Adams and his Red Wings, Lindsay's sense of satisfaction, of honour satisfied, is palpable. "Adams never won anything after that. He never won a thing."

CHAPTER ELEVEN

The Quiet Pride of Red Kelly

"Jack Adams walked Andra [Kelly] down the
aisle and gave her away. And then, six months later,
he gave me away."

—Leonard (Red) Kelly, 1993

MOST ACCOUNTS OF THE DEATH of the NHL Players Association echo Ted Lindsay's view that Gordie Howe and Red Kelly were largely responsible for sealing the association's fate. Howe has seldom, if ever, gone out of his way to dispute that view. But Kelly, formerly of the Detroit Red Wings and the Toronto Maple Leafs, formerly of the Canadian House of Commons (Liberal, York West) and the NHL coaching ranks, and now president and chief shareholder of CAMP Systems of Canada, a Toronto aircraft-maintenance firm, doesn't entirely share Lindsay's interpretation. Although he agrees the association's demise in 1958 was regrettable, Kelly believes his own role has been misrepresented.

A thoughtful, mild-mannered man with a slow, crinkly-eyed smile and a touch of red still showing through the grey, Kelly clearly remains vexed by the events of nearly forty years ago. There's no doubt in his mind that the fatal blow was the trade of Lindsay to Chicago. Until then, he, Howe and the other Detroit veterans had been onside with the association—if only because they believed in Lindsay and his persuasive arguments. But in Lindsay's absence, their lack of experience in such worldly matters made them nervous, uncertain about the justice of their case and easy prey for management's manipulations.

"I wasn't really into the association very much," Kelly acknowledges. "I was playing hockey; that was my major concern." In that, he and Howe were identical; they left the politics to Lindsay. When Kelly cites the change in Howe's attitude to the association after Lindsay was banished, he's also talking about himself.

"Gordie would go along with whatever Ted said in those years, they were that close. But then [after the trade], we didn't really know what was going on any more, we weren't in touch. We didn't know these two lawyers in New York, who didn't know beans about hockey. In those days, you didn't want to hurt the game or its reputation. Oh, there were lots of things that were wrong . . ."

For months before and after the trade, Kelly, Howe and their teammates had been under relentless pressure from Adams to abandon the association. Buffeted by the two sides' conflicting claims, confused by the rapid pace of events during 1957 and demoralized by Lindsay's departure, they decided to seek independent legal advice. "The best thing, we figured, was to get a lawyer to advise us which way we should go."

Even the fact that the players had the temerity to hire their own lawyer drew Adams's wrath: "He thought we should have taken his word for it."

But in the end, the association foundered on the classic dilemma of struggling labour groups: the reluctance of their members to go out on strike. Although no strike had yet been called, it would have been the ultimate weapon once the association had been legally certified as a bargaining unit on behalf of the players.

Kelly and Howe wanted to take a gentler, kinder approach. "I've been reading some books [about the pension issue]," Kelly says, "and they don't explain this. They just say we led the players out of the association, which broke it. I didn't think we were doing that. We agreed 100 per cent with what the players were trying to get, but we didn't want to strike, we wanted to negotiate. I thought we should sit down and talk and iron things out."

Kelly was dismayed when the management-player talks fizzled out completely after a few meetings. Once the NHL had intimidated the players into dropping their court action, negotiation yielded only a few small concessions, such as a $7,000 minimum salary, and minor increases in pension benefits and playoff earnings. There was no progress at all on sharing television revenues. That wasn't what Kelly or the others had intended, and he wonders now about the wisdom of surrendering the strike threat.

"There was a TV market coming up that they were starting to talk about, and I guess the weapon was the strike. Maybe if the strike had gone on, something would have happened. Who knows?"

Howe has expressed second thoughts, too, but even more vehemently. In a rueful tone, he told June Callwood in the 1992 Vision-TV interview, "We weren't like the players this past year, who stood up for themselves and who struck for what they wanted. Maybe we should have done that. But we didn't have enough guts or enough leadership."

Although he showed plenty of guts in every game, leadership was never Howe's strong suit: his instinct was always to defer to whichever authority was nearest at hand. At first, Kelly was the same way. But before long, Kelly would experience his share of adversity and mistreatment, which would toughen his gentle nature so that he was no longer a boy in a man's world. This was a transition that all the Red Wings of the 1950s would have to make sooner or later—even Howe himself.

Of all Howe's teammates throughout the championship years in Detroit, Kelly was the most like him in personality. Both came from families with farming backgrounds, although Kelly's was much more affluent; he grew up on his parents' tobacco farm near Simcoe, Ontario, north of Toronto. Both were shy, soft-spoken, polite, modest, self-effacing young men—when newly arrived in the NHL, Kelly had a reputation for addressing sportswriters as "Sir"—yet both were single-mindedly devoted to hockey and passionately determined to play it professionally. And both, when they first set out to pursue that passion, experienced deep pangs of homesickness.

In Kelly's case, he left home at fifteen to board at the private high school his father and uncles had attended—St. Michael's College School, run by the Basilian fathers in downtown Toronto. Lying awake at night in the dorm with the other boys, Kelly remembers, "I'd get homesick as all get-out when I heard the streetcars clanging down Bay Street. I was used to having the family around me, and it was always quiet on the farm."

The homesickness lasted until the hockey season started. Hockey was the reason Kelly was at St. Mike's in the first place: "I was born to play hockey," he still says. But at first, it seemed young Red's ambitions might exceed his abilities. He tried out for the St. Mike's junior A team and was cut on the first day. He tried out for junior B and was cut again. Finally he caught on with the midgets as a forward on the third line; the team ended up winning the Ontario midget championship. Graduating to the junior Bs and then to the As, Kelly played in two national finals for the Memorial Cup. In 1946, St. Mike's lost the championship to the Winnipeg Monarchs, but in 1947 they defeated the Moose Jaw Canucks in a wildly spirited series played entirely in the west. Although St. Mike's won four games to none, each game grew progressively tighter and tougher, and Kelly experienced harder hits than at any other time in his career.

The Canucks' three stars were Metro Prystai, Bert Olmstead and Emile Francis. Kelly recalls a life-size photograph of young Prystai in a Moose Jaw store window, portraying him as Captain Marvel in a cape and dubbing him "Marvellous Metro." He also remembers being a target for bottle-throwing fans during the series, and being refused restaurant service as a member of the invading eastern enemy. When the St. Mike's boys came back from Saskatchewan with the Cup, Toronto threw a big ticker-tape parade for them, and the display of civic joy surprised Kelly. "This was an Orange town back then, and people didn't normally like the Micks."

Like Lindsay, who was two years ahead of him at St. Mike's, Kelly somehow got overlooked by the Maple Leafs. "They didn't think I was good enough, so they didn't put me on their list." Although Toronto normally snapped up every St. Mike's player of quality, Kelly was signed for the Red Wings by Carson Cooper while still in junior B.

Howe had already played one season with Detroit when Kelly joined the team in 1947, becoming the Wings' spare defenseman until a player named Doug (Crash) McCaig broke his leg. Kelly went on to be the cornerstone of the Wings' formidable defense, and a dangerous rusher, quarterbacking their offense. His high-scoring output was exceptional for a defenseman in those defense-minded days. Named to the all-star team every year between 1950 and '57, and to the first team six times, Kelly won four Lady Byng trophies, having emulated Quackenbush's classy, finesse style of playing the position. He became the first recipient of the Norris trophy when it was introduced in 1954 to recognize the NHL's best defenseman.

Looking back at what he calls those "great years in Detroit, great teams, a great bunch of guys," Kelly sees the high point as the Wings' 1952 Cup triumph in eight straight. He and his fellow defensemen at the time, Leo Reise, Bob Goldham, Marcel Pronovost and Benny Woit, used to figure they could give Sawchuk enough protection that the opposition would get only four or five good scoring opportunities per game; and even then, chances were good that Sawchuk would come up with a big save.

That year was a high point for Kelly in another way, too: he began his remarkably romantic, remarkably long and (at the time) much-publicized courtship of Andra McLaughlin, now his wife of thirty-five years. Unwittingly, it was Gordie Howe who brought them together.

At sixteen, Andra McLaughlin was already the glamorous darling of North America's leading skating show, the Hollywood Ice Revue, also starring "Canada's Sweetheart," 1948 Olympic champion Barbara Ann Scott. The Revue often visited the Detroit Olympia, and in their endless quest for publicity, the show's promoters had cooked up a newspaper romance between Howe and Scott. At the time, Howe was already dating Colleen. The truth was that Gordie and Barbara Ann, the quintessential all-Canadian hero and heroine, had never actually met, except in the gossip columns.

That didn't stop the Revue's stage manager from trying to stage-manage a real-life meeting between the two at that star-crossed Detroit rendezvous, Carl's Chop House. Howe was game but didn't want to attend alone, so he asked Kelly to accompany him. When the two players arrived at the restaurant, it turned out Barbara Ann couldn't make it after all; but the stage manager asked them, "Would you like to meet one of the other stars, Andra McLaughlin? She's here with her mother and brother."

Ushered along with Howe to the McLaughlins' table, Kelly could do little but gape. With characteristic understatement, he recalls, "I didn't say much, but I kind of got taken with Andra." She, meanwhile, was checking out his teammate, since Barbara Ann had told her, "Take a good look at Gordie Howe—supposedly I'm engaged to him." Howe's lack of loquaciousness was easily a match for Kelly's, so we have to assume the McLaughlin women did most of the talking that night.

The attraction between Red and Andra quickly became mutual. "We went out, and then we got to writing each other, and that's how it started. And eight years later, we were married."

Eight years?

There were obstacles. Some existed already because of their careers: both of them were on the road so much that they seldom found themselves in the same city at the same time. Mostly, they had to make do with letters. Andra estimates that, in eight years, they actually dated as often as most couples would in three months. They went so far as to get engaged and even set a wedding date more than once, but every time, something happened to interfere. Complicating the relationship was Andra's family: they weren't thrilled with the idea of her marrying this Canadian hockey player, no matter how famous he was.

Andra, at twenty-three, had to make a decision about whether it would be easier to live without skating or without Red. In 1958, she agreed to let her parents send her away on an African safari for a year, and at that point, she and Red broke up. Andra sent back her engagement ring; Kelly despaired.

They'd been out of touch for fourteen months when his phone rang in Detroit one morning at the beginning of July 1959. Andra had just returned to New York and she'd made up her mind: she could live without skating.

She immediately flew to Detroit, arriving that afternoon. It was a Wednesday, and after talking it over, they decided to get married on Saturday. With the church already decorated for another wedding, 250 invited guests showed up on two days' notice. Kelly's parents drove all night from Simcoe to be there; when Red had called to tell them he was getting married, his father, who'd heard this news before, asked skeptically, "Yeah? Who to?"

Ma Shaw offered the newlyweds a temporary love nest, saying, "You know, this is the first time I've ever had a girl staying in this house. Would never have allowed it, but you're married now."

The McLaughlins senior hadn't been present for the ceremony. The Red Wings' very own patriarch, however, filled in for Andra's father. "Jack Adams walked Andra down the aisle and gave her away," Kelly says. "And then, six months later, he gave me away."

Adams's trade of Kelly to the Toronto Maple Leafs in 1960 has the dubious honour of being called by veteran journalist Trent Frayne the "dumbest trade ever made by one of the all-time great traders." Making it even dumber and stranger was the fact that in twelve previous seasons with the club, Kelly had been Adams's favourite Red Wing, next to Howe himself. Murray Costello tells a story illustrating how Kelly could do no wrong in Adams's eyes.

"Monday morning was movie day, right after the weekend games. We'd be sitting there along the benches and Adams would come in and roll the old 16-millimetre game movies. Adams was getting older. He had those thick glasses and we figured he was half-blind. He was always giving people shit, I guess that was the style in those days. The night before, we'd got beaten by Boston. In the film, Milt Schmidt was coming down the wing, cut to centre and made the big move, stuffing it between the legs of the defenseman, who stumbled as he turned—you could see the big number four on his back, which was Kelly. Schmidt stepped around Red and went in and scored on Glenn Hall.

"'Run that back!' Adams growled. He played it over three times and everybody was wondering what he'd say, because Red was his favourite guy. He turned to the bench. There was Gordie, and sitting next to him Warren Godfrey, a cocky dead-end kid from Cabbagetown chewing gum, who was number five, and then Kelly.

"Adams turned on Warren and went into one of his tirades. He bellowed, 'Jesus Christ, Godfrey, if I've told you once I've told you a hundred times, you don't let those assholes get around you! You don't take the puck, you take the man! When the hell are you going to learn?'

"With Gordie on one side of him and Red on the other, Godfrey took it up and down and nobody said a word—nobody was going to correct Adams. But they were all laughing behind their hands."

Kelly insists today, however, that he came second in Adams's affection after Howe. To illustrate, he cites the late season of 1953, when Howe was going for his 50th goal of the season and he himself was going for his 20th, a tremendous achievement for a defenseman. Playing against Boston with five games left in the season, Kelly took a shot from the point and immediately was hit and knocked down. The puck went into the Bruins' net.

"The official scorer gave me the goal. But Adams, up in high heaven, had the official scorer come over because Gordie was going for number 50. Adams said Gordie scored it, and he tried to get me to say so. I said I didn't see it—I was flat on my back and didn't see it go in, so I didn't know *how* it went in. It could have been Gordie's, but I couldn't tell you yes or no. The official scorer said he saw it all the way and wouldn't change it. Adams never fought for me on anything like that. But he tried to get me to lie."

Nonetheless, when Adams stripped Lindsay of the captaincy in 1956, he chose Kelly to replace him. Kelly had the gumption to turn him down at first, arguing that he was happy where he was and the change would be bad for the team, since it would affect Lindsay's play. Adams came back to it again, and Kelly turned him down again. Finally, Adams raised the subject a third time.

"He came to me and said, 'No matter what happens, Lindsay's not going to be captain. So if you don't take it, it's not going to make any difference.' So I became captain for a year, and the next year it was Howe."

By that time, Lindsay had been traded, the battle over the players' association was at its height, and Adams's hatred of Lindsay continued unabated. As some of the players were coming out of Mass one Sunday morning, Lindsay's name came up, and Adams turned to them and said, right there on the church steps, "You mention that sonofabitch! I want you to know, I get down on my knees every night and thank the Good Lord I got rid of that sonofabitch!"

But then Kelly led the Detroit players in obtaining a lawyer of their own, and Adams, ever in need of scapegoats, began training his shortsighted, suspicious eyes on his red-haired boy. In the end, Kelly's special status with Adams would afford him no protection after all.

"Adams had his good points," Kelly now says judiciously. "It wasn't all one-sided. But he turned on Lindsay, he turned on me, he turned on a lot of players, without any real reason. He thought he had reasons, but he imagined them sometimes."

In Kelly's case, the final "reason" was a broken foot. The injury occurred in practice towards the end of the 1959 season, and the team doctor put Kelly's foot in a cast all the way up to the knee. Without their defense ace, the Red Wings went on the road and lost their next three games. Adams and coach Sid Abel, who had replaced Jimmy Skinner midway through the previous season, were desperate to make the playoffs. A year earlier, the team had finished third, just a point out of fourth place, and had been easily eliminated in the 1958 semifinals by Montreal, four games to zero. Now the Red Wings were facing the even more dire prospect of missing the playoffs for the first time in twenty-one years.

In their anxiety, Adams and Abel approached Kelly to ask if he'd play the final games of the season. Dr. Karibo, who was a friend and next-door neighbour of Adams's, had said the cast could be removed and the foot and ankle taped. Kelly replied, "Well, I can try."

The ankle was so stiff that he couldn't turn on it properly. Kelly had little manoeuvrability; he had to give an opposition attacker the hole on one side, and so naturally his play was well below par. Naturally, too, the team didn't admit he was playing on a broken foot. "I didn't care if people didn't understand. The team knew, *they* understood why I couldn't play as well."

He played the rest of the season, but the Red Wings missed the playoffs anyway, losing their final two games to New York and Toronto, and finishing dismally in last place. During the off-season, Kelly strengthened his foot and ankle by exercising and running barefoot along sandy beaches. But it bothered him that press reports kept appearing in Detroit, blaming him for the

Wings' bad year. "I knew that stuff was coming out of the front office. Yet I'd done everything I could do."

With Kelly fully recovered, the Red Wings recovered too in the 1959-60 season, and were tied for second at the midway point. While in Toronto for a game early in the new year, Kelly gave a fateful interview to Trent Frayne, writing for the old *Star Weekly*. Frayne suggested to him that his strong play was the big reason for the Wings' improvement. Kelly tried to slough the matter off, but Frayne, sensing a story, persisted in asking about the off-season rumours out of Detroit that Kelly's legs were gone and he was all washed up.

"Well, I guess it won't hurt to tell you now," Kelly said finally, his pride provoked. "You don't tell everybody about a broken foot, because you don't want other guys swinging at it." And he gave Frayne the story.

Back in Detroit, Kelly's revelation was picked up and embellished by Marshall Dann, writing in the *Free Press*: "Was Red Kelly forced to play on a broken foot?" the Detroit headline screamed.

Andra Kelly, now pregnant with their daughter, Casey, hadn't even seen the newspaper when her friend Pat Lindsay phoned and asked, in her husky, humorous voice, "Have you got your bags packed?"

"I hadn't said anything about being 'forced'," Kelly explains. "Management had asked me if I'd play, and I'd said yes, I'd try. But now I'm traded—boom—right after that."

On February 4, 1960, after a game against the Rangers at the Olympia, Kelly was summoned to Adams's office, where he found Jolly Jawn sitting with Red Wings' president Bruce Norris, both of them wearing grimly businesslike expressions.

"I sat down, and they weren't calling me 'Red' any more. 'We've just traded you to the Rangers,' Adams said. 'You report at the Leland Hotel at 8:00 A.M. tomorrow to take the bus to New York.'

"I said, 'I'll think about it.'

"'What do you mean you'll think about it? Be there!'

"I said, 'I'll think about it, and I'll let Mr. Patrick [Rangers' G.M. Muzz Patrick] know.'"

Kelly went home and stayed up all night talking his decision over with Andra, and with the many teammates, friends and supporters who phoned or dropped by the house. In the morning, he went to church, then phoned his off-season employer at the Renew Tool Company to confirm that he would be able to start full-time work right away. Finally, he phoned New York: "I told Muzz I wasn't reporting, and it had nothing to do with him or New York. I said I was retiring."

Adams was apoplectic. He'd swapped Kelly and forward Billy McNeill to New York for Bill Gadsby and Eddie Shack. Already Shack had mouthed off to the press about how glad he was to be leaving the Rangers. And to top it all off, McNeill, whose wife had recently died, was also refusing to report. The magician's deal was in tatters. He threatened to suspend Kelly, which led to a phone call from Clarence Campbell himself.

"Now Red," Campbell intoned, "I'd like you to think this over. Mr. Adams wants to suspend you, and if he does that, you'll be out of hockey for life—in any capacity, playing, coaching, even refereeing."

"Mr. Campbell," Kelly replied stubbornly, "I *have* thought it over. I've played hockey ever since I was knee-high to a grasshopper, I've given it everything I have. But if that's the way it's going to be, that's the way it's going to be, because I'm not reporting."

"I'll hold Jack off," Campbell offered, "and give him a few days to cool down."

"It won't matter, Mr. Campbell. I'm not going to New York."

The decisive intervention was a phone call from King Clancy in the Maple Leafs' front office. Toronto wanted Kelly, fifteen years late.

Wearing a Homburg to hide his red hair and make himself less conspicuous, and carrying only an umbrella and a small overnight bag, Kelly crossed into Windsor and flew to Toronto for secret talks with Clancy and coach Punch Imlach. Kelly had made up his mind. He was danged if he was going to cooperate with the men who'd betrayed him.

"They'd tried to blame me for the Red Wings not making the playoffs. When they won, they didn't say it was because of me, it was always thanks to somebody else. But when they lost, I was the guy they blamed—the management, who knew I was playing on a broken foot, who I played any and every position possible for, under any circumstances, with no regard whatsoever for myself but regard only for the team—and they'd come out and say a thing like that.

"But when Toronto called, I thought, 'What the hang?' Hockey was my life. That's tough to give up—you've been playing and, all of a sudden, boom. I wasn't ready to stop, I'd just got married. I'd played junior in Toronto, my farm was near there. Somebody wanted me. Wasn't that nice?"

Clancy got Adams to agree to a bizarrely lopsided trade: Kelly for a comparatively undistinguished defenseman, Marc Reaume. It was another example of a trade that didn't serve the Red Wings, only Adams's need to get rid of a player he could no longer control.

But for Kelly, the move was a stunning personal victory, both then and later. He not only surmounted the hurt and humiliation that Adams had tried to inflict on him; in the long run, he extended his career by seven more seasons with an emerging contender, a club that would own the Stanley Cup through the early 1960s, and even squeezed in two terms as an MP while playing hockey. By finally standing up to the bosses, the gosh-darn farm boy had come of age.

In his first game for Toronto at Maple Leaf Gardens, where he'd played so often for St. Mike's, Kelly started at centre against Jean Beliveau. Out for the opening face-off, Kelly describes himself as feeling like a violin whose strings had been tightened to the breaking point. He hadn't played for ten days. When the puck was dropped, it was if someone had cut the strings. "The puck went straight down the ice past the Montreal net, and I went after it like a bat outta . . . Plante came out to field it, but when he got to the puck, there I was. All he could do was duck, and I went flying straight over him. They had a photograph of it up in the Gardens for years."

Kelly's will to win was stretched even tauter when he played against his old team. But in his first meeting with Detroit, it was Howe who taught him a lesson in how much the world had changed.

"The puck is shot into the corner and I'm going for it, Gordie right with me. He's got one arm stuck around me like this, and his other arm around here [demonstrating the way Howe had him tied up]. I'm going to be the first one on the puck, but I can't move. All I'd do is tear a groin or something if I tried to tear away, because he's got ahold of me. Gordie's right by my ear and he says, 'Red! How's the wife?' And I go to turn and say, 'Oh, she's—' and *whump*, he pretty near puts me through the boards. I think I left my footprints right there in the wood. And I say, 'You sonofa . . . , that's the last time you do *that*.'

"But that's Gordie. Cute, cute. And that's acceptable in his game. I'm the opposition; I should have expected it. I did from then on."

Over the next seven seasons, Kelly won four more Stanley Cup rings with Toronto, matching the four he'd already won with Detroit. More than his numerous trophies and all-star selections, those Stanley Cup victories are Kelly's greatest source of pride. His grand total of eight makes him, outside of those who played for the Montreal Canadiens, the player with the most Stanley Cups in a career.

During that career, and later during ten seasons as a coach with Los Angeles, Pittsburgh and Toronto, Kelly had plenty of opportunity to observe and assess Howe. He arrived at some long-term conclusions about his former teammate, both as a player and as a person.

"Gordie was powerful, and he could do lots of things on the ice. He could be mean—the elbows and the whole deal. I saw him break a guy's nose once when we played the Rangers. Not a very big guy, but he'd been whacking Gordie on the shins, and Gordie had told him to leave him alone. Suddenly the guy comes onto the ice and *whump*, he's down with a broken nose. No penalty or anything, nobody knows what happened, the referees never saw it. But that was Gordie."

That was the "cuteness" Kelly feels was Howe's trademark, as opposed to the sheer will to win, the killer instinct, of a Lindsay or a Richard.

"Gordie was different from the Rocket. On a given occasion, the Rocket could rise to greater heights. All-round, Gordie would be the best. But the Rocket could be more dynamic.

"I guess it just depends what kind of killer instinct you mean. I played against the Rocket, on his side of the ice, and when he came down offensively, he was just dynamite. He was the hardest guy I ever had to stop in my whole career. I played with Howe and against Howe, against Milt Schmidt. There were some great players through the years, but the hardest to stop was the Rocket coming down that opposite wing, then cutting across to the net—he could cut at right angles—and when you tried to stop him, he'd just grab your stick with one hand and shove you aside. He did that to me, and I couldn't figure it out. Most guys I would get, but he'd take my stick and shove it, and he'd be right over to the net, and he had one hang of a shot. He was strong *and* quick.

"Yet I never had problems getting along with the Rocket. He hated Howe and he hated Lindsay, but he never played dirty against me, and I never played dirty against him."

As one who was "brought up to win," and believes you're not really happy if you don't, Kelly makes tough judgements on those grounds.

"Gordie played on three Stanley Cup teams. We won a total of four there in Detroit, but only three with Gordie playing. The first one, he got knocked out in the first game. And they've never won a thing since.

"So I'm saying, what is a great hockey player? If you have the greatest hockey player in the world, how come you don't win? It's a team game, isn't it? That's how I look at it."

Kelly muses some more, then remarks softly, with only the faintest of smiles, "What's the game of hockey about? To win the Stanley Cup. It didn't matter whether I was an all-star or won a trophy, my goal was to win the Cup, and everything else would take care of itself. That was how I felt: if the team wins, everybody wins. But if I win a trophy and the team loses, everybody doesn't win."

Kelly's judgement of Howe may be coloured slightly by the events of February 4, 1960, the dark night when Adams turned on him. While staying up into the wee hours at home, Kelly noticed that the one teammate who didn't call about the trade—and whom he certainly expected to call, given their long association on the ice and at Ma Shaw's—was Howe.

Nearly thirty years later, Kelly had a strange intimation of something he couldn't quite put his finger on. He was at a dinner at the Waldorf Astoria to receive an achievement award from the Canadian Society of New York; it's an annual award, which has been given in the past to Howe and, in another year, jointly to goaltenders Ken Dryden and Vladislav Tretiak. Each recipient is permitted to invite four special guests and their spouses; Kelly invited Ted Lindsay and Marty Pavelich from his Red Wing days, and former linemate Frank Mahovlich and Eddie Shack from his Maple Leaf days. There were many hundreds of other guests present, including Howe as a previous winner.

"Gordie got up to say a few words. And I don't know what he was saying, really, but it made me look, because he was sort of apologizing, in front of this whole crowd of a thousand people there at the Waldorf. I thought it was like an apology, and my wife thought it was . . . but I really don't know."

Apologizing for what?

"I would suspect, knowing the team, that Adams probably talked to him about my being traded. When I thought about it, I thought more than likely he could have been asked [his opinion]."

Furthermore, says Kelly, "Gordie would not exert himself in any way that would cause any problems. He'd go along with whatever they'd say."

Kelly emphasizes that this is only a subjective impression, not proven by anything on the record. And certainly Howe is far more outspoken today in his criticism of NHL management than he was in 1960. Be that as it may, Kelly feels vindicated in the matter by his own subsequent career achievements. "I surprised Howe a little, I think, when I went to Toronto and played as well as I played. For a guy whose legs were gone, I covered a lot of territory."

CHAPTER TWELVE

The Long March
into the Record Book

> "Have you ever done something where you feel you've
> been there before? . . . The first time's an accident,
> the second time you're stupid. So the second time,
> I didn't want to be stupid."
>
> —Gordie Howe, 1992, on fighting Lou Fontinato

WITH THE DETROIT DYNASTY DECIMATED by trades and time and
Jack Adams, Gordie Howe *became* the Red Wings. As the 1950s
gave way to the 1960s, he represented, as no other player could,
those Stanley Cup years of the past. He carried the fans'—and
management's—fond hope that their team could be rebuilt into a
powerhouse once again: all it would take would be the right
combination of talent to complement their aging yet seemingly
ageless superstar.

It almost happened, but not quite. As Dave Keon, the Maple
Leafs' all-star centre, once remarked, the NHL had four strong
teams in the early 1960s: Toronto, Montreal, Chicago and Howe.
Although Howe continued to prove his astonishing productivity
and durability year after year, placing among the top five scorers in
every single season of the 1950s *and* 1960s, winning his sixth
scoring title and sixth MVP trophy in 1963 at the advanced age of
thirty-five, he had to carry on those sloping shoulders a team that
had come to depend on him too much.

This didn't change the fact that, by the early 1960s, Howe had
proven beyond all reasonable doubt that he was the greatest all-
round player in the history of hockey. As partisan a foe as Canadiens' G.M. Frank Selke called him that, stating, "I don't know
what the Wings would do without him." Selke added, "There isn't
another club in hockey that depends so much on one player."

This wasn't Howe's doing, needless to say, but management's. Whether it was Adams, Jimmy Skinner or Sid Abel, they all expected Howe to achieve more than any mortal could. At times, they seemed to forget he *was* mortal. At the start of the 1957-58 season, right after he'd traded Lindsay, Adams announced his Howe-centric strategy to the media, and he would repeat this refrain with variations over the next several seasons.

"Sure, we're building this club around the Big Fellow," Adams proclaimed. "And I think this season, his twelfth, could be his best. As a matter of fact, you could put Howe on any team in the NHL and know it would win the title."

How wrong Adams was: life wasn't that simple any more. The Red Wings not only failed to win the regular schedule that year, but finished just one point ahead of fourth-place Boston and were swept by the Canadiens in the semis.

The following season, 1958-59, when Red Kelly broke his foot, the team finished a miserable last. Sawchuk's goals-against average had ballooned to three. It just wasn't the same team any longer: how could it be? On top of his previous trades, on top of the animosity and discord he'd sown, Adams had now dealt off quality players like Dutch Reibel and Bill Dineen without getting much of value in return. For the time being, team morale had sunk far below the level of the Tommy Ivan years.

Howe couldn't dispel the Red Wings' malaise all by himself. As Kelly argues, hockey is a team game. Howe knew that: he often said so himself, and he played it as a team game. Yet the Detroit management seemed to expect miracles from him nonetheless. If he passed to his teammates because he thought they had a better chance to score than he did, Adams and the coaches would get on his back about not shooting enough. If he stick-handled to keep possession until he saw an opening, he'd get a similar lecture. Jimmy Skinner, before he was switched from coach to scout, said publicly, "Gordie is as close to perfection as we'll ever see, but he's been too unselfish lately. He's passing sometimes when he might barrel in and shoot goals for himself." Howe was being expected to produce even more than his average of 35 to 40 goals a season—whereas for anyone else, a 20-goal year was considered to be excellent. And conversely, not enough was being expected of the rest of the team.

Adams insisted Howe have possession of the puck, and shoot it, as much as possible. This was Adams's law, laid down at practice and in the dressing room. Murray Costello remembers hearing it time and time again.

"Adams would give us his pep talk and kick the oranges off the table—they'd be spread all over the room, and the trainers would hustle around to pick them up—and he'd say, 'All right, for you young guys: if you're on the ice with the Big Guy and you happen to get the puck, your job is to get it to the Big Guy as quickly as you can.'

"And this kid Cummy Burton says, 'But Mr. Adams? What if the Big Guy just gave it to you?'

" 'Well then,' Adams shouted, 'for Christ's sake! You just give it back to him as fast as you can!' "

"When Gordie was on the ice, he carried the mail," Costello remarks, "and that was it."

Such heavy reliance on Howe resulted in other Detroit players failing to develop to their full potential. Either they'd be under-utilized, or they'd be looking for Howe on the ice instead of trusting their own instincts about how to respond to the play. In addition, the club neglected new player development, with results that would show up increasingly as time went on.

Yet an overreliance on Howe was perhaps inevitable to a degree since, when he carried the mail, he so often delivered. His skills awed even the men he played against. Glenn Hall, who stands third in all-time NHL shutouts, backstopped Howe for two seasons before facing him for another fourteen at Chicago and St. Louis; he calls Howe "super-skilled" and "the ultimate player." Still closely involved in pro hockey—for the past decade, he's been goaltending coach with the Calgary Flames—Hall compares Howe to today's NHLers: "It doesn't matter who you put him up against, he's the greatest. There are some tremendously skilled players today, but none of them can match him."

After the Red Wings' peak years had passed, Howe continued doing everything superbly, no matter how low his team sank in the standings. And he continued loving what he was doing. "The superstars always enjoy playing the game," Hall observes. "If there's a common denominator among them, it's the *desire* to play, and play well. Gordie was like that—always tremendously easy-going, enjoying practice and every aspect of the game."

Hall marvelled at how well Howe "saw the ice": it was as if Gordie knew what was going to happen, and where, and when. "He was like Gretzky that way, and Lemieux, Orr, Lafleur, the Rocket—it's a gift. The thinking mind can't keep up with the action and relay the message in time to react. Those guys don't *think* of the play they're going to make, they instinctively take advantage of their opportunities." And by trusting his instincts, Howe avoided signalling his intentions on a play, retaining the advantage of surprise over his opponents.

Another veteran of defending against Howe was Bob Baun, a pillar of the Toronto Maple Leafs' tremendous blueline corps during their Stanley Cup years in the 1960s. Baun feels Howe's physical equipment played a part in his success—and not only his strength and size: "He probably had the best athletic body I've ever seen. With the sloping shoulders and the big upper body, he had lots of movement." Blessed with height and long legs, Howe had great flexibility and mobility, Baun says, whereas players like himself or Bobby Hull "were almost muscle-bound."

Howe's ability to coordinate all that equipment explains why he was exceptional at every sport, from golf to water-skiing to fishing. "He could pick the eyes out of a snake with a spinning rod at fifty paces," Baun asserts, "and he had lightning-fast reflexes." Like Hall, Baun comes back to that indefinable second sight, "that wonderful extra sense, like Gretzky, that very few athletes have, of always seeming to know where everybody was. Before you could anticipate, he'd *be* there."

Usually there are two or three options on every play; the great hockey players somehow know to pick the right one. "Howe was tremendously smart that way," Hall explains. "Whichever way the puck bounced, he'd play it right." As a goalie, Hall both feared and admired Howe's versatility. "He could beat you in a lot of ways. If you gave him a little spot, he'd take it."

Hall gets no argument from Johnny Bower, who also tended goal against Howe throughout the 1960s. "I had all kinds of problems with him," Bower admits cheerfully. "Forehand, back-hand, left-hand shot, right-hand shot—he could shoot both ways, eh? He'd throw me off balance by switching hands. Nobody could take the puck off him, he was too strong."

Howe had experimented with the newfangled slapshot (breaking Adams's favourite wooden stool in the process). He soon decided not so much that the shot was too wild and inaccurate, but that it required the shooter to look down a split-second too long, breaking visual contact with the play swirling around him and leaving him no other option than shooting. "Gordie had a good slapshot," Bower observes, "but he didn't go all the way back with it. It was more of a *snap*shot, with the stick only a quarter of the way back. He had better control that way. That's why he scored so much, eh? He knew exactly where he was."

If Howe's opponents were in awe of him, his teammates were often in the same state, especially new arrivals; they watched him closely and tried to emulate him. Howe led mostly by example, at least in the earlier part of his career. Although generally encouraging to rookies, he didn't usurp the coach's role. He'd become freer with tips and advice to young teammates later, in his elder-statesman years with the Wings in the late 1960s and then in the World Hockey Association. But in the 1950s, he was seldom vocal. Metro Prystai remembers him as still shy and quiet: "He didn't say too much on the ice, and not even in the dressing room. I think where he was a leader was by what he *did* out there."

Often, what he did out there was just too amazing, too difficult to replicate. Fellow players, coaches and spectators still talk about Gordie's incredible one-handed goal against the Canadiens—all the more incredible because he beat not only Jacques Plante on the play but also the player who had emerged as the best defenseman in the league by that time, Doug Harvey.

Howe carried the puck into the Montreal zone, picking up speed with the long, loping stride that created the dangerous illusion he wasn't moving very fast. Harvey, skating backwards, was the last man back. Howe faked him inside, then cut around him to the outside, and Harvey instantly knew he was beaten. In desperation, Harvey reached backwards with his stick and jammed it over Howe's shoulder and down in front of his chest, between his legs, to try to slow him as he drove to the net. But Harvey could do little more than hang on. Moving in on Plante, Howe took his left hand from the upper shaft of his stick, raised his massive arm and lifted Harvey right up onto the toes of his skate blades to move him out of the way. Howe now had only one hand on his stick, halfway down the shaft. He threw a leg out, sweeping the puck, as if he were going to cut across in front of the net. This caused Plante to move sideways with him—but as soon as Plante moved away from his post, Howe, with that one hand, hoisted the puck into the opening, straight up into the mesh in the top of the net.

Howe's teammates on the bench saw the net bulge upwards and looked at each other: "Holy Jesus, did you see that?" The next day at practice, several of the younger Red Wings—Johnny Bucyk, Bucky Hollingworth, Murray Costello and Cummy Burton among them—tried to see if they could duplicate what Howe had done. They placed pucks on the goalline and tried to hoist them, with one hand, up into the net. But they found they couldn't even get them up off the ice. They just didn't have the strength and power that resided in Howe's big, meaty hands and wrists, or the manual dexterity.

Such superhuman feats fostered Howe's aura of invincibility. So did his steady productivity, week in and week out, year in and year out. Prystai recalls: "When I first played for Chicago, everybody was always talking about Howe, Howe, Howe, and I'd wonder why. But when I went to Detroit and played with him and saw what he did game after game after game, then you wondered whether the guy was human. He killed penalties and was a threat out on the ice all the time and scored 40-45 goals, when there were only half a dozen guys who scored more than 25 a season."

That productivity, even more than his deferential nature (Clarence Campbell once said approvingly, "His attitude was one of deference to authority or to anyone senior to himself"), practically guaranteed Howe would never be traded, even by trade-happy Adams. He was too much the franchise player.

It wasn't only that Howe was the fans' hero, either. Adams had risked offending the fans before, by disposing of such crowd favourites as Lindsay, Sawchuk and Pavelich. It was his dependability. "He was just so *reliable*," Costello says. "The whole operation revolved around Gordie. He was productive, he could play defensively, he could kill penalties, he'd play fifty minutes a game if you wanted him to. He was just a bull—you couldn't wear him down. And he didn't get injured, he was that strong."

Productivity, reliability, endurance, strength. In addition to these qualities, there was a darker quality that Howe consistently displayed. It blossomed most violently on the night of February 1, 1959, in the old Madison Square Garden.

Strangely, the Lou Fontinato fight sticks out in people's minds more conspicuously than any single event in Howe's career. All kinds of people remember that fight: far more people than could possibly have been there at the time, and even more, it seems, than remember his breaking Richard's career goals record. And everyone seems to have his or her own (sometimes widely differing) version of how it happened.

That fact may be some kind of tribute to *Life* magazine, which covered the event as if it were a heavyweight championship bout, with a three-page photo spread. Or it may simply testify to the grip that hockey violence, like war, holds on our imaginations. For certain, the fight was more like a slaughter—although not of the innocent.

The storm between Howe and "Leapin' Louie" Fontinato, the defenseman who had built a reputation as the premier battler of the New York Rangers, and perhaps the league, had been gathering for some time. Fontinato had taken on many of the other NHL heavyweights, such as Fern Flaman, at one time or another. The Rangers' coach, Emile Francis, used to send Fontinato out to run at stars like Howe and Beliveau to throw them off their game. Sooner or later, a Howe-Fontinato set-to was inevitable. "It was coming," Bob Baun says, "and all of us in the league knew it."

In one warm-up to the incident, Fontinato split Howe's lip with a high stick. Howe retaliated by lashing out unthinkingly and received a penalty. As he sat morosely on the bench with an ice pack over his mouth and nose, Fontinato skated by and taunted him, "What's the matter with your nose, Gordie? What's the matter with your lip?"

Never one to forget an insult, verbal or physical—and this was both—Howe settled in to wait for an opportunity to get his own back. It was a question of personal pride and honour. It was even, as he saw it, a kind of intelligence test.

"Have you ever done something where you feel you've been there before?" he asked June Callwood rhetorically. "Well, I was there before. The first time's an accident, the second time you're stupid. So the second time, I didn't want to be stupid. When Louie came back at me, I got in there first and cut his ear. That was meanness, but it was a return favour. They put a turban on him, and I said, 'What's the matter with your ear, Louie?' So this battle had been going on a *long* time."

On the fateful night, the final showdown was triggered, ironically enough, by Red Kelly, whom everyone considered so mild-mannered and gentlemanly. But, as Howe reminds us, "Red was a Golden Glover." Kelly was mixing it up in a serious way behind the New York net with his future teammate in Toronto, the Rangers' Eddie (Clear the Track) Shack. Howe likes to portray himself as the innocent bystander to this merriment.

"So I'm leaning on the net, watching this lovely fight going on, and it finally dawned on me, 'Louie's out here.' And when I turn around, sure enough, his gloves and stick are back at the blueline, and he's ten feet away and coming in at me, obviously, to say hello. So when he swung the first one at me, I was ready for it. He missed. Then I got lucky on that one, because Louie's a big kid, and a tough boy too."

For the rest of the story, we must turn to franker, less euphemistic accounts. According to New York hockey writer Stan Fischler, who was perched in the Garden press box practically right above the fracas, Howe had already intervened to help out Kelly and was "disposing of the irritant [Shack] with consummate ease." So Fontinato was actually charging to Shack's rescue, as a policeman should. Other observers, such as Lefty Wilson and NHL historian Charles L. Coleman, confirm this. In fact, Howe had clobbered Shack on the ear with his stick. But Fontinato would rue his bravado.

With one hamlike fist, Howe got a good tight grip on the neck of Fontinato's sweater. With the other, he began pounding Fontinato in the face, over and over—"whop, whop, whop, just like someone chopping wood," according to a Red Wing player quoted in the *Life* story. With one of those punches, Fontinato's nose was broken for the fifth time.

Over at the Detroit bench, Lefty Wilson heard the fight, as well as seeing it: "With every blow, you could hear something break—*squish, squish*. Finally Andy Bathgate jumped in and stopped it."

The officials had decided to let the two fighters go at it. One published account claims the savagery lasted a full minute, although that seems hard to credit—Fontinato is, after all, still alive. Howe suffered a black eye and a few stitches, so Fontinato was hardly defenseless, but Leapin' Louie was by far the worse for wear. "Fontinato was a mess," Fischler wrote. "His nose was smashed and his ego was demolished." So was his reputation as a tough guy.

New York coach Phil Watson later said the bloody beating Howe administered to Fontinato broke the Rangers' collective spirit that season. They lost their bid for a playoff berth, while Fontinato wound up in the hospital, bandaged like an Egyptian mummy. This was the image that appeared in *Life*, shocking gentle American readers by portraying the vicious side of hockey; on the facing page, the magazine ran a photo of Howe in the Detroit dressing room, shirt off and muscles rippling.

The irony of it all, as Lefty Wilson points out, was that, before the game, he'd taped Howe all around the rib cage: "He had a muscle that had rolled over a rib, and he was hurting pretty good. If Fontinato had come up under Howe [instead of going for his head], he'd have dropped him. But Fontinato didn't know that."

The fight was Howe's last major bout—not because he lost the stomach for it, but because it put the word around the league that challenging him face-to-face was not an intelligent move. It also led to descriptions such as this, from the twenty-fifth-anniversary program issued by the Red Wings on Howe's final season with the club: "He is everything you'd expect the ideal athlete to be," an unidentified opponent was quoted on the subject of Howe. "He is soft-spoken, [self-]deprecating and thoughtful. He is also one of the most vicious, cruel and mean men I've ever met in a hockey game."

Howe declined the honour. "Hockey is a man's game," he replied unapologetically at the time. "You have to take care of yourself." He always insisted his treatment of Fontinato was self-defense—his father's edict, "never take any dirt from nobody," in action yet again. Howe himself once phrased the concept with more elegance: "Unless a player keeps asserting himself, the other players take it as a sign of weakness and start to climb all over you." But he also admitted, after twenty-five seasons, that he'd done some things on the ice he wasn't proud of.

In a more relaxed and candid vein in 1989, Howe revealed in *After the Applause* that he'd known perfectly well what he was doing all along. "You've also got to remember that I was crazy," he is quoted as saying. "I was never afraid of getting hurt . . . It's one thing to be rough, but to be rough *and* crazy means the other guy is never going to get the last hit . . . I'd play with him, tease him, but he knew that sooner or later he'd pay."

All the same, brawling toe-to-toe wasn't normally Howe's style. He himself was subjected to endless nasty harassment and chippy play and cheap shots. "They look me up," as he once put it, especially players new to the league, who hadn't learned to behave themselves. So, like some stern school principal, he developed a consistent and time-honoured method of disciplining them. He'd note their numbers, bide his time. A period or a few games or even a year later, when the offender had forgotten the incident and wasn't expecting anything, Howe's elephant-like memory would kick in and he'd level the guy with an invisible elbow or lightning thrust of his stick to some tender part of the anatomy. More often than not, the retribution would occur behind the play, when the officials were distracted elsewhere. For the young upstart, it was always a learning experience, administered by "a recognized master," as *Toronto Star* sportswriter Jim Hunt once wrote, "of the art of high sticking."

Howe's artistry with his stick was witnessed from the stands by a young Bob Baun during a game against Boston. While Howe was carrying the puck, Bruin defenseman Larry Hillman took a run at him: "Gordie let the puck drop right at his feet, brought his stick up and put a perfect Z on Larry's forehead, like the mark of Zorro. Next thing you knew, he was back stick-handling. He never lost control of the puck, and it happened so fast the ref didn't notice."

Alex Delvecchio, who continued to centre Howe through much of the 1960s, had a nicer way of putting it. "If you got

Gordie really mad, he'd give you a little wood, but only if you got him mad. Yes, he was dirty, but in a clean sort of way."

Of course, Delvecchio didn't have to play against him. Pierre Pilote, the Chicago Black Hawks' all-star defenseman, did. "Nobody takes a chance with Gordie," Pilote stated, "because you never know what he can do to you. He plays the game for keeps. He doesn't expect you to take it easy on him, and he doesn't take it easy on you."

Players who forgot that hard-earned knowledge could get a surprise. Baun's defense partner, the equally rugged Carl Brewer, once fell on top of Howe after a struggle behind the net. Tempted to get in one last shot while he had the chance, Brewer resisted when he heard Howe say, "Okay, Carl, the play's over." There was another pile-up later in the game, and this time it was Howe on top. Assuming they had a sportsmanlike understanding, Brewer relaxed, waiting for Howe to get off him, and suddenly had the wind knocked out of him with a hard blow to the ribs.

"Cute," as Red Kelly would say.

On March 3, 1959, just over a month after the Fontinato fight, the Red Wings paid their franchise player the singular honour of holding a Gordie Howe Night. Between the first and second periods of a game against Boston, the club presented him with a treasure trove of gifts worth an estimated $10,000—more than the average NHL salary in those days—ranging from clothing, luggage and a Miami vacation to toys for the kids and a 130-piece layette (Colleen was pregnant with their fourth and last child, Murray).

The biggest and most expensive gift was a new station wagon, built there in Detroit, and bearing Michigan licence plate GH-9000. It came rolling out onto the ice wrapped in cellophane. When the wrapping was removed from the front windows, Howe literally doubled over in shock and clutched his head: Ab and Katherine Howe were sitting in the front seat.

It was the very first time Ab had come to Detroit, the first game he'd witnessed his son play in the NHL. And it was the first time for Katherine since coming to watch over him after the 1950 head injury. Gordie's eyes filled with tears. Overcome with emotion, he watched his parents step out of the car and broke down completely as his mother put her arms around his neck and hugged him in front of the packed, cheering house.

The fans screamed for a speech. Howe, unaccustomed as he was, gave it his best shot.

"Don't mind the odd tear," he said, after a long pause. "It's a long way from Saskatoon. I want to thank you for the biggest thrill in my life. Things have been like this ever since I hit Detroit. I want to thank the late James Norris, Bruce Norris, Jack Adams and Sid Abel."

"And Ted Lindsay!" someone in the crowd yelled.

"Yes, of course, Ted Lindsay," Howe replied.

Indeed, Lindsay was there too, flown in from Chicago.

With his mother and father in the stands, Howe was too wrought up to score during the next two periods. Recounting the event many years later, he said it had never dawned on him that his parents might actually be there for Gordie Howe Night. "Maybe I was a little slow at thinking, but when I got to the rink, I thought, 'Wouldn't it be nice if Mom and Dad were here.' And they *were* there—they were in the car when it rolled out on the ice. And you're supposed to be a big tough guy, and it broke me up, it just broke me up."

That recollection ties in with another story of Howe's about Ab. Reminded once by interviewer June Callwood that Doug and Max Bentley's mother used to say her daughters were better hockey players than her sons, Howe responded, "I had trouble with my dad that way. He insisted that [brother] Vic was a better hockey player. Vic played about sixty games in the NHL—I played more *years* than he did games! But Dad watched Vic a lot playing for the Saskatoon Quakers."

In fact, Vic was brought up from the minors for a total of only thirty-three games with the New York Rangers between the 1951 and '55 seasons; finally, finding it too difficult to play in his famous brother's shadow, he retired from hockey and moved to Moncton, New Brunswick, to become a railway policeman. But Howe's telling of that anecdote is a reminder that praise and affirmation from Ab seldom came easily, even—and perhaps especially—after thirteen seasons of NHL stardom.

To lesser players, a night in their honour would signal the twilight of their careers, an expectation that they would soon be gone. Howe continued to carry the mail *and* the Red Wings all through the team's ups and downs of the 1960s. He wasn't completely isolated in his glory. He had other fine players for teammates (Sawchuk, Marcel Pronovost, Bill Gadsby, Doug Barkley) and in some cases linemates (Delvecchio, Norm Ullman, Vic Stasiuk, Parker MacDonald); and for the first half of the decade, the Wings rallied to become serious contenders once more. There was even the splendid 1964-65 season when Howe was reunited with Ted Lindsay, who came out of retirement to help his old team recapture the league title.

There was another reunion: Howe's coach throughout that decade was the third man from the original Production Line, Sid Abel. Under Abel's tutelage, the Wings rebounded from last place in 1959 to finish fourth and earn a playoff berth in both of the next two seasons. In 1961, they succeeded in going all the way to the Stanley Cup finals against a new powerhouse, the Black Hawks of Bobby Hull, Stan Mikita, Pilote and Hall, extending Chicago to six games before losing.

But to some observers that year, Howe finally seemed to be slowing down, feeling his age. In an era when the average NHL career lasted six seasons, and ten was considered a good run, he'd now completed fifteen. The 1960-61 season was his poorest for goal production since 1949—23—and, interestingly, his lowest in penalty minutes, too—30. Was there a linkage here between scoring and mischief? Sportswriters short of copy speculated that Howe was tired and washed up, and started writing his obituary.

The obituaries were premature. He was hardly senile: only the season before, he'd won his fifth Hart trophy, a league record— surpassing Eddie Shore, who won four. And even in this supposedly slumping season, he had 49 assists and placed fifth in scoring, with 72 points. He also shared the lead in playoff scoring with Pilote. For any other player, it would have been considered a terrific year.

Perhaps Howe was missing the stimulus of his ancient rivalry with the Rocket, who had retired, at thirty-nine, at the beginning of the 1960-61 season. No longer could Howe's competitive nature take gleeful delight in tweaking the Rocket's pride, as when he'd scored his 100th goal on Maurice Richard Night in 1951; or his 400th on December 13, 1958, when the Rocket unintentionally assisted him, lifting his stick to deflect the puck into the net. Howe had called the Rocket his pacemaker, "the man who led the way for the rest of us." Now all Howe had to look forward to was breaking Richard's records: previously, they'd been moving targets; from now on, they were sitting ducks.

It was true Howe had been temporarily slowed by a bloody collision with Eddie Shack in a game in January 1961 at Maple Leaf Gardens. Knocked out cold, Howe suffered a concussion and a gash in his forehead requiring twelve stitches. Shack received a major penalty for high sticking. But although Howe missed three games because of the injury, he insisted Shack shouldn't be blamed for intent to injure.

There was one other factor detracting from Howe's performance in the 1960-61 season. Bernie Geoffrion did what Howe was unable to do throughout his entire career: equal Richard's 50-goal record. The next season, Bobby Hull too would tie it, but like Geoffrion he would not break it. So the record, shared by the three players, would continue to stand like some seemingly impregnable fortress refusing to fall to its besiegers, until finally Hull went over the top in 1966.

In the 1961-62 season, Howe regained his momentum, bouncing back as he had eleven years earlier after his life-threatening head injury. He confounded the obit-writers by collecting 33 goals and tying young Stan Mikita for third in scoring, behind Hull and Andy Bathgate. Late that season, on March 14, 1962, Howe reached a major milestone of his career: his 500th goal.

He scored it at Madison Square Garden against Gump Worsley, a frequent victim of his big markers, who was in his last season with New York before being traded to Montreal (and who once, when asked which team gave him the most trouble while he was with the Rangers, replied "the Rangers"). Howe and Delvecchio were out killing a penalty when Delvecchio broke Howe loose with a quick pass up the right side. Doug Harvey, traded to New York as delayed punishment for his involvement with the players' association, was once again the last man back. Howe faked Harvey to the right, went to his left, lost control of the puck momentarily, then kicked it ahead. Catching up to the puck, Howe bore in on Worsley, who had come out to cut off the angle, and fired it under the goalie to become the second player in NHL history to reach 500 goals.

Howe was now within clear sight of Richard's all-time record of 544. The only question was whether he would take one season or two to demolish it. Barring a comeback, Richard would have the bitter experience of sitting helplessly by and watching his career landmark fall—just as Howe would, with Gretzky, three decades later.

A remarkable thing happened to the Detroit Red Wings before the 1962-63 season: they were relieved of the burden of Jack Adams. After their spirited performance against Chicago in the 1961 finals, the team had fallen out of contention once again in 1962, finishing fifth, behind the Rangers. President Bruce Norris was persuaded the fault lay with Adams's failing judgement and outdated approach to the game. Needing a younger G.M. with a surer touch, Norris appointed Abel to succeed his former mentor while continuing as coach. Adams was retired at full pay and put out to pasture as president of the Central Professional League, where his experience would be useful—and where he couldn't do any more harm to the club that, in earlier days, he'd moulded and guided to so many victories.

At that point, Howe still had tender filial feelings for his old boss. He approached Norris to satisfy himself that Adams was being properly taken care of. Then he proceeded to have one of his last truly great years of the Original Six era. That year was 1963, and Howe's achievements spanned two different hockey seasons.

The 1962-63 season was dramatic for the tightness of the league standings—by the end of the regular schedule, only five points separated fourth-place Detroit from first-place Toronto—and the excitement of the individual scoring race.

Against many of the most brilliant offensive stars ever to compete in the NHL, all of them younger than he, Howe scored 38 goals and 48 assists for 86 points, to win his sixth and final scoring championship—5 points ahead of second-place Bathgate, 10 ahead of third-place Mikita, 13 ahead of Frank Mahovlich and Henri Richard, 19 ahead of Beliveau, 20 ahead of Bucyk, 22 ahead of Delvecchio, a full 24 ahead of Hull and Murray Oliver. On the eve of his thirty-fifth birthday, Howe had played all seventy games of the season and had far outdistanced most other players in penalties, compiling 100 minutes (which was still considerably less than the 273 racked up by his wild-man teammate, defenseman Howie Young). And he was now a mere four goals short of equalling the Rocket's career record.

But Howe's season wasn't finished. He led the Red Wings to an impressive upset in the Stanley Cup semifinals and a highly creditable performance in the finals. After spotting second-place Chicago the first two games of their opening round, Detroit surprised the odds-makers by winning the next four straight to advance against the Leafs, who had eliminated Montreal.

In the finals, it was the late 1940s all over again: Punch Imlach's team played basic, hard-hitting, positional hockey, nothing fancy, and had too much defense and too much depth for the Red Wings, as well as tremendous goaltending from Bower. But the Wings kept it close; while they won only one game, they never lost by more than two goals. And Howe and Ullman ended the series tied for the lead in playoff points. Deservedly, Howe was accorded his sixth Hart trophy as the league's MVP.

His next season, 1963-64, would be superlative for different reasons. With 540 career goals, Howe was staring Richard's record in the face and trying not to blink (not easy for him). He got off to a blazing start, with two goals against Glenn Hall in the first period of the season's first game, and another in the next game against Boston, putting him within one of the record. Then he was struck by a severe case of self-consciousness. Exactly as ten years earlier, when he'd been chasing the Rocket's 50 goals in a season, Howe's teammates continually tried to set him up; but the media and crowd attention, and the self-generated daily pressure, made him nervous, throwing him off his game. For the next four outings, he was held scoreless. But that was just as well: his next chance to match his career rival would be at home—on October 27, 1963, against the Canadiens.

One of the photographs of Howe's record-tying goal shows Montreal's Gilles Tremblay making a grim, all-out, teeth-gritting effort to ride Howe off the puck right in front of (as fate would have it) Gump Worsley. Tremblay is just a little too late, and Howe, who has taken a relay in the slot from Bruce MacGregor after a pass from Gadsby, is just a little too strong. In the foreground, Worsley is flopping to his left as the puck enters the net. In the background, Henri Richard is standing in the open gate at the Montreal bench. He's staring in dismay—and not only because his older brother's record has just been equalled. The Canadiens' John Ferguson was in the penalty box at the time, and Richard was supposed to stay on the ice until the penalty was over; but somehow, there had been a mixup of signals at the Canadiens' bench, and Henri had gone off before he was supposed to, giving Detroit the two-man advantage that helped set up Howe's goal.

The partisan crowd of 14,749 went wild in a five-minute standing ovation. Programs fell from the Olympia's upper tier like propaganda leaflets. But for Howe, the pressure wasn't over: now he had to score number 545 to overtake the Rocket.

As Wayne Gretzky found in pursuit of number 802 in March 1994, it wouldn't be quick or easy. From October 27 to November 10, 1963, Howe played five games without scoring—an unusual slump by his standards, and all because he was on the spot once more. The stress on the team, on the Howe household and inside Howe himself became almost unbearable. But, on November 10, the Canadiens came back to the Olympia, recreating the conditions under which Gordie had tied the record. The only difference was that Charlie Hodge would be in goal instead of Worsley, who had the relatively good fortune to be injured this time around.

In the second period, Detroit was short-handed, and Howe was out killing the penalty with Gadsby and Billy McNeill. As the three broke quickly out of their own end, the Montreal attackers were trapped behind the play, and only Jacques Laperriere and Dave Balon remained back. McNeill scooted up the right side with the puck, cutting to the middle and crossing the blueline. He passed to Howe on his right, who immediately snapped a wrist shot from the top of the face-off circle, aiming for Hodge's short side. The goaltender lunged to his left, but too late—the puck whistled by between him and the post, hip high. The all-time goals record had a new owner.

Above the crowd's unremitting roar, Howe told Sid Abel, "I feel ten pounds lighter." This time, the standing ovation continued for ten minutes as debris rained down. After slamming the post with his stick in disgust, Hodge went to the Montreal bench to wait out the uproar, while Canadiens' captain Jean Beliveau skated over to congratulate Howe. After the game, Beliveau presented Howe with an oil portrait painted by former Montreal Alouettes' football lineman Tex Coulter. "Am I glad you finally scored," Beliveau told Howe. "I've been carrying this around for days."

No one was gladder or more relieved than Howe. Although he enjoyed the tumult, and the tributes and telegrams that poured in from all over the league and the continent, he had hated the process of getting there. One reporter phoned Ab Howe in Saskatoon to ask what he thought of his son's breakthrough: "What took him so long?" Ab chortled.

But from now on, every NHL goal Howe scored would be golden, embellishing his record and putting it farther and farther beyond the reach of others—for the time being, at least. The time being would last thirty-one years. In an interesting parallel, both Richard and Howe were in their eighteenth seasons when they reached goal number 544. The Rocket took 978 games, Howe 1,126.

It's less often remembered that another NHL record was reached that night. Detroit won the game 3-0, and the shutout was Terry Sawchuk's 94th, tying the career record set by George Hainsworth with Montreal and Toronto in the 1930s. By the time he died on active NHL service in 1970, Sawchuk would boost his record to 103, where it still stands today, untouched.

In a postscript to Howe's triumphant year, Canadian sportswriters voted him Canada's outstanding male athlete of 1963— making him, surprisingly enough, only the third hockey player to receive the honour to that point. In Toronto, however, curmudgeonly Gordon Sinclair, the Jack Adams of journalists, demanded to know on radio station CFRB why the honour had gone to an American. Howe (unlike Adams) had made a point of keeping his Canadian citizenship after settling in Detroit, even though his wife and children were American: it was the reason he gave for turning down requests to campaign on behalf of vice-presidential candidates Richard Nixon and Hubert Humphrey. But Sinclair's fulminations, incorrect as they were, took the edge off Howe's award from his home and native land just a little.

In the 1964 playoffs, the Red Wings duplicated the previous year's pattern: having finished fourth, they again defeated second-place Chicago and advanced to the finals against Toronto. Howe scored a total of 5 goals against the Black Hawks, as Detroit came from behind to win the semifinals in seven games. In the process, he toppled yet another of Richard's records: his second goal gave him the lead in career playoff points, with 127.

The Leafs-Wings final also went to seven games, and seldom has such a vivid contrast in coaching philosophies existed as the one between Punch Imlach and Sid Abel. Imlach was the puritanical, punitive, unforgiving slave driver who got his charges up early for a gruelling practice, even if they'd played the night before, and *especially* if they'd lost. Abel, free to run things his way now that Adams was gone, believed his players played better after a little R & R, and took them to the racetrack.

Abel's relaxed approach was almost proved right. By the sixth game, his Wings were leading three games to two and could almost taste the champagne from their first Stanley Cup in nine years. "For the first time in the series I really feel we can beat them," Abel told Bruce Norris.

Late in the third period, however, with the score tied at 3-3, and Detroit just a goal away from victory, Bob Baun took a low, heavy shot from Delvecchio on his ankle. "My leg just turned to cream cheese," Baun said later; he had to be carried off on a stretcher. The ankle was broken, but Baun, injected with Novocain, leaped back out onto the ice in the overtime period and fired the celebrated goal that sent the series into a seventh game in Toronto. The Leafs, many of their best players wounded, taped, trussed and frozen, but playing over their injuries as Imlach fully expected them to, triumphed 4-0, equalling the three consecutive Stanley Cups of their predecessors in the late 1940s. The leader in playoff points was thirty-six-year-old Howe, who totalled 9 goals and 10 assists: a great individual performance, but not quite enough for the Cup.

In 1964-65, the Red Wings won their first league championship since 1957. With a fine new goaltender, Roger Crozier, in place of Sawchuk (who was now in Toronto), and a stirring comeback by a player who had starred on that 1957 team, thirty-nine-year-old Ted Lindsay, they seemed for one season more like the Red Wings of old.

Even while playing three seasons with the Black Hawks, Lindsay says, he'd still been a Red Wing at heart: "I was just existing in Chicago, not living." After retiring in 1960, he returned to Detroit to help run the business he owned with Marty Pavelich. During four years away from the NHL, Lindsay kept in shape by playing hockey three times a week with Pavelich and some college players. Then, in spring 1964, he participated in a charity game between Detroit and the Red Wing Oldtimers. Howe was lent to the Oldtimers so the Production Line could be reunited. "Taking Gordie off their team was like taking a leg off some of those Red Wing players," Lindsay says. The Oldtimers shocked the younger men by nearly beating them, and Lindsay began to get ideas.

"In the summer I went to see Sid, and said I wanted to end up associated with the Red Wings in some capacity. He said, 'Why don't you come back and play? I think you could help us.' I thought he was joking. But he was serious, and after a couple of days I said yes, I'd give it a try."

At training camp, Lindsay practised on the early shift, between 8:00 A.M. and 10:00 A.M., so that he could get into the office for a full day's work. "People thought I was just trying to stay in shape. Sid told the media, 'A young rookie's going to make his debut tomorrow night.'"

For the season opener against Toronto, Lindsay emerged onto the ice at the Olympia to a tumultuous standing ovation: "It was very emotional. And it was a great year, lots of fun. I had the young legs of [linemates] Bruce MacGregor and Pit Martin to keep me going."

But it was Lindsay who got himself going—dropping Tim Horton with one punch in the opener and, along with a 10-minute misconduct for that one, and 173 penalty minutes for the full season, scoring a decent 14 goals and 14 assists as Detroit finished first, four points ahead of Montreal. Lindsay scored 3 more goals in the semifinals against Chicago, while Howe got 4. But Hull, Hall and company were too fired up for the Red Wings to handle, and the Black Hawks edged the Wings out in seven games.

Lindsay would have played another season for Detroit if he could, but Abel didn't put him on the protected list, and Toronto wouldn't pass him on waivers. Since he didn't want to leave his business behind again, Lindsay decided to retire. "Maybe I was lucky," he says now, with a deep chuckle. "I wasn't hurt, and I got out of it with all my faculties."

But by missing the next season, he did miss one last crack at the Cup. Dropping to fourth in the standings, Howe and the Red Wings nonetheless revenged themselves on the Black Hawks in the first round of the 1966 playoffs, then held a reunion with first-place Montreal in the finals, just as in the old days. They even beat the Canadiens for the first two games at the Forum, with Crozier brilliant in goal. But Montreal won the next four—two of them by only one goal—and Detroit waved good-bye to the Stanley Cup yet again. It was the Red Wings' last appearance in the Cup finals to this day, nearly thirty years later.

The team now began a long slide in the general direction of oblivion. In Howe's final five seasons with the club, 1966-67 to 1970-71, Detroit would finish last twice, and second-last twice. In the meantime, he himself would soldier on, continuing his long, lonesome march into the NHL record book.

CHAPTER THIRTEEN

The Mushroom Treatment

"So much in sports is pure hogwash. Team spirit is so
often what comes in a player's envelope twice a month."
—Colleen Howe, *My Three Hockey Players*

HOWE HAD NOW COMPLETED TWENTY full seasons with the
Detroit Red Wings. In 1946, the year he'd broken in, Boston's
Dit Clapper had established a new record for longevity; Howe had
equalled it and would soon surpass it.

At thirty-eight, he didn't have a whole lot left to prove in the
NHL. On his way to the 1966 playoffs, he'd scored his 600th career
goal, against the Canadiens—and Gump Worsley, naturally—on a
pass from Gary Bergman, a rookie defenseman playing his first
game: "Gump fished the puck outta the net and handed it to me,"
Howe reported afterwards. "He didn't say anything . . . just kind
of gave me a look."

By now Howe held most of the league scoring records that
mattered. And yet he'd continue playing in Detroit for another five
seasons. He'd play on, despite the cumulative wear and tear on his
aching body, which kept him longer and longer on the rubbing
table or in the whirlpool bath. He'd play on, despite the nagging
stiffness and chronic pain of arthritis in his wrists and knees;
despite the three hundred stitches (and counting) in his face alone;
despite the seven missing teeth and the threat to those that
remained; despite the long history of physical and spiritual scar
tissue from torn knee cartilages, battered ankles, a broken wrist, a
dislocated shoulder, concussions, and broken ribs and toes (not to
mention brain surgery); and despite the knee injury he suffered in

the 1966 pre-season, which dogged him for weeks and induced a twelve-game scoring slump, his worst since his rookie year. He tried to follow the guideline he'd learned early on from a team doctor: you can play over pain, but never over an injury.

On the positive side, he had a great deal of reinforcement for continuing to play. He acknowledged that he still received pleasure and satisfaction from doing it, even though it meant tolerating levels of pain that would discourage others. And he still *could* do it. Just as his stated reason for excelling at skiing and other sports was "so I won't make a darn fool of myself," he'd have stopped playing hockey if he'd been playing badly: his pride and competitiveness would have called a halt. But he wasn't playing badly, far from it. He would remain among the league's top five scorers for several seasons yet, even while his team was declining around him.

In addition to this reinforcement from within, he was receiving much reinforcement from without. On July 22, 1966, the media and civic authorities of Saskatoon threw a gala Gordie Howe Day, showering him with recognition and praise, and in the process strengthening his links to his hometown family—links that had weakened during years when he hadn't returned as often as in the past. For the first time in eighteen years, all of Katherine and Ab Howe's nine children were home together.

There were hockey celebrities and luncheons and mass auto-graphings and a three-mile parade through the Saskatoon streets with marching bands, and Gordie, Colleen, Marty, Mark, Cathy and Murray waving from an open convertible. A 350-acre athletic and camping complex was somewhat formally christened "Gordon Howe Park," and a $1,000 hockey scholarship was established in his name by the Kinsmen's peewee hockey league, in which he'd played as a poor West End kid. Prime Minister Lester Pearson, Opposition Leader John Diefenbaker, the premier of Saskatchewan, Ross Thatcher, the governor of Michigan, George Romney, and old Jack Adams all sent messages of congratulations.

The big day ended with a rally and stage show at the Arena. Robert Trickey, Howe's public-school coach, was there. So was leather-lunged Father Athol Murray of Notre Dame College, who pronounced a glowing tribute: "We honour this guy tonight— with all my heart, fella—as a great Canadian!" Toe Blake, Jean

Beliveau and George Armstrong, the Maple Leafs' captain, were among the NHL stars who sent telegrams. Armstrong's ended, "P.S. Please quit soon."

Howe was touched by all the acclaim, and his response was characteristic. "People have been so great, so kind to me . . . I don't think I'll ever get over it. So I just want to say once again, people behind me, thank you for all the kind words. I know if I can live up to even 10 per cent of it, I'll be a very happy man. And I hope I never go astray in such a way that some youngster maybe gets into a little trouble and says, 'Howe did it, and I can do it too.'"

Seldom was a hockey hero with so much honour in his own land. Or possessed of so much unnecessary humility.

After all the fuss, Howe went back to Detroit and continued doing what he knew best. He also continued to believe he was the league's best-paid player. After all, he'd been told so by the Red Wings' management.

When the Rocket had retired in 1960, it was widely assumed he had been receiving the NHL's highest salary—in the realm of $30,000. Now Howe was supposedly the best-paid; by 1963, he was making about $28,000 plus bonuses, which might total $9,000 in a good year. Players such as Doug Harvey ($27,000) and Frank Mahovlich ($25,000) weren't far behind in salary, and in fact Beliveau was likely receiving as much as, if not more than, Howe. But it was difficult to tell, since all six teams guarded salary figures with obsessive jealousy, and players were strictly forbidden to discuss them publicly, or even with each other. Only the boldest and most enterprising defied management to confide in a trusted teammate. But they certainly wouldn't betray the team by confiding in opposing players, discovering how much *they* were making; that would have been disloyal.

One player who fought this cult of secrecy, because he well understood how it served only the owners' interests, was Toronto's Bob Baun. He was a middle-class city boy who'd grown up in Scarborough and had always been a go-getter; in addition to having a healthy self-respect, Baun had unusual ties to the Maple Leafs' front office, in the form of friendships with several directors of Maple Leaf Gardens, including Don Giffin, Stafford Smythe and Harold Ballard. Knowing how very lucrative the hockey club was, Baun didn't hesitate to bargain hard for a better salary, even before the era of player agents. Every year at contract time, he'd carefully prepare a presentation to management, enumerating his strong points from the previous season and arguing his case for a decent increase. Most importantly, he'd share what he knew with his teammates.

One thing he knew, Baun says today, was that "Gordie just loved to play so much, it almost didn't matter what he made. He and the Rocket had kept everyone else low. This was generally understood around the league, but there was so little fraternization in those days, you didn't really know the details. That was how the league kept control."

Management used Richard and Howe against the other players, saying, in effect, 'They're the best, so why should you get more than they're getting?' Conversely, Baun explains, Howe was quite happy with his annual $1,000 raise, because he was told other players were receiving only $250. "They'd give him a pat on the back, like a big Saint Bernard, and tell him he was four times better than anybody else, so they were giving him $1,000."

The older players accepted this state of affairs; they assumed it was normal, or at least unavoidable. But in the 1960s, younger ones like Baun became angry about it and started comparing notes about their earnings. Curiously, the proliferation of hockey schools had something to do with it: NHL players from different teams would find themselves coaching together in the off-season, and, says Baun, "You'd meet an opposing player and his wife and think, 'Hey, he's not such a bad guy. They're real people.'"

Eventually, Baun compiled quite an information file on salary levels; so he was a natural choice to become first president of the revived NHL Players' Association in 1967.

Starting with the 1967-68 season, the NHL expanded to twelve cities, and suddenly it was a whole new hockey game when it came to money. With six additional teams competing for star players to build a franchise around, and new owners coming in with new money and more open minds, the players finally had some bargaining power. Even the dinosaurs in the cozy Original

Six owners' club began to realize they'd have to ante up; Howe's salary quickly escalated in stages to about $35,000, then $45,000.

The Oakland Seals picked Baun first in the expansion draft. When he went to play in California, he negotiated an enormous salary jump, from $25,000 with the Leafs to around $60,000, plus a house. The next season, Baun was traded to Detroit: "I said to myself, 'Finally I'm going to get to know the Big Fellow.' I thought maybe we could get some things going in Detroit, see if we could make some money."

Baun had certainly known the Big Fellow on the ice. There had been the time, for instance, when Toronto and Detroit had played a home-and-home series one weekend in 1959. On the Saturday night at Maple Leaf Gardens, Baun nailed Howe twice and hurt him. In the dressing room after the game, fellow defensemen Tim Horton and Allan Stanley warned Baun, "Look out, we're going into Detroit tomorrow night, and that big sonofabitch is going to be waiting for you!"

The next night at the Olympia, Baun remembers, "I got sort of a half-assed breakaway in the third period. Well, who should be back there but big Gordie. He took the net away from me, so I went behind the net, thinking I'm going to make a great play out to the front. Gordie came with me, took me up against the fence and gave me that elbow—he didn't move it six inches, but it was just like being hit by a sledge hammer. My head went into the glass, I was down on one knee, and suddenly I was like a sperm whale, a fountain of blood spurting out the top of my head."

Howe took off down the ice and pulled up inside Toronto's blueline. Baun skated semi-deliriously after him: "In the old days, we didn't have any padding in the back of our pants, so I gave him a two-hander with my stick and lifted him a foot and a half off the ice. Broke my stick, too. But I didn't wait around to see what he was going to do next. I went right into our dressing room and got sewn up. Twenty-three stitches."

When Baun arrived in Detroit in the summer of 1968, however, such frivolities were more or less forgotten. Howe had heard Baun was knowledgeable about contract matters; Baun said yes, he had a pretty good idea what everybody in the league was making. "That's part of my business," he told the Big Fellow. "I want to know what my ability is worth. And I might be making more than my ability, but that's because I put a presentation together and sell myself."

"What do you think I make?" Howe asked.

"I think you're making $49,500."

"You're practically dead-on," Howe replied, incredulous.

He was even more incredulous when Baun told him what he was making: $67,000.

"I wanted to let him know," Baun says simply. "I thought we could open things up very quickly."

Baun, age thirty-two, gave Howe, age forty, a talking-to about self-worth: "Gordie, you have to have confidence in your abilities. Bruce Norris certainly does. You tell him what you want to make, and he'll sign it. You've been proving yourself for twenty-some years and you've got every scoring record there is. You just have to believe in your ability and what you're worth to the hockey club."

Baun figured that worth at about $150,000.

Having been schooled from earliest memory not to think too highly of himself, Howe said, "No way!" But he was excited.

On reflection, he allowed his native caution to reassert itself. "The story Gordie told me," Baun says, "was that he turned chicken when he went in to sign his contract, so he put in $100,000, and Bruce Norris signed it back. Gordie said to Norris, 'Here I've been playing all these years for you, and you just give me that now?' And Bruce said, 'Gordie, you never asked for anything more. I'm a businessman.'"

Later that year, Howe and Baun would discover Norris had signed Carl Brewer for even more money than *either* of them was making.

Howe's disillusionment and bitterness over Norris's attitude, and his sense of humiliation, are still fresh after all these years. He said in 1992, "Yeah, I was all brains. You know, ignorance is one thing—we never talked about it among the teammates, until Bobby Baun . . . Bobby said, 'The whole league knows it. They think you're stupid and they're laughin' at you.' That hurt."

After he agreed to the salary increase Howe had asked for, Bruce Norris said something else that angers Howe to this day: "I hope that makes Colleen happy."

Howe replied, "Colleen doesn't come into this. She's never scored a goal in this league, so why bring her into it—*I'm* the one you've got to make happy. And how can I be happy when I don't know how many years this has been going on?"

In fact, Colleen did come into it, and would increasingly from then on. There was already a long history of animosity between Colleen Howe and the Red Wings' front office, particularly where Bruce Norris was concerned. Colleen has related in her memoir how, many years earlier, she'd first met the Red Wings' new president at his year-end team party. Norris drove her to tears by drunkenly accusing her of having affairs, claiming he knew all about her "ski trips." The truth was, Colleen says, that unlike other hockey wives, she refused to stay at home boring herself to death, or dutifully attending every Red Wings' home game, so she'd go on skiing weekends with the children or other couples. Because Howe was on the road so much, she even attended social events without him, unusual for those unliberated times. But Bruce Norris had no business speaking to her as he had that night.

Colleen Howe was a hockey wife and hockey mother with a difference; in many ways, she was a woman ahead of her time. In addition to keeping the home front organized during her husband's frequent absences, she drove her three hockey-playing sons to their games and tournaments in freezing arenas throughout Michigan, Ontario and Quebec. But not content to cheer them on from the sidelines, she also organized Detroit's first junior hockey team playing out of the Olympia, on which Marty and Mark played. In the process, she often clashed with team management over the scheduling of games, or the arena's physical condition, which she considered disgracefully dirty.

Because she asserted herself and didn't bow and scrape, she was labelled a "pushy, interfering wife": in the boys' club of professional hockey, she just didn't know her place. She once likened her efforts to include wives at men-only NHL functions to trying to desegregate the Masonic lodge. Jimmy Skinner admitted that when he saw Colleen coming down the hall at the Olympia, he'd hide in the men's room.

An immensely energetic, ambitious person, with a competitive spirit to match her husband's, Colleen threw herself into organizing Howe's off-ice career, systematically marketing his fame as a way of supplementing their income. In the early days, when Jack Adams had sent him out to father-son banquets to promote the Red Wings, Howe had been so shy and tongue-tied he'd talked mainly to the kids instead of their dads. But now he'd developed into an effective, homespun public speaker who had a winning way with all ages. Colleen made sure he was remunerated properly by service clubs, business groups and the like, just as pro baseball or football players were. At the same time, he remained available to charities at no charge and was generous with his time, his presence often giving an enormous boost to the fund-raising efforts of such causes as the March of Dimes for disabled children.

With the help of an attorney friend, Colleen negotiated Howe's first major endorsement contract in 1964, with the T. Eaton department store chain. She calls it the first long-term contract of its kind for any hockey player. Eaton's committed to paying Howe $10,000 a year for ten years in exchange for his endorsement of their Truline sports equipment. Each summer, he'd spend several weeks travelling across Canada to Eaton stores, appearing in their sports departments and autographing photographs of himself for fans and customers.

In those days, $10,000 was a considerable amount of money. Gradually the Howes, who had owned a succession of homes in Detroit since their marriage, accumulated enough disposable capital to buy a large, elaborate cottage property with extensive water-sports facilities at Bear Lake in central Michigan, and to begin investing in various business ventures.

While there's no question that the Red Wings had taken advantage of Howe's naive and trusting nature over the years, the family was now comfortably off. This was particularly true once Gordie took Baun's advice to demand his market value from Norris. For comparison purposes, at the time Howe began pulling in $100,000 in salary, a director of education at a big-city school system in Canada was earning $30,000 a year, and a senior journalist at a major daily about $20,000.

Of course, NHL pensions, including Howe's at $15,000 Canadian a year, would turn out to be pathetically small—at least until the retired players concluded their successful court action in July

1994. But Colleen had the foresight to ensure the Howe family would have a few hedges against poverty. Her husband had always given her credit for keeping him organized, and for broadening his vocabulary by getting him to take up crossword puzzles, which became his obsession during long waits in airports and hotel lobbies. Now, he also saw her as his salvation financially. "If I'd been smart," he told June Callwood years later, "I'd have got married at fourteen to her. She knows what's true value."

Howe turned forty during the NHL's first expansion year. Like many veterans, he had his career extended and his performance enhanced by the resulting dilution in the quality of play. Opposing shooters found the new teams, with the chief exception of St. Louis (where Jacques Plante and Glenn Hall shared the goaltending), easy pickings for the first few seasons.

Howe rebounded from 25 goals in the previous year to 39 in 1967-68, and 44 the next season. With 59 assists, that gave him 103 points for 1968-69 in a seventy-six-game schedule (he played them all)—the only time throughout his NHL career that he broke the 100-point ceiling. He was third in scoring that season, behind Boston's Phil Esposito and Chicago's Bobby Hull.

Howe also scored his 700th goal—in Pittsburgh on December 4, 1968, against the weakling Penguins and their goaltender, Les Binkley—with only 4,414 paying customers to witness the historic event.

By now, former teammate Bill Gadsby had taken over as Detroit's coach, with Sid Abel as G.M. Howe was part of a new dream line—an updated version, if you like, of the Production Line—with Alex Delvecchio at centre and Frank Mahovlich at left wing. The three stars thrived on working together and were immensely productive, scoring 114 goals among them. But alas, the Red Wings were woefully weak in other areas and still failed to make the playoffs in the NHL's East Division, which contained all the Original Six teams.

The Wings improved to third in the division in 1969-70 but were immediately eliminated in four games by first-place Chicago. Gadsby was long gone, fired by the increasingly erratic and alcoholic Bruce Norris. Howe was making more money than he ever had, but having less fun, and feeling worse pain. At the end of that season, he checked into the University of Michigan Medical Centre for a two-hour operation for traumatic arthritis in his left wrist, from which bone fragments were removed.

He wore a cast for the next six weeks, but still managed to get in some golf that summer. Now forty-two, he came out as usual for training camp to start the 1970-71 season, his twenty-fifth. Nobody knew for sure then—not even Howe—that it would be his last as a Red Wing.

It was not a great year for either Howe or his team. For the first time in twenty-two years—since 1949—his name didn't appear among the top five scorers in the league. His 23 goals, 29 assists and 52 points were more than respectable, and they still put him a long way from the bottom of the scoring list. But he'd missed fifteen games due to a rib injury and a variety of other painful causes; and in the other sixty-three games, he felt he hadn't played consistently. The team finished dead last in the reorganized, seven-team East Division.

Meanwhile, the Detroit front office was in a state of chaos. The highly unpopular Ned Harkness, who had coached Ken Dryden during a successful career at Cornell University, had been brought in as coach but couldn't handle the transition to the NHL. Norris moved Harkness to G.M. when Abel, angry that Norris wouldn't let him fire Harkness, resigned in January 1971. Norris then made former player Doug Barkley coach. It would be musical chairs at the Olympia for some time yet; the team's troubles were just beginning. That's mostly another story, except for a certain announcement on the day after Labour Day, 1971.

Howe played golf that morning at Detroit's Plum Hollow Golf Club, which hosted the Gordie Howe Golf Tournament each year to benefit the March of Dimes—and in the afternoon announced his retirement as an active NHL player.

Howe had agonized over the decision all summer. Explaining his reasoning, he acknowledged he'd been unhappy with his performance during the past year. He didn't want to risk playing another season, because he was no longer confident his skills could rebound to their former level.

Howe formulated the question of his continuing to play as a moral issue: "Last year I felt like I was cheating. It seemed like I was making excuses all the time for the way I was playing. I just can't go on like that. I've got to be honest with myself and with the fans."

The operation on his left wrist a year earlier had restored the full use of his hand, but he still carried a great deal of pain in his wrists and legs: "My legs didn't bounce back last year the way they used to. I remember saying they were hurt or that I was bruised. But those were just excuses. Lies, utter lies. I wasn't kidding myself. I only got 23 goals because of one hot streak. I could still execute the big play, but I couldn't do it often."

Typically, he talked about the fans, and what they had a right to expect of him. And typically, he talked about Colleen, and what she expected. "My wife told me to play another year if I wanted, but she didn't want to see me suffer like I did last year, when they should have benched me."

Howe said during his retirement announcement that a whole new life was opening up for him. And for a little while, it seemed as though that might be exactly what would happen.

The Detroit organization announced he'd been appointed a vice-president of the club, which seemed a grand enough position for a hockey figure of his stature. His salary was rumoured to be $75,000. He wouldn't be G.M., exactly, or a coach, exactly, although he'd be assisting the coaches in some unspecified way at training camp in Port Huron, Michigan, and with the Red Wings' farm clubs. But he'd also been made a vice-president of the holding company that owned Bruce Norris's insurance companies and other interests. Howe said sincerely, as only he could, that he was really looking forward to learning the insurance business.

In the meantime, the tributes and honours poured in. As sports columnists and politicians and hockey moguls described his retirement as "the end of an era," the cliché seemed entirely apt.

The mayor of Detroit, Roman S. Gribbs, declared a Gordie Howe Day, calling him "a legend" and proclaiming, "If a city ever loved a sports hero, then Detroit has truly loved Gordie Howe." A lavish luncheon was laid on at the Olympia. President

Nixon sent a telegram. Clarence Campbell and Tommy Ivan and Sid Abel attended.

Only Jack Adams was missing. He'd died three years earlier, while still in harness at the Central Pro League. His epitaph might well have been the anecdote that Howe once told about riding in the car with the other pallbearers after Adams's funeral: one of them, another former player, said, "Well, he was a miserable old sonofabitch. Now he's a *dead* miserable old sonofabitch."

On Gordie Howe Day, Clarence Campbell told the assembled dignitaries, "Never in the history of this game has there been such an obvious and dramatic loss by a single sport . . . Hockey has been fortunate to have Gordie. When he came into the league, hockey was a Canadian game. He's converted it into a North American game."

Having accomplished so much, having been so important to so many people, having received such recognition, admiration and affection on a local, national and international scale, Howe set off optimistically to perform his new job with the Red Wings.

There was just one problem: there was nothing for him to do. Before long, he'd term it "the mushroom treatment: that's when they keep you in the dark and come in once in a while to throw a little manure on you."

CHAPTER FOURTEEN

The Second Coming

"Nothing can replace blood kin."
—Gordie Howe, 1992

HOWE HAD ALWAYS REMAINED CLOSE to his mother, even though they lived so far apart; naturally he took it very hard when she died in the summer of 1971. Katherine and Ab Howe were staying at the time in the cottage at Bear Lake, Michigan, minding the Howe children while Gordie and Colleen were away. Mrs. Howe fell down a flight of stairs and struck her head, dying immediately. She was seventy-five. After rushing back to the cottage, Howe phoned his brothers and sisters; he was so distraught that, at first, he could only say she'd been hurt very badly. It was impossible to believe she was no longer alive.

Some say his mother's death had an influence on Howe's decision to retire a few weeks later. She'd always told him hockey wasn't worth killing himself for; when it became too much for him, he should just give it up. He'd always promised her he would, when that time came. Now he kept his promise.

Adjusting to retirement ranks high on the stress scale—right up there, for many people, with the death of a loved one, or a divorce, or getting fired. The trauma of retirement is doubled for professional athletes. They must learn to live without the adrenalin-producing drama and ego-building adulation that sport gave them. And they're young enough when they retire that they still need to work (or at least they did, before the recent advent of megabuck salaries). The big question they must answer, now that their bodies won't allow them to play for pay, is what will they do? What can they find to replace the rewards, financial and emotional, of performing in front of roaring crowds?

For Howe, the answer seemed more promising than for most retiring players of his era. As a reigning superstar for so many years, he was still in the public eye, still in demand. And he had an executive position as an obviously valued employee of the organization he'd worked for all his adult life.

Although the Red Wings hadn't given him a job description, Howe was depending on certain vague promises and broad hints he'd heard from management. He was to have a hand of some sort in running the hockey club; he was also supposed to be trained as an insurance executive, perhaps moving onto the board of Norris's holding company. He was forty-three, and a place at the top of the insurance business seemed to offer a fitting future to a man with a lot of working years left.

Considering Howe's education and experience, insurance might have seemed less fitting than a future as a hockey coach. But Howe repeatedly said he wasn't interested in coaching. After a story came out that G.M. Ned Harkness had offered him an interim coaching job after Doug Barkley resigned, Howe explained why he'd turned it down: "I had told everyone, including my wife Colleen, that I'd never take a coaching job when I resigned, and I wasn't going to go back on my word."

A few years earlier, around the time of Gordie Howe Day in Saskatoon, he'd sounded far more interested in the idea of coaching. "I want to spend as many years in the National Hockey League as I can," he said then. "It's been awful good to me, and it's everything I have in life . . . That's why I'm aiming for a coach or scout or something to stay in the game of hockey."

But Colleen already seemed to have different ideas. In an interview, she acknowledged, "Gord has always expressed an interest in the coaching end of hockey, although I feel that Gord is primarily adapted to working so closely with public relations and people that I'm almost hoping he'll get into that field, rather than coaching, and maybe this will take some of the tension away."

In the end, her view prevailed. Or perhaps Howe just realized his easygoing, self-effacing personality wasn't suited to the rigours of coaching. Jack Adams had once suggested Howe might make a good coach, while wondering aloud whether he "might be too nice" for the job.

In any event, "public relations" could describe what Howe ended up doing as a vice-president. But the work, such as it was, bore no resemblance to a thought-out PR strategy. His job never amounted to more than window-dressing; the Red Wing executives seemed to have no idea how to put Howe's unique stature and immense personal popularity to the service of the hockey club.

His only active duties involved attending public functions: " 'Go represent the club,' they'd tell me. Half the time, they didn't even have the courtesy to tell me in advance where I'd be going."

The Red Wings were paying him a lot of money to do virtually nothing. The greatest scorer and all-round player in hockey history went into his office every morning and sat in his chair watching the paint dry. It wasn't even a very big or impressive office. Colleen called it "tacky" and said that, whenever the team wanted him to pose for a photographer, they'd move him into someone else's quarters, so that in every shot there would be pictures of someone else's children in the background.

On one occasion, Howe was despatched to an awards event at which the club had purchased a table for ten. Arriving to discover he was the only person sitting there, he walked out rather than stay and feel humiliated. Later, he was upset to discover he was supposed to have received one of the awards.

The Red Wings' lack of courtesy and professionalism was reflected in another story Howe once told to a journalist. The club phoned him at home one evening and said the team had to be represented at a luncheon in New York the next day. He was to get himself onto a flight to New York in the morning, attend the luncheon and return in the afternoon. Colleen and the rest of the family were away at the time, and when he hung up, Howe realized he didn't know how to arrange the trip; he'd never had to book his own flights before. He'd flown hundreds of times, but the club, or Colleen, had always handled ticketing arrangements.

Howe's new job was even more demeaning on the insurance side. No executive training materialized, and soon he found he was no longer even listed in the company's annual report as a vice-president. When he learned at the beginning of 1972 that his involvement in the insurance business had been postponed for two years, he was so unhappy that he flew down to Norris's residence in Miami to get some answers in person. Temporarily mollified, he came away with a new title—vice-president of public relations for the Red Wings—and told the media, "I'm my own man now. Bruce has given me complete control of what I do and no one is going to interfere."

Perhaps no one did interfere. But nothing really changed, either. The sole bright moment during this period was the ceremony on March 12, 1972, to retire his number nine jersey officially. This was one occasion when the club executives did justice to their greatest star—although they had to be persuaded by a Detroit friend of the Howes, businessman Chuck Robertson, to upgrade the event from a modest ritual to a full-fledged ceremony that ended up involving the White House. Between periods of a game between Detroit and Chicago, they literally rolled out the red carpet, one with a giant white number nine in the centre. Before a capacity crowd, Howe stood shoulder-to-shoulder with Colleen, Mark, Cathy and Murray (Marty had a hockey game that day in Toronto), Ab Howe, Ted Lindsay and U.S. Vice-President Spiro Agnew, who brought personal greetings from President Nixon. Not too many hockey players could have drawn a presidential emissary.

Bobby Hull brought greetings from all the NHL teams Howe had mistreated over twenty-five seasons. Hull took the gum out of his mouth long enough to say, "I've played against the greatest of us all, and I've enjoyed every high-sticking minute of it."

To Bruce Norris, Howe turned over the jersey he'd made famous, stating there was just one condition on which it could be brought out of retirement: if one of Gordie's sons ever played for the Red Wings.

The two eldest of those sons were now busy preparing to launch their own pro hockey careers. In 1972-73, Marty Howe, eighteen, was in his second season as an outstanding defenseman with the Toronto Marlboros in the Ontario Hockey Association junior A league. He was joined on the Marlboros that year by forward

Mark, seventeen, who had already been selected for the U.S. Olympic team, and who moved up from the Detroit Junior Red Wings after a tough year marred by knee surgery. Mark's demands on signing included a $10,000 compensation payment if his teammates ever shaved his head in an initiation ritual, as they'd shaved his brother's the year before, and (for good luck, at his father's urging) team jackets for himself and Marty. At season's end, the Marlboros would win the Memorial Cup.

Youngest son Murray, twelve, was busy playing as often as five times a week in Detroit's minor hockey program, and Cathy, thirteen, was busy with her music and friends and school.

And of course Colleen was forever busy. Recently she'd invested their capital, through a friend, in apartment complexes, a herd of polled Hereford cattle in western Michigan and a cattle ranch. Soon she and Gordie would establish a company called Gordie Howe Agri Labs, which distributed Silo-Guard, a product for treating cattle feed. Colleen wrote that in the two years after her husband retired from playing hockey, their estate almost doubled. She was also heavily involved with charitable work, heading Detroit's Arthritis Foundation that year.

In fact, the only Howe who wasn't productively busy was the famous one. He'd just been inducted, in August 1972, into the Hockey Hall of Fame—two years early, since the normal three-year waiting period had been waived for him and for Jean Beliveau. But in the apparent absence of any further contribution he could make to the Detroit organization, whether in the Red Wings' front office or in Norris's insurance empire, Howe felt a powerful longing to get out on the ice and make himself useful, in the one area where everyone damn well *knew* he excelled—where, in fact, there could be no conceivable argument against his involvement. He craved it. He needed it. He deserved it.

Incredibly, he was denied it. Ned Harkness told Johnny Wilson, the coach who had succeeded Barkley (and Howe's old teammate from twenty years earlier), to forbid Howe to go out for practice—or even to go into the dressing room. There seemed to be an assumption that Howe's presence would somehow disrupt the team, instead of helping and inspiring the players. Perhaps Detroit's struggling and unproven management team was feeling insecure; perhaps they were afraid the players would listen to Gordie Howe instead of to them. But the Red Wings weren't doing particularly well, and it's difficult to imagine that Howe could have made things any worse.

If Howe wasn't welcome on the ice, where was he welcome in the organization? Nowhere, it seemed. Then they told him to keep his wife away from the Olympia, and from the Junior Red Wings, which she'd worked tirelessly over the years to establish, and that did it.

"I may have disturbed a few people at the Olympia," Colleen recalled later. "I really don't know. It was never my intention to do so . . . So, if I did step on someone's toes and they didn't like it, I can't worry about that now. I have to do what I feel is right."

Feeling that both he and his wife were unwelcome in the organization to whose success and prosperity he'd contributed so much, Howe became not only unhappy and depressed but angry—and restless. It might be difficult to keep that promise to his mother after all.

The phone call in the spring of 1973 caught Howe at a vulnerable moment. Instantly, he knew it was the right moment. He listened as his old adversary, Doug Harvey, told him the Houston Aeros of the World Hockey Association were about to make Mark Howe their number-one pick in the WHA draft. Harvey was by then an assistant coach and scout with Houston in the upstart league, which had begun challenging the NHL's monopoly of pro hockey a year earlier. At eighteen, Mark was still too young to play in the NHL, but the Aeros didn't care—they were going to test the age regulation and prove it didn't apply to the WHA.

The Aeros also picked Marty in the twelfth round. Immediately, Clarence Campbell, still NHL president, and still counting on Howe to defer to his authority, got on the phone to ask him to prevent his sons from signing with the rival league. Howe thought about it overnight, then replied that he wouldn't dictate to them, or deny them an opportunity they'd been working hard for: after all, he wouldn't have wanted his own father to interfere in that way.

Something else was ticking over in Howe's mind. Houston's coach was his old teammate Bill Dineen. One day, Dineen was discussing the boys' future with their dad by long distance when Howe casually asked, "Say, Bill, how would you like to have three Howes?"

There was a long pause at the other end of the line, then Dineen replied, "Hell, yes!"

Solid-gold superstars like Howe, or Bobby Hull, who signed with the WHA's Winnipeg Jets, were exactly what the new league needed to build attendance and credibility. And the WHA owners were ready to dig deep into their pockets to outbid what NHL owners were willing to pay.

The gleam in Howe's eye became a vision after he discussed it with Colleen. She feared the effect on his health. But she knew, better than anyone, how long and fervently her husband had been dreaming of playing hockey professionally with his sons. A few years earlier, she'd organized a charity game between the Red Wings and the Junior Red Wings, and Howe had played on a line alongside Mark and Marty, with Murray and Gordie's brother Vern on defense—five Howes on the ice at once. Gordie had told her then, "Wouldn't it be wonderful if this was for real!"

It had always seemed impossible before: Marty and Mark were too young, their father too old. But now the opportunity was there. It was really the old man's choice. Was he still up to it or not?

If Colleen had worried previously about the "tension" that coaching would have brought into their home and relationship, she now knew the depression induced by Gordie's "non-job," as she called it, was worse. Seeing the familiar happy grin lighting up his face again, she told him to go for it, and threw herself into the ultimate negotiation—solidly securing her family's financial future.

The Howes flew to Houston to check out the city and the team owners, and liked both. Howe himself was ecstatic. He said he felt "like a new kid again. My name got thrown into the hat, and they offered me money, and I felt like saying, 'Colleen, sign it!' It looked *so* good."

With the aid of Gerry Patterson, a business associate, Colleen obtained a four-year package deal for all three of her hockey players, worth some $2 million spread over four years. "The biggest family package in the history of sports," she proudly termed it.

Much easier to refuse was a halfhearted offer from Bruce Norris to keep Howe in Detroit, accompanied by the insulting inference that he'd actually have to work to earn the money. When Howe collected the last of his twenty-nine years' worth of paycheques from the Red Wings, it came to only $50: the team had deducted some travel expenses that Howe had incurred with Norris's travel agency.

In Houston, the attitude was far more generous and expansive. The salary package was based on roughly a million for the two boys and another million for their father. But it wasn't just the money. All the Howes found the Texas oiltown's citizens enthusiastic and hospitable. A giant banner hanging from a downtown skyscraper read WELCOME TO HOWESTON.

Originally, Father Howe was to play only for the first year of the contract and then ride a desk for the next three. But that idea soon went out the window. He received a clean bill of health from his doctor, who found him in remarkably youthful condition and compared his exceptionally low pulse rate to that of a dolphin. "He's kept himself in splendid physical shape," the team doctor stated. "He's one of those one-in-a-lifetime professional athletes. You have to compare him with George Blanda or Arnold Palmer."

After working himself slowly and stiffly back into his game, the old man began enjoying himself again. On the morning of the season opener against a team called the Cleveland Crusaders, however, Howe was in traction in the hospital for treatment of back spasms. Somehow he got himself to the arena and into uniform for the game, and he acquitted himself as only he could in a losing cause.

Since there were three of them on the team, the Howes had to have their full names sewn onto the backs of their blue and white sweaters. For that opening game, Gordie's sweater announced "GORIDE HOWE." As an antidote to taking himself too seriously, it worked. It almost rivalled the story he liked to tell about the Saskatoon old-timer who years before had asked him: "Where do you go every winter anyways? I never see you around here any more."

Outside of cities where WHA teams played, it's doubtful if any but the most hardcore hockey trivia buffs remember many details of the WHA's seven seasons, even though numerous big-name players, from Howe and Hull to Dave Keon, Carl Brewer, Gerry Cheevers and Wayne Gretzky, played in the league at various times. Some may not even remember that the WHA's answer to the Stanley Cup was called the Avco World Cup, or that the Houston Aeros captured it in 1974, the Howes' first year, four games to none over the Chicago Cougars. Mark Howe was named WHA rookie of the year that season. For the record, his father scored a nice, round 100 points, on 31 goals and 69 assists, good enough for third in WHA scoring—and for the league's most valuable player award. The next season, they named the award after him.

Howe enjoyed the champagne shower in the dressing room after the victory; it had been an awfully long nineteen years since a team he'd played on had won that other Cup. In 1974-75, the Aeros triumphed again, this time over the Quebec Nordiques, and Howe, at the age of forty-seven, scored 99 points during the regular season.

But what he enjoyed most of all was the fun and excitement of playing with the boys—all the boys, but especially his own two. He was once more a boy himself. "I got the love of the game back," he'd say. "That's why I played so well. I felt like a kid again."

And he exulted in the camaraderie, the joking around in the dressing room, the fulfilment of his need "to be on the ice, to sweat and bleed with the boys." He told a CTV television crew that had travelled to Houston to film the miracle on ice, "All the old-timers will tell you, the number-one thing you miss about the game of hockey is its closeness, its companionship. It's such a team game, it's unbelievable how close you get to certain individuals. Honestly, that's what I missed."

At the same time, the eternal boy could metamorphose at any moment into a fiercely proud or fearsomely protective father. One of Howe's biggest thrills in the WHA was assisting on Marty's first professional goal. He threw the puck out from behind the net, glimpsed a pair of Aeros' stockings and a left-handed shot, and then the mesh bulged, almost hitting him in the cheek. Figuring it was Mark, Howe turned to congratulate him on his 20th goal, but instead he was overwhelmed with delight to see a huge grin plastered across his other son's face: Marty had finally scored.

But woe betide any opposing player foolish enough to mess with either son. More than once, a player who tripped or slashed Mark got hammered by Gordie and Marty swooping down on him from opposite sides. Another player who hit one of the boys saw Gordie coming after him and pleaded, "I didn't mean it!"

And there was the time a WHA thug clobbered Mark and landed on top of him. Gordie told the offending player, politely, to let Mark up. "When he didn't," Marty recounted, "Gordie [his sons called him by name only on the ice] reached down, stuck his fingers into his nostrils and pulled him off the ice. The guy's nose must have stretched half a foot."

"I don't know why I do these things," Howe commented, laughing, "but it seemed the right thing to do at the time." He did, however, provide a simple explanation, one that governed his behaviour both on and off the ice: "Nothing can replace blood kin."

Howe applied that principle with a vengeance in autumn 1974, when he and both sons were members of Team Canada, WHA version, in an eight-game series against the Soviet Union national team. After breaking even with a win apiece and two ties in Canada, the teams flew to Moscow for the final four games. The Soviets, already in awe of Howe's fame, were equally astonished to discover his elbows, especially after anyone mistreated his boys. When Mark was crosschecked in game seven, Howe sent the Soviet offender into orbit around Luzhniki Arena. The outcome of that particular game ended in dispute—Team Canada claimed a victory on Bobby Hull's last-second goal, but the officials called it a tie—and the Soviets took the series 4 games to 1, with 3 ties.

In 1977, after two more seasons with Houston, time ran out on the Howes' contract and on the team itself. Like many another WHA franchise, the Aeros slid into financial trouble and eventually into hockey oblivion. A new group of investors had bought the team in summer 1975, making the grand gesture of naming Howe president; but less than two years later, they couldn't meet the payroll. A brief controversy arose when Colleen disclosed that her three players had been paid, while the rest of the team had not.

As much as they'd enjoyed the city and the money, the Howes now had to look around for a new home. Father and sons wanted to keep playing together, and Colleen put her mind to finding them the best deal.

The sentimental favourite was Detroit, the presence of Bruce Norris notwithstanding. It would have been a homecoming for the entire family, a return to the city where Colleen and the children had grown up, where Howe himself had come of age professionally and personally, where they all still had many friends and many memories.

Colleen provided the Red Wings with a proposal for a major new role in the organization for her husband. As far as the Howes were concerned, even the general manager's job was a possibility.

After Howe's vice-presidential experience several years earlier, it's difficult to imagine such an arrangement working out. And from the Red Wings' point of view, if they made Howe general manager, who would really be running the club, given his subservience to Colleen in business matters? In the end, Norris squelched Colleen's proposal by hiring someone else as G.M. instead: Ted Lindsay.

This was adding insult to injury. Lindsay had been in the Howes' bad books for years. He'd pooh-poohed the WHA in 1974, suggesting the league played poor hockey if a forty-six-year-old could score 100 points and become its most valuable player. There had been other sore points, too, such as Lindsay's criticism of the Howes for accepting paycheques from Houston when the other Aeros went without. For a long time, Lindsay and his old friend, and his old friend's wife, didn't speak.

Colleen says that, as G.M., Lindsay refused to negotiate with her and blocked Howe's return to the old team by refusing to deal for the NHL rights to Mark, which belonged to Montreal. Lindsay, for his part, says bluntly the refusal lay with Norris, who wouldn't have any part of negotiating with Colleen: "Norris hated women. His joy in life was to belittle any woman in the same room with him."

Colleen then tried to negotiate something with the Boston Bruins, but in the end had better luck with the WHA's New England Whalers, with whom she'd been talking since the final season in Houston. She netted Gordie a ten-year personal-services contract worth an estimated $5 million for both playing and front-office duties, and the family settled in Hartford, Connecticut, in summer 1977. But despite the lucrative deal, the failure to return in triumph to Detroit went down hard. Colleen was still mourning it fifteen years later, in a 1992 interview with the *Detroit Free Press*. "We were extremely happy in Hartford," she stated. "We would have been happier in Detroit."

But the Howes were becoming an adaptable family. They put down roots in Connecticut, and eventually Colleen invested in a restaurant there, co-managed a large team of Amway salespeople and Cambridge Diet Plan distributors, and ran for Congress as a Republican. The men played hockey.

During the first season, their coach was Harry Neale, now a colour commentator on CBC's *Hockey Night in Canada*. Neale found Howe—and Colleen—still highly protective towards their two sons. Neale has related how, when he didn't play Marty much, Colleen confronted him and said: "When I come to a game I come to see my *three* boys play."

Neale also told the story of Howe's going for his 1,000th career goal (NHL plus WHA, including playoffs) in December 1977. Between shifts, Howe would sit on the bench, his left hand in a bucket of warm water for his arthritis, his right hand in a bucket of ice because of an injury, but he refused to stop playing until he scored that goal—which finally came, after a wait of several games, in Birmingham, Alabama, of all places, against John Garrett of the Birmingham Bulls. "After he got the goal he had his hand X-rayed," Neale recounted in Dick Irvin's *Behind the Bench*, "and sure enough, there was a small crack in there. If Mark or Marty had a hangnail Gordie would tell them they shouldn't be playing. But when he had a broken hand he wouldn't stop playing, or practising, until he got the goal."

That persistence, that dedication, that *obsession*, didn't end even there, although by the time of the 1,000th goal, Howe was already forty-nine. In all, he played three seasons in New England, and by the third—1979-80—the team had been renamed the Hartford Whalers, and Howe had come full circle, playing once again in the NHL, which had absorbed five teams from the now-defunct WHA.

This was his final season. Even Marty and Mark were now veterans of professional hockey. Their father had prevailed through thirty-two big-league seasons, during which he'd played in five different decades, spanning the eras of six Canadian prime ministers from King to Trudeau, and eight American presidents from Truman to Reagan. By the end of it all, his NHL goals record had reached 801. His NHL and WHA record combined had reached 975 and his career total, including playoffs, was 1,071.

During his last season, the fifty-two-year-old grandfather of two scored just 15 goals, but he played in all eighty games and continued to practise what he called "religious hockey": it's better to give than to receive. Opposing players less than half his age were still keeping a self-preserving distance from those elbows, and his last coach, Don Blackburn, was saying, "I never know what he'll do with the puck because there is no limit to his creativity." Jean Beliveau put it succinctly: "Gordie, he still has that instinct."

By that time, the wonder of it was that he was playing at all. He was no longer being judged as a mere hockey player. Ken Dryden, a star of a younger generation who had retired the year before Howe returned to the NHL, comments: "By the time I got to know him, Gordie Howe the player was eons ago. He was already a miracle. Anything he gave by then was a bonus."

How he kept going such a miraculously long time can be explained by a mysterious conjunction of physical and emotional factors: his extraordinary physique, strength and conditioning; his rejuvenation through the experience of playing with his sons; his deep devotion to the game: "I was totally in love with what I was doing. Even as a grown man, I could have played hockey all day."

And that's the key: by continuing to play hockey, Gordie Howe was doing the main thing he had really wanted to do in life.

Even after his playing career ended, hockey continued to be what he was all about. Once he signed his autograph for a young fan over a photograph of one of his sons.

"That's not *you*," the boy exclaimed.

"No," Howe replied, "but that's my *work*."

In his hockey-playing sons, the living legend had left a living legacy.

A Little Thing Called Fun

"Off the ice, I struggle as you do,
  but off the ice you never see me . . .
  We are not heroes. We are hockey players."
  —Ken Dryden, *The Game*

THERE'S A STORY THEY LIKE TO TELL about Gordie Howe. One summer, during a fishing trip in Alberta, he was driving with his tackle up to a lake north of Edmonton. Approaching an old man fishing off the side of a bridge, he slowed his car to a stop, rolled the window down and stuck his head out.

"How're they bitin', old-timer?" he called.

The stranger didn't look up from his rod. "Pretty good, Gord," he replied.

I'm reminded of that kind of public recognition when I finally get to Gordie on an evening in August 1993, nearly forty years after my friend and I argued passionately over him and the Rocket. I'm sitting across the table from Howe in a restaurant in Abbotsford, British Columbia. Beside him is Colleen Howe; beside me is publisher Rob Sanders. We're there to discuss the possibility of collaborating on Gordie's long-overdue autobiography.

But Howe can scarcely take part in the conversation. He's too busy accommodating the steady stream of restaurant patrons, young and old, who keep stopping at our table and asking, some shyly, some boldly, for his autograph. As a result, the strongest impressions I retain from that evening are visual ones: the hugeness of Howe's hands, the hands that administered the legendary wrist shot and the punishing beatings and that now shrink neighbouring objects by comparison, making our cups and saucers and cutlery resemble a dollhouse tea set; his fingernails as big as dollar coins; his wrists the girth of ankles; yet everything in perfect proportion. And pain. He seems a veritable mountain of pain, from his elongated, muscled neck and precipitously sloping shoulders to his long, thick, gnarled limbs gathered stiffly under the table, all aching so much that he's constantly wincing and massaging his massive wrists and thighs and kneecaps to get some relief.

It is strange and regrettable that, so many years after his retirement, Howe still hasn't published his autobiography. Not only has Gretzky already come out with his life story, but the list of former NHL players who have collaborated with co-authors is as long as Howe's arm. Some, such as Gump Worsley and Johnny Bucyk, are close to him in age, but other retirees in print—Stan Mikita, Gerry Cheevers, Phil Esposito, Brad Park, Mike Bossy, Paul Henderson, Larry Robinson, Tiger Williams, to name a few—are considerably younger. Already two biographies of Mario Lemieux have appeared. Even Eric Lindros has told his story, at the ripe old age of eighteen, back before he'd played a single game in the NHL.

It seems wrong that hockey's greatest living player still hasn't recounted his career from start to finish; he is moving farther and farther away from the source of those personal memories and reflections that legions of fans would love to read about. And it's not as if writers and publishers haven't tried to collaborate with him. Trent Frayne and Roy MacGregor are two highly respected and experienced hockey writers Howe could have worked with over the years, but didn't.

For whatever reason, I don't have any better luck than they did. But later that evening, in the Hotel Vancouver, I come across a plexiglas showcase displaying a gilt-edged souvenir plate. The plate bears a hand-painted portrait of Wayne Gretzky in action, uniformed in the colours of the Los Angeles Kings. And hovering above Gretzky's head, emerging from the heavens like some biblical vision, is none other than the weathered, hawk-nosed profile of the man I've just had dinner with. The portrait seems to be saying, "And Howe begat Gretzky . . ." It confirms my conviction that any man who becomes an icon in his own lifetime deserves a book to himself. Hence this unauthorized biography.

And yet I still hope Howe writes his own story some day. It could be more than just another variation on his "Mr. Hockey" persona, the public Gordie. It might reveal something of the private Gordie: the "big kid" Bob Baun enjoyed so much when he and his family were invited up to the Howes' cottage for water-skiing and sailboating and trail-bike riding and Monopoly and card games from early morning until night, and Howe always had to lead the pack or win the race or be the best at whatever game it might be, and yet was so infused with excitement and enthusiasm for everything he did that Baun developed "a great feeling towards him."

Or it might reveal the man Baun experienced on another occasion, which he calls "the best night I ever had with him," at the Howe home in Detroit.

"Everybody else was at the cottage, and it was this beautiful warm summer night. He had a big pool in the backyard, and there was just Jean Beliveau, Gerry Patterson, Gord and I. We'd had a few beers, and we were like big porpoises in the pool, having the time of our lives swimming and diving. One of us would do a double flip and the others would have to do a double flip, all like big kids, and it was a wonderful insight into both Gord and Beliveau—the real Gord and the real Beliveau—and how much they admired each other. That evening, a writer would have got the story of a lifetime."

Few of us have been privileged to share such intimate, unguarded moments with the real Gordie Howe. But sometimes, the kids he instructs at hockey clinics do receive a glimpse into what he's all about.

First, he'll offer them his philosophy about playing hockey: that if you give everything you have out on the ice, you'll be able to sleep soundly at night—you'll be able to say, "Whatever you saw me do out there, good or bad, that was the best I had."

And then he'll give them his reminder that "In between, there's a little thing called fun. That's why we call hockey a game."

Professional Career Record

YEAR	REGULAR SEASON TEAM & LEAGUE	GP	G	A	PTS	PIM
1945–46	Omaha USHL	51	22	26	48	53
1946–47	Detroit NHL	58	7	15	22	52
1947–48		60	16	28	44	63
1948–49		40	12	25	37	57
1949–50		70	35	33	68	69
1950–51		70	43★	43★	86★	74
1951–52		70	47★	39	86★	78
1952–53		70	49★	46★	95★	57
1953–54		70	33	48★	81★	109
1954–55		64	29	33	62	68
1955–56		70	38	41	79	100
1956–57		70	44★	45	89★	72
1957–58		64	33	44	77	40
1958–59		70	32	46	78	57
1959–60		70	28	45	73	46
1960–61		64	23	49	72	30
1961–62		70	33	44	77	54
1962–63		70	38★	48	86★	100
1963–64		69	26	47	73	70
1964–65		70	29	47	76	104
1965–66		70	29	46	75	83
1966–67		69	25	40	65	53
1967–68		74	39	43	82	53
1968–69		76	44	59	103	58
1969–70		76	31	40	71	58
1970–71		63	23	29	52	38
1973–74	Houston WHA	70	31	69	100	46
1974–75		75	34	65	99	84
1975–76		78	32	70	102	76
1976–77		62	24	44	68	57
1977–78	New England WHA	76	34	62	96	85
1978–79		58	19	24	43	51
1979–80	Hartford NHL	80	15	26	41	42
	NHL Totals:	1767	801	1049	1850	1685
	WHA Totals:	419	174	334	508	399
	NHL & WHA Totals:	2186	975	1383	2358	2084

(★ INDICATES LEAGUE-LEADING FIGURE)

Awards and Honours

Art Ross Trophy (NHL leading scorer): 1951, 1952, 1953, 1954, 1957, 1963 (6)

Hart Memorial Trophy (NHL most valuable player): 1952, 1953, 1957, 1958, 1960, 1963 (6)

Gary L. Davidson Trophy (WHA most valuable player): 1974

Lester Patrick Trophy (outstanding service to hockey in U.S.): 1967

NHL First All–Star Team: 1951, 1952, 1953, 1954, 1957, 1958, 1960, 1963, 1966, 1968, 1969, 1970 (12)

NHL Second All–Star Team: 1949, 1950, 1956, 1959, 1961, 1962, 1964, 1965, 1967 (9)

Inducted into Hockey Hall of Fame (Canada): 1972

YEAR	PLAYOFFS TEAM & LEAGUE	GP	G	A	PTS	PIM
1945–46	Omaha USHL	6	2	1	3	15
1946–47	Detroit NHL	5	0	0	0	18
1947–48		10	1	1	2	11
1948–49		11	8	3	11	19
1949–50		1	0	0	0	7
1950–51		6	4	3	7	4
1951–52		8	2	5	7	2
1952–53		6	2	5	7	2
1953–54		12	4	5	9	31
1954–55		11	9	11	20	24
1955–56		10	3	9	12	8
1956–57		5	2	5	7	6
1957–58		4	1	1	2	0
1958–59						
1959–60		6	1	5	6	4
1960–61		11	4	11	15	10
1961–62						
1962–63		11	7	9	16	22
1963–64		14	9	10	19	16
1964–65		7	4	2	6	20
1965–66		12	4	6	10	12
1966–67						
1967–68						
1968–69						
1969–70		4	2	0	2	2
1970–71						
1973–74	Houston WHA	13	3	14	17	34
1974–75		13	8	12	20	20
1975–76		17	4	8	12	31
1976–77		11	5	3	8	11
1977–78	New England WHA	14	5	5	10	15
1978–79		10	3	1	4	4
1979–80	Hartford NHL	3	1	1	2	2
	NHL Totals:	157	68	92	160	220
	WHA Totals:	78	28	43	71	115
	NHL & WHA Totals:	235	96	135	231	335

Sources and Acknowledgements

THIS BIOGRAPHY OF GORDIE HOWE is unauthorized. Nothing in it is based on any interview I conducted with the subject or his wife; indeed, no such interview took place, although I did meet with the Howes on one occasion to explore the possibility of an authorized work.

During the course of his long and extraordinary career, Howe has been the subject of numerous print and broadcast interviews, newspaper and magazine profiles, radio and television programs, and even several books. The written, audio and video record on him is therefore quite extensive, and I have drawn upon it as acknowledged below. I have also consulted many former NHL players, both teammates and opponents, whose careers touched his; and many knowledgeable observers of Howe and his era in hockey, mainly fellow writers and journalists. From all of those people I received much helpful information and insight, and I thank them individually below. I hope this book justifies the time and trouble they took to talk with me and share their memories, ideas and opinions. I enjoyed their company.

Although several biographies of Howe have appeared previously, they are either out of print or seriously out of date, or both. Anyone attempting to fill the need for a current biography, however, owes a debt to the pioneering work of two earlier writers in particular: Jim Vipond, whose *Gordie Howe: Number Nine* (McGraw-Hill Ryerson) first appeared in 1968 and was revised in 1971; and Don O'Reilly, whose *Mr. Hockey: The World of Gordie Howe* (Henry Regnery Co.) was published in 1975. Both of these books, written before Howe's playing career ended, have provided a solid foundation for others to build on, especially in regard to his early life.

Several books were invaluable in documenting the historical context for Howe's career. *The Trail of the Stanley Cup* by Charles L. Coleman (1976), published in three volumes by the National Hockey League, is an essential reference work covering every NHL season in detail up to the league's expansion in 1967. D'Arcy Jenish's *The Stanley Cup: A Hundred Years of Hockey at Its Best* (McClelland & Stewart, 1992) provides a sound historical overview. *The Habs: An Oral History of the Montreal Canadiens, 1940-80* by Dick Irvin (McClelland & Stewart, 1991) superbly documents the Montreal-Detroit rivalry of the 1950s in the words of the players themselves. *The NHL Official Guide and Record Book, 1993-94* (NHL, 1993) is a gold mine of facts and statistics.

A few breakthrough books have made the term "hockey literature" no longer an oxymoron, and I was both inspired and profoundly informed by them. The first of these, of course, is Ken Dryden's *The Game* (Macmillan, 1983), a Canadian classic. Another is a book I relied on for its wealth of historical information and particularly its elucidation of the first attempt to form an NHL Players' Association: the passionately written *Net Worth: Exploding the Myths of Pro Hockey* by David Cruise and Alison Griffiths (Penguin Books, 1992). Also in this category are *Home Game: Hockey and Life in Canada* by Ken Dryden and Roy MacGregor (McClelland & Stewart, 1989); and MacGregor's incisively unsentimental *Road Games: A Year in the Life of the NHL* (MacFarlane, Walter and Ross, 1993).

Several titles provided me with colourful anecdotal and period detail: Trent Frayne's *The Mad Men of Hockey* (McClelland & Stewart, 1974); Jack Batten's *The*

Leafs in Autumn (Macmillan, 1975); Dick Irvin's *Behind the Bench: Coaches Talk about Life in the* NHL (McClelland & Stewart, 1993); Phil Loranger's *If They Played Hockey in Heaven: The Jack Adams Story* (Marjoguyhen); and Stephen Cole's *Slapshots: The Best and Worst of 100 Years of Hockey* (Penguin Books, 1993).

Tiger: A Hockey Story by Dave (Tiger) Williams and James Lawton (Douglas & McIntyre, 1984) and *Mario* by Lawrence Martin (Lester Publishing, 1993) are two fine and contrasting examples of hockey biography that set a standard to aspire to. I would also like to acknowledge with thanks the contribution of *Gretzky: An Autobiography* by Wayne Gretzky, with Rick Reilly (HarperCollins, 1990).

Readers will note that this book does not enter the maze of detail surrounding the retired NHL players' successful court battle to recover their pension money. This is a deliberate choice, since that whole, complex subject has already been exhaustively documented in other recent books, such as Bruce Dowbiggin's *The Defence Never Rests* (HarperCollins, 1993) and in various studies of that much-examined man Alan Eagleson. Nor does this book presume to know the real reasons in Gordie Howe's mind for not attending Gretzky's games when the latter was shooting for Howe's all-time NHL goals record, even though Howe had willingly been there to witness and applaud when Gretzky broke his NHL points record in October 1989. It was frequently alleged in print that Howe was angry because he felt Gretzky should have thrown his weight behind the pension fight; but Howe's actual thinking on that subject may have to await publication of his own book.

Colleen Howe's own two books, *My Three Hockey Players* (Hawthorn, 1975) and *After the Applause*, with Gordie Howe and Charles Wilkins (McClelland & Stewart, 1989), were naturally consulted for this biography.

Among broadcast materials, I am greatly indebted to the long, candid and highly sympathetic interview with Howe conducted by June Callwood and first aired by Vision-TV in 1993 on the program *June Callwood's National Treasures*.

Other broadcast sources include a CBC Radio documentary prepared at the time of Gordie Howe Day in Saskatoon in July 1966 and aired later that year on the prairie edition of the program *Between Ourselves*, hosted by Frank Willis; and a television documentary entitled *Back Where It All Began*, made by CFQC-TV in Saskatoon on the occasion of the 1993 Howe homecoming. The CTV network broadcast a Howe documentary in the series *Target: The Impossible* in 1974, which is an interesting record of his return to professional hockey in the WHA; and Peter Gzowski did a lengthy and lively interview with Gordie and Colleen on CBC Television's *Ninety Minutes Live* on February 2, 1978.

Most of the audio and video resources I consulted are in the collection of the National Archives of Canada in Ottawa, whose staff were extremely helpful. The Archives personnel also obtained for me various Detroit Red Wings game films from the 1950s showing Howe in action, including fascinating documentaries on the 1950, 1952, 1954, 1955 and 1956 Stanley Cup playoffs.

I could not have written this book without the cooperation, advice and helping hand of many individuals. At the beginning of the project, Ottawa authors Roy MacGregor and Lawrence Martin kindly gave me the benefit of their ample experience writing books on hockey and its practitioners. Roy's name opened some important doors, most helpfully that of Murray Costello, director of the Canadian Amateur Hockey Association in Ottawa, who opened many more and was a delightful raconteur of Howe and Red Wing tales.

Ken Dryden was generous with his time and his extraordinarily thoughtful reflections. Our conversations helped me to understand the scope of the task I had set myself, and to formulate my approach to it.

In Saskatoon, I was assisted by several people who had known Howe as a boy: Frances Hodges, Buck Crawford and one of Howe's sisters, Joan Clark. Former teammates Metro Prystai and Gerry (Doc) Couture accorded me valuable interviews. Lynda McLean-Woodward, principal of King George Community School, which Howe once attended, was gracious and helpful.

I would like to thank several Saskatoon media people who went out of their way to assist me in various ways: Dale Heath of CFQC-TV, Ned Powers of the *StarPhoenix* and broadcaster Lloyd Saunders.

In Detroit, I received the considerate and indispensable cooperation of Ted Lindsay and Marty Pavelich, two of the Red Wings who were closest to Howe when he was still a teen-ager. Ross (Lefty) Wilson and Lil Wilson welcomed me to their home and lent me memories and photographs. Bud Lynch gave me some deep background on life at the Olympia.

Pat Zacharias, Jeanette Bartz and Steve Fecht of the *Detroit News* and Rose Anne McKeen of the *Detroit Free Press* facilitated my obtaining many of the period photographs appearing in the book.

In Toronto, I was fortunate in having generous access to Red Kelly and his views, supplemented by the recollections of his wife, Andra Kelly; I was also assisted by their daughter Casey Kelly. Johnny Bower and Bob Baun were both exceptionally helpful and filled crucial gaps in the story. Among my journalist colleagues in Toronto, I'd like to thank Jim Proudfoot of the *Toronto Star*, Trent Frayne, June Callwood and Ted Mumford. Thanks also to Jean Bradshaw in the *Star* photo department.

Unique professional insights came by long-distance telephone from Ted (Teeder) Kennedy, Glenn Hall and Harry Lumley.

Several fellow writers shared their imaginative visions of my subject. John Bemrose, Guy Vanderhaeghe and Sean Rossiter provided me with fresh and original angles that made this a better book. Sean Rossiter, Mike Harling and Maja Grip also read the manuscript and saved me from myself in many instances.

My publisher, Rob Sanders of Greystone Books, and his associates at Douglas & McIntyre provided me with wonderful encouragement and excellent staff support. Barbara Pulling was a sensitive, creative and exacting editor who improved the manuscript enormously. Tom Brown and Terri Wershler did a great job on the book's design and production. Thanks also to Bill Hemy and Mike Alexander for their help with the visual materials.

My literary agent, Dean Cooke of the Livingstone Cooke Agency, helped keep me going.

Finally, I want to thank from the bottom of my heart Graham and Andrew for getting me back into my boyhood love, hockey, and Suzette for her love and unfailing support.

Index